POPULAR NARRATIVES
AND ETHNIC IDENTITY

POPULAR NARRATIVES AND ETHNIC IDENTITY

Literature and Community in *Die Abendschule*

BRENT O. PETERSON

Cornell University Press

Ithaca and London

First published 1991 by Cornell University Press.

International Standard Book Number 0-8014-2548-4
Library of Congress Catalog Card Number 91-17895
Printed in the United States of America
*Librarians: Library of Congress cataloging information
appears on the last page of the book.*

⊗ The paper in this book meets the minimum requirements
of the American National Standard for Information Science—
Permanence of Paper for Printed Library Materials, ANSI Z39.48-1984.

For my parents

Contents

Preface

The issue of identity, whether ethnic, gender, national, or racial, has of late become fashionable in a wide variety of disciplines—in history, literature, anthropology, and political science, and above all among the practitioners of "literary theory." As well it should have, for when the world we have known for so long is on the verge of utter collapse; when the boundaries around almost every political entity lose even the dubious validity of convention, and the ideas that once delimited nations and states are no longer meaningful or enforceable; when people who were united begin to go their separate ways, while others "reunite"; and when, at the local level, the once unchallenged roles of man, woman, husband, wife, adult, and child no longer make much sense—what could be more appropriate than asking, "Who are we?" or, as I would prefer to phrase the question, "How do we learn to be what we become?"

Yet, as interesting as any specific answer might be, it is just as important to examine what is at stake in even posing the question. Done well, analysis of any group from any time or place could provide an opportunity to reconsider both questions and answers, but the most productive intervention into the current discussion of identity, which has for far too long been concerned almost exclusively with the so-called marginal groups of contemporary society, might well come from a study of people who did not view themselves as being either on the edge of society or opposed to it, who could, in fact, be regarded as occupying the social, political, and ideological center. The reasons should be obvious. First, how the group that ends up controlling society decides who belongs and what belonging and therefore exclusion mean is of profound political and cultural significance. Second, if the process of identity formation is an important object of inquiry, useful explanations of the phenomenon should be broadly applicable—for men as well as women, for majorities and minorities, for conservatives and radicals, now and historically.

This book is a longitudinal study of nineteenth-century German immigrants that broadens the discussion and analyzes the arguments current among feminists, materialists, postmodernists, and others—including traditional scholars and those who are merely interested. The book treats identity as acquired consciousness and contends that what German immigrants read was intimately connected with their continually shifting sense of who they were. It analyzes the immigrants' reading practices in an effort to determine how the popular narratives that were their principal form of entertainment functioned, both as models of the immigrants' search for identity and as representations of the discursive universe in which their search took place. The documentary basis for the project is material that appeared between 1854 and 1900 in *Die Abendschule*, a once well-known German family journal published in St. Louis, Missouri. German-Americans and the broader question of what I term "historical ethnicity" provide new means of exploring the constitution of identity, the nature of subjectivity, and questions of agency. The relevance of the magazine and its readers to today's debates becomes all the more apparent when we realize that both the German immigrants in America and the texts they read were inscribed with the tensions of cultural pluralism, class and gender issues, and the continuing redefinition of "high" versus "low" literature.

The "narrative" behind my decision to write a book on *Die Abendschule* involves both a long-standing plan and a fairly serendipitous accident. I began work on the manuscript 1986 at the University of Minnesota, where I arrived in 1982 without any training in literary studies. Some years before—in Münster in the course of expanding a paper on the causes of German emigration for Richard Tilly's Institut für Sozial- und Wirtschaftsgeschichte—I had been struck by the sheer bulk of literature in the German-language newspapers and periodicals I was reading. When I decided to pursue graduate study, in German rather than in history, it struck me that a dissertation centered on those German-American journals might be interesting. I even proposed the topic in my application to graduate school, only to lose sight of it again while spending some years starting to learn what the discipline of literary studies was all about. Despite the fashionable lure of "theory," however, and despite the impossibility of continuing to write in the same naive mode as before, I still wanted to write literary history.

At this point both, Gerhard Weiss and Jochen Schulte-Sasse were extremely supportive, and it was Professor Schulte-Sasse who had previously encountered *Die Abendschule* and who suggested that it might be a possible focus. Luckily, Concordia College in St. Paul owns a nearly complete run of the journal, and the head librarian of their Buenger Memorial Library, Glenn Offerman, was genuinely pleased to see that someone was interested in reading through them for the first time in decades. Concordia's reference librarian, Charlotte Knocke, was also enormously helpful, and the Concordia Historical Institute of St. Louis allowed me full access to their collection of *Die Abendschule*, which included papers and memorabilia donated by the heirs of Louis Lange, the magazine's longtime publisher.

I am also grateful to Ruth-Ellen Joeres, M. J. Maynes, and Rudolph J. Vecoli for the encouragement they provided in the course of this and other projects. Steve Suppan, Bob Shandley, and Jack Goodman read and offered valuable comments on various drafts that led to the present book. A special grant from the Graduate School of the University of Minnesota enabled me to make a research visit to the archives of the Concordia Historical Institute, and the fellowship I received from the Graduate School allowed me to spend the academic year 1987–88 reading and writing. Heartfelt thanks are also due to my editors at Cornell University Press, especially to Bernhard Kendler, and to my copy editor, Peggy Hoover.

And I would even like to thank *Die Abendschule.* In addition to the enormous good fortune of ready access, the magazine turned out to be a gold mine. Every time I got stuck, every time I was unsure of my ideas, I really needed only to work through another volume; almost without fail the next text was just what I needed to explore a hunch or to see more of what was happening. It was not always fun, but it was invariably interesting, and even I hope valuable—and not just to me.

Finally and most important, thanks to my friends and family, who were always there when I needed them.

Portions of Chapter 5 have been issued elsewhere in different forms, and I am grateful for permission to reuse the following material here: "The 'Political' and the German-American Press" was published in the *Yearbook of German-American Studies* 23 (1988): 41–48; "Refunctioning History, Raabe Bowdlerized, or *Unseres Herrgotts Kanzelei* as an 'ethnic myth of descent'" appeared in *The German Quarterly* (Summer 1991): 353–67.

BRENT O. PETERSON

Princeton, New Jersey

POPULAR NARRATIVES
AND ETHNIC IDENTITY

Reading an Ethnic Identity

Few experiences can be as disorienting as migration, for migrants generally leave behind not only their homes and occupations but also, and in varying degrees, their families, friends, and acquaintances, as well as the whole range of institutions they would likely name if asked about their identity. For who are individual human beings if not the stories they tell to themselves and others—the narratives they construct at the intersection of various roles—in personal relationships, at work, in clubs, in churches, and, particularly in modern times, in nations and states? If asked to explain who they are, some people would also consider class to be an especially important or particularly intractable variable, whether inherited or enforced by economic imperatives, while others would scarcely understand either a question or an answer with that focus. Another group might talk of race or gender. Indeed, one could easily expand any list of relevant factors. Furthermore, in any particular instance most people would probably relate a story slightly different from the one they would produce if prompted by other circumstances, and it is almost certainly true that any given individual's set of possible narratives would be considered inconsistent, even contradictory, if considered as a whole.

Migrants—that is, men and women who by definition suddenly find themselves in another context, where their old narratives of identity have become inoperative—must be able to fabricate new identities. Unlike the people who stayed behind, whose settled lives mean that questions are fewer and answers are easier, migrants occupy economic, political, and cultural space where they can neither repeat the same old stories nor abandon them completely without incurring a considerable personal cost. Dealing successfully with the dislocations of migration therefore involves, among other things, acquiring a whole new set of narratives. It is not enough to move, to get a job, and then to find a place to live, worship, and relax; most migrants also have to relearn who they are—both as individuals and as members of a new and different collective.

For the nineteenth-century German immigrants who are the focus of this study, migration necessarily entailed refurbishing, recontextualizing, and rearticulating an identity whose inadequacy at some level had prompted their leaving Germany in the first place. Potential emigrants were either unhappy with the identities society had accorded them or unable to maintain those identities in the face of the social and economic pressures that can be summarized as urbanization, industrialization, and modernization.[1] Of course, having come from Germany and being able to speak German provided most of them with a base on which to build their new identities, but neither the often vague sense of national origin nor the language that German immigrants shared, though perhaps only partially, with millions of other Germans was by itself an identity. For even if they did not reject their heritage altogether, once they had settled in the United States, German immigrants, like their counterparts from every other region of the world, had to acquire a new set of stories—specifically, they had to learn what it meant to be German-American. It will be argued here that German immigrants to the United States acquired their identities, and perhaps eventually rejected them, with the aid of what they read—that is, with the aid of narratives that not only modeled potential identities, but that also both

---

[1]The concept of modernization, which is connected to urbanization and industrialization, has long since been a bone of contention among historians. For a report on the controversy (the book's subtitle indicates the stakes in the battle), see Richard J. Evans, *Rethinking German History: Nineteenth-Century Germany and the Origins of the Third Reich* (London: Unwin Hyman, 1987), esp. the chapter titled "The Myth of Germany's Missing Revolution," 93–122. Whether or not something like modernization took place (and the debate is as much about the term's definition as about its explanatory usefulness), contemporaries were indeed troubled by a sense of loss. I therefore argue below that the texts they read were inscribed with the yearning for a perhaps mythical past—that is, with an antimodernism that was not strictly dependent on empirical evidence of change, and certainly not the kind of change that fits neatly into sociohistorical categories. Indeed, the narratives that were read and produced at the time are probably the best sources for finding out what the shorthand notations—urbanization, industrialization, and modernization—actually meant to the people who felt threatened by those phenomena.

constituted and represented the discursive universe in which the immigrants' search for identity took place.

To be sure, German immigrants' recourse to narratives was only part of a much larger set of social and cultural changes that had an impact on such texts. Ever since the eighteenth century, narratives, particularly written narratives, played an increasingly significant role in the process of socialization. Narratives—whether published in calendars, pamphlets, or the penny press—provided an alternative to the models of identity that were traditionally transmitted orally or through the example of local figures of authority. The growing significance of narratives was the result of changes in the technology of printing, in the scope of public education, in the degree of literacy, and consequently in the size of the potential reading public, which for the first time in human history made truly popular literature possible.

Whatever the ultimate outcome of that process, an immediate result was that a new layer of meaning was added to the variety of overlapping and at times contradictory identities people shared. Now they were not only members of families who had jobs, belonged to clubs and churches, and lived in particular times and places, but also readers—that is, people whose commerce with texts located them in a specific cultural-political space. What makes the expansion of the reading public all the more significant is that literature, whether conceived of as individual texts or as an institution in society, was by the middle of the eighteenth century beginning to address a new and very different set of concerns. For example, one consequence of the gradual secularization and rationalization of society that accompanied the Enlightenment was that literary texts were no longer written primarily in the service of the state or the church, but rather were addressed to individuals struggling to attain a degree of personal and political autonomy. The shift in the locus of moral authority away from churches and absolutist states to a bourgeois public sphere, which was almost wholly constituted in and through literature, also meant that neither the system of feudal obligations and urban corporations nor organized religion could continue to provide people with an adequate sense of who they were. Thus, particularly in the nineteenth century, what people read became an important source of the "imaginary" material they used both to fashion their own identities and simultaneously to outfit themselves with the norms and values they needed to act in society. Conversely, that search for identity was inscribed in the narratives themselves, particularly as some of these texts were published in media produced by and for an emerging immigrant community.

This book contributes to an ongoing discussion of the significance of changing reading practices. It contends that what nineteenth-century German immigrants read was intimately connected with their continually shifting sense of who they were. The documentary basis for the project is *Die Abendschule* (The Evening School, or somewhat less restrictively, as the magazine referred to itself when trying to impress English-language advertisers, *The Evening Companion*),[2] a Christian family journal published first in Buffalo, New York, and then in St. Louis, Missouri, from 1854 to 1940. Its continuous publishing history means that *Die Abendschule* provides an ideal vehicle for a longitudinal study of the way popular narratives functioned within a developing community of readers—in this case, among a significant segment of the millions of German immigrants who streamed into the United States during the second half of the nineteenth century. The German-language press was the one place where these immigrants, who were both disoriented by migration and modernization and separated from the rest of American society by language preference, could learn how to deal with their new situation with relative ease. Indeed, it might well be argued that "German" magazines actually taught immigrants how to become "German-Americans," but to read these journals simply to uncover their supposed pedagogical intent would radically foreshorten any consideration of the discursive forces at work in the texts they published. The more fundamental issues are whether the narratives published in *Die Abendschule* can be profitably read as representations of the material that immigrants used to manufacture their own identities and whether these texts can therefore provide access to the constantly evolving mental framework of German-American life as immigrants reacted to changes in the culture and society that surrounded them.

The first chapter presents an overview of *Die Abendschule*'s development in the course of the forty-seven-year period covered by this book, from 1854 to 1900. Changes in the journal's title and the eight different masthead illustrations under which the magazine appeared in those years help reveal the image of itself that *Die Abendschule* presented to its readers. In addition, since these masthead il-

[2]From a prospectus for advertisers titled "Abendschule," presumably 1895. Concordia Historical Institute, St. Louis, Missouri, August Lange Papers, doc. 648 (hereafter cited as CHI, AL followed by document number).

lustrations all contain variations on the common theme of people reading, I argue that publications like *Die Abendschule* fostered a particular mode of reading. By analyzing the magazine's iconic suggestions about how its readers were supposed to read, I also explore how a medium can attempt to shape its own specific community of recipients. In *Die Abendschule* that process essentially involved the magazine's insertion, or to use the more precise literary term, its inscription of the implied readers into the multiple subject positions of the bourgeois family—namely, as reading fathers and listening mothers and children, who were all caught up in the changes that affected both the family and the status of German immigrants in the United States. Chapter 1 also presents a brief overview of the history of the family journal, paying particular attention to *Die Abendschule*'s German relatives, especially to *Die Gartenlaube* (The Garden Bower), which was by far the most successful example of the genre, and to its overtly Christian counterpart, *Daheim* (At Home).

The second chapter, "Ethnicity and Ethnic Literature," discusses various ways of framing the twin questions of who *Die Abendschule*'s readers were and how to label what it was that they read. It begins with a look at how the readers of texts like those published in *Die Abendschule* have previously been identified—for example, in the case of the foreign-language press in the United States—as members of specific ethnic groups. After examining the little evidence that remains concerning the magazine's actual subscribers, and after describing the position that those subscribers occupied within the culturally, socially, and religiously diverse population of German immigrants in the United States, the chapter turns to the problem of how scholars in the disciplines of history, literature, and anthropology have described ethnicity. This discussion includes the more recent approaches to ethnicity that have grown out of the debate over modernism and postmodernism, and I examine specifically the manner in which ethnicity and ethnic literature have been appropriated in the postmodernist discussion of agency. After this more general treatment, the chapter focuses on the ways in which the categories of ethnicity and ethnic literature have been applied specifically to German-Americans, both as purported members of an ethnic group and as producers of a distinct literature and culture. In addition, because nineteenth-century German-Americans often thought of themselves as the legitimate heirs of German culture in the United States, I ask to what degree their claim meant that German-Americans competed for precedence as the mediators of "German" culture with the nascent discipline of *Germanistik*. The implicit question is whether "German" culture encompassed the life and literature of German-Americans or whether it was limited to the fragments of "high" culture offered up in academia. Inasmuch as the study of German literature in the United States has generally marginalized German-American literature in favor of the German "classics," the chapter includes a discussion of why the discipline of German might profitably study the popular narratives that German-Americans read and wrote, as a model for other immigrant languages and indeed for English-language popular narratives as well. The chapter's most radical move, however, is the redefinition of ethnicity as a category defined by reading rather than by the national or cultural origin of the authors of ethnic literature. It is that redefinition that ultimately justifies the extended critique of previous attempts to define the object of inquiry in ethnic studies.

The third chapter deals with the founding of *Die Abendschule* and its development through the end of the American Civil War, when the magazine finally began to assume an identity that would carry it through to the end of the century. The chapter explores the specific historical factors that produced this particular journal with its own peculiar sense of mission. An important part of the discussion of the journal's early years is a close look at the magazine's contents, which ranged from light fiction and popular biographies to reports of recent scientific advances and news summaries. Not coincidentally, the first work of fiction published in *Die Abendschule* was also the magazine's first serialized novel—that is, the first example of a genre that, in 1854, was already one of the defining features of the German-language press, both in the United States and in Germany. This particular text, an anonymous seven-part work titled *Die hölzernen Teller* (The Wooden Plates), is interesting in its own right, but it is also useful as a concrete methodological test case. Given the practical and theoretical difficulty of separating methodology from the object of inquiry, the chapter examines various competing claims about the significance of popular literature against the background of *Die hölzernen Teller*. The reason for this lengthy discussion, which ranges over positions as diverse as ideological criticism (*Ideologiekritik*) and literary sociology and includes recent feminist and psychoanalytic treatments of popular narratives, is to assess the strengths and weaknesses of those theories for *Die Abendschule*'s texts. It thereby lays the groundwork for an analysis of the much larger body of texts published in the magazine in the years after the Civil War.

Two subsequent chapters explore the way in which both the overt contents and the models of identity generated by the texts published in *Die Abendschule* changed over time, as new discourses and various external events impinged on the journal's representation of reality. Chapter 4 deals with early versions of the magazine's attempt to provide its readers with the outlines of a coherent German-American identity. In effect, the chapter describes the impossibility of resolving the question of immigrants' identities in the first decade after the American Civil War, when both the magazine and its readers were torn between the fundamentally irreconcilable demands of being "German," "American," and "Lutheran" simultaneously. There was still no such thing as German-American identity—in any context—because the decision to embrace any single position would have necessarily involved the loss of cherished elements of the three alternative bases. In part, the difficulty was brought on by the essentially defensive posture of the embattled Missouri Synod Lutherans who made up *Die Abendschule*'s primary readership; the Synod stressed its doctrinal differences with Roman Catholics, Mormons, and Methodists, and especially its opposition to the "wrong" kind of Lutherans. At the same time, even the Missouri Synod's apparently well-defined identity was often at odds with both its "German" roots and its "American" surroundings. The resulting juggling act became all the more necessary—and all the more impossible—in 1871, when the cathartic "event" that can be abbreviated as German unification once again reopened the question of German immigrants' identities. Essentially, Chapter 4 examines a group of fictional and nonfictional narratives—mainly novels and popular histories—for traces of the continuous negotiations that occurred between competing subject positions, and it pays particular attention to the norms and values at stake in each of the three separate but at times also overlapping identities mentioned above.

Chapter 5 analyzes the gradual emergence of a more inclusive definition of German-American identity, and asks what it must therefore have meant for readers of *Die Abendschule* to attempt to integrate "Lutheran," "German," and "American" into some form of "German-American" identity. Of course, the same immigrants were also defined by numerous other identities—their jobs, ages, genders, etc.—but, to judge by the narratives they read and by the discursive strategies represented there, the religious rifts that had once divided the German immigrant population seem to have gradually declined in significance. This was particularly true within the German-American middle class, whose members were apparently busy constituting themselves as a subgroup distinct from and in opposition to the often socialist German-American working class. A significant aspect of their relatively successful act of intragroup demarcation—which was achieved, in spite of all odds and countervailing pressures, by formulating an essentially nostalgic, precapitalist locus for their identity—is that it demonstrates how popular narratives could refashion the discourse of history into a continuously rearticulated "ethnic myth of descent." Yet, although such myths were at least temporarily successful in keeping the terrible reality of social and economic change at bay, the versions of German-American identity represented in *Die Abendschule* nevertheless soon proved inadequate for the task of dealing with either the changes in the society at large or with the challenge launched by the country's embattled elite.

By 1900 the middle-class German-Americans who read *Die Abendschule* were not only threatened by the tempo of social and economic change; they were also trapped in the increasingly narrow discursive space between the so-called new immigrants from southern and eastern Europe, who were denigrated for supposedly advocating the same dangerous ideas previously espoused by "German" radicals, and the "American" attempt to exclude these newcomers as "undesirable aliens." Since "hyphenation" no longer provided a viable identity—that is, because it was no longer possible to succeed in the culture at large as a *German*-American, or as any kind of *something*-American, *Die Abendschule*'s narratives attempted to appropriate the norms and values of the "Anglo-Saxon" establishment, people whose history was nothing if not "German." In the process the German-Americans who took their cue from *Die Abendschule* gradually became more "American" than the "Americans." Paradoxically, by "successfully" discarding the exclusive identity they had once fought so hard to establish and maintain, the same German-Americans also jettisoned every reason for their own continued existence as an ethnic group. German-American identity had gradually been reduced to little more than a nostalgic language loyalty and regular visits to the local beer garden.

This book ends with 1900, because by the turn of the century there was so little left for German-Americans to give up that the supposed "tragedy" of 1917–18 had almost already happened. *Die Abendschule*'s success had ultimately undermined the entire project of helping its readers come to terms with their environment by giving them the tools with which to forge a German-American identity. A brief conclusion and summary assesses the specific traces of German-American identity that did survive the disaster of World War I, particularly as those remnants were preselected by more than five decades of popular narratives.

As intrinsically interesting as the content of German-American identities may be, this book is more than a thematic analysis of the narratives that *Die Abendschule* published in the latter half of the nineteenth century. Its purpose is rather to explore in paradigmatic fashion the complex set of relationships between literature and community—between what people read and who they became. Ultimately, the book shows how reading the popular narratives published in *Die Abendschule* enabled some German immigrants to deal, both individually and collectively, with their own ambiguous subjectivity in a rapidly changing and "foreign" new world. In so doing, the book provides a framework for analyzing the discursive, that is, the narrativized verson of reality inhabited by other migrants who lived, and still live, in other times and places. For migration, whether from one country to another or "merely" from the country-side to one of the rapidly growing industrial cities that were springing up in Europe in the nineteenth century and are still emerging in the rest of the world, has been one of the most common experiences of the last 150 years of human history.

Even if we conclude that the German immigrants who read *Die Abendschule* made a series of bad choices, and even if they ultimately tried to hold on to a world that was irrevocably lost, understanding their experiences could nevertheless be part of one of the most important projects in the field of American history, as well as of considerable interest to virtually every foreign language department in the United States. The plight of nineteenth-century German-Americans and the strategies they used to deal with their situation are examples of the almost universal phenomenon of cultural dislocation, and we can scarcely hope to answer questions as significant, as urgent, and as seemingly unrelated as the status of the English language in the United States or the situation of *Gastarbeiter* in the Federal Republic of Germany—to say nothing of the immensely difficult and to some degree dubious undertaking of combining "two Germanies" into a coherent whole—without considering where such problems are located in a much larger historical context. Once we understand how German immigrants came to know who they were, we might gain some additional insight into the far larger problem posed by the contemporary production of national, social, cultural, economic, ethnic, and gendered identities.

Imagining *Die Abendschule*'s Family of Readers

In a poem written to celebrate the new year of 1856, an anonymous writer painted an idealized picture of German-American family life, which in this case revolved around *Die Abendschule*, the conservative Christian family journal in which the poem had been published:

Und alle Hausgenossen sind ganz Ohr,	When the entire household is one big ear,
Der Vater sitzt am Herd auf seinem Stuhle,	And father is sitting by the stove on his stool,
Und lieset mich der lieben Jugend vor:	Reading me aloud, to his loved-ones dear,
dann fühlet sich belohnt die Abendschule.	Then feels rewarded *The Evening School*.[1]

Aside from the dubious poetic quality of my translation, which is arguably not much worse than the original, the point here is that the poem's verbal image corresponded precisely to an illustration that graced the journal's masthead during the first year of its existence (Figure 1). In fact, the verbal image of a father or grandfather reading to his (extended) family coincided in varying degrees with the pictures in each of the eight different illustrated mastheads under which *Die Abendschule* appeared between 1854 and 1907.[2] The

[1]"Zum Neuen Jahr 1856," *Illustri[e]rte Abendschule* II, 24 (5 January 1856), 185–86. Because the magazine's pagination is continuous, subsequent references to *Die Abendschule* will be identified hereafter only by volume and page number. Unless otherwise noted, all translations are mine, and, except for this one bit of "poetry," I have omitted the German originals. Readers who are unwilling or unable to track down copies of *Die Abendschule* are directed to the earlier version of this study (Ph.D. diss., University of Minnesota, 1989).

[2]In checking a number of contemporary German and American journals (*Daheim, Die Gartenlaube, Grenzbote, Über Land und Meer, Scribner's,* and *Harper's Monthly Magazine*), I was struck by the paucity of masthead illustrations. While some mastheads were illustrated, the practice was by no means universal. In addi-

Figure 1

constant theme of these mastheads was reading, represented either as an individual activity or more frequently as the center of a family gathering. In effect, *Die Abendschule* was showing its readers how they were supposed to read; the journal's mastheads were a kind of primer devoted to the complex set of relationships between the magazine's readers and the texts they read. What these images portray is reading—and specifically, as will become clear shortly, reading *Die Abendschule*—as a social activity that was just as important as the content of what was actually being read.

Such a claim may seem exaggerated or even out of place in the first chapter of a book that concentrates on verbal rather than visual texts, but one must understand what reading meant to the readers of *Die Abendschule* before it makes any sense to talk about what they read. Until well into the nineteenth century, for example, there is no compelling reason to restrict reading practices to the activities of isolated individuals. Literary images of families reading together are at least as old as Martin Luther, whose family life was an important model for the German Protestant readers of *Die Abendschule*. In the introduction to his version of Aesop's fables, for example, Luther wrote: "One can have a good time [*fröhlich sein*] and still discuss one of these fables in the evening at the table with one's children and servants in a manner that is both useful and enjoyable [*nützlich und*

---

tion, the illustrations in these other journals were seldom, if ever, changed. Not having studied their individual histories, I can offer no explanation for the difference.

lüstiglich]."[3]The Enlightenment could also be characterized, at least in part, by group reading practices, which were often modeled in the texts of the period,[4] and even the titles of nineteenth-century periodicals like *Die Spinnstube* (The Spinning-Room), a calender issued by Protestant pastor Wilhelm Oertel, testify to the role of the person who read aloud (*Vorleser*) at quilting bees and similar functions in village life.[5] In fact, such written evidence, coupled with the images provided by *Die Abendschule*'s mastheads, shows that the generic term "reader" might better be regarded as a plural.

One could certainly posit a transitional, group-reading phase in the shift from story-telling, which Walter Benjamin characterized as the face-to-face exchange of experiences, to narration, which he described as both isolated and isolating.[6] Group reading also needs to be incorporated into the transition from intensive to extensive reading that Rolf Engelsing locates at the end of the eighteenth century.[7] Rather than reading and then constantly rereading the same book, or concentrating on a very limited number of books—generally the

[3]Martin Luther, "Etliche Fabeln aus Äsop, 1530," *Ausgewählte Schriften*, ed. Karin Bornkamm and Gerhard Ebeling (Frankfurt am Main: Insel, 1982), 5:166.

[4]See, e.g., Joachim Heinrich Campe, *Robinson der Jüngere: Zur angenehmen und nützlichen Unterhaltung für Kinder* (1779–80; Stuttgart: Reclam, 1981), where a father/teacher reads aloud to his assembled charges from his own version of Defoe's well-known tale. In the first edition of the text the group is also pictured, seated together under an apple tree with the father/teacher/reader at their center (p. 3). Eighteenth-century *Lesegesellschaften* would be another example; see Horst Möller, *Vernunft und Kritik: Deutsche Aufklärung im 17. und 18. Jahrhundert* (Frankfurt am Main: Suhrkamp, 1986), 261–68.

[5]See Klaus Müller-Salget, *Erzählungen für das Volk: Evangelische Pfarrer als Volksschriftsteller im Deutschland des 19. Jahrhunderts* (Berlin: E. Schmidt, 1984), 113–14, and Rudolf Schenda, *Volk ohne Buch: Studien zur populären Literatur im 19. und 20. Jahrhundert* (Munich: DTV, 1977).

[6]Walter Benjamin, "The Storyteller: Reflections on the Work of Nikolai Leskov," *Illuminations* (New York: Schocken Books, 1969). When talking about telling stories, Benjamin refers to "the ability to exchange experiences (*Erfahrungen*)" (p. 83). To this he contrasts modern narration: "The birthplace of the novel is the solitary individual" (p. 87) and "The reader of the novel . . . is isolated, more so than any other reader" (p. 100).

[7]See Rolf Engelsing, "Die Perioden der Lesergeschichte in der Neuzeit: Das statistische Ausmass und die soziokulturelle Bedeutung der Lektüre," *Archiv für Geschichte des Buchwesens* 10 (1970): cols. 945–1002, as well as his *Analphabetentum und Lektüre: Zur Sozialgeschichte des Lesens in Deutschland zwischen feudaler und industrieller Gesellschaft* (Stuttgart: Metzler, 1973). In spite of Engelsing's argument, it was probably only with the emergence of the *Familienblätter* in the second half of the nineteenth century, when cheap texts became readily available to a mass audience, that large sectors of the population began to read extensively.

Bible and various religious tracts—people began to read more widely. They read texts one after the other, and they only read them once. In the space between Benjamin's and Engelsing's alternatives, however, the subject positions depicted in *Die Abendschule*'s mastheads suggest that reading was for much of the nineteenth century a social act that was not limited to a single individual's interaction with texts—that is, not limited to reading per se. *Die Abendschule*'s readers were assigned roles in a specific, historical institution, namely, in the emerging bourgeois family.

Both the reality of family life and the idealized projections of that life changed significantly between 1854 and 1907, particularly as the changes Karin Hausen has identified in the role of the eighteenth-century woman were consolidated and became more widespread.[8] On the basis of her extensive reading of contemporary encyclopedias, medical handbooks, and pedagogical treatises Hausen argues that whereas eighteenth-century women were still regarded as important members of a family unit of production, the "ideal" nineteenth-century woman was increasingly confined within a nuclear family that was constituted as a refuge from the "male" world of work. On the other hand, at least in Germany, Wilhelm Heinrich Riehl's idyllic views of the extended family, which included apprentices supervised by the woman of the house, remained largely unchallenged until the end of the nineteenth century.[9] In addition, the image of the family in *Die Abendschule* was also embedded in the discourses that defined gender identity and the German-American community. Yet, in spite of all these complications, one place to see how the image of the family—and of the reading practices that were part of that collective role—developed over time can be read from

[8]Karin Hausen, "Die Polarisierung der 'Geschlechtscharaktere': Eine Spiegelung der Dissoziation von Erwerbs- und Familienleben," in Werner Conze, ed., *Sozialgeschichte der Familie in der Neuzeit: Neue Forschung* (Stuttgart: Klett, 1976), 363–93. Hausen's essay, which has become something of a classic, is available in English in Richard J. Evans and W. R. Lee, eds., *The German Family: Essays on the Social History of the Family in Nineteenth- and Twentieth-Century Germany* (Totowa, N.J.: Barnes and Noble, 1981), 51–83. See also E. J. Hobsbawm, *The Age of Capital, 1848–1875* (New York: Scribner's, 1975), 230–50; and Michael Mitterauer and Reinhard Sieder, *Vom Patriarchat zur Partnerschaft: Zum Strukturwandel der Familie* (Munich: Beck, 1984).

[9]On Riehl, see Jochen Schulte-Sasse and Renate Werner, "E. Marlitts 'Im Hause des Kommerzienrates': Analyse eines Trivialromans in paradigmatischer Absicht," in Schulte-Sasse and Werner, eds., *E. Marlitt, "Im Hause des Kommerzienrates"* (Munich: Fink, 1977), esp. 418–24.

the progression of icons contained in successive mastheads from *Die Abendschule*.

At the very least, *Die Abendschule*'s masthead images suggest that more might be involved in reading the journal than simply settling down, alone and in an easychair, with the latest issue. Thus, if there was a community created by the literature published in *Die Abendschule*, it was apparently intended to exist in a specific form, as the result of a particular mode of reading. As the series of mastheads clearly demonstrates, however, these prescriptive images of reading practices also changed over time. These eight mastheads therefore provide an opportunity to survey the whole course of the magazine's development in summary fashion, before subsequent chapters examine various portions of that history in greater detail.

In assessing *Die Abendschule*'s masthead images, this chapter pays particular attention to the subject positions suggested to the journal's readers. Admittedly, the use of the term "subject position" here—and the notion of the "subject" that it implies—could open up a theoretical discussion so involved that *Die Abendschule* itself— its texts and their readers—would disappear from view for hundreds of pages. While not denying the importance of the still unresolved discussion of subjectivity, this book makes a contribution that is not strictly theoretical; its purpose is rather to explain the significance of a particular set of popular narratives in the discourse of German-American identity. To the extent that the analysis is paradigmatic, however, it can show how even traditional topics in the field of literary history can take part in contemporary theoretical debates, basically by insisting that literary history is not simply a subsidiary space where ideas from the loftier realm of "theory" are mechanically applied to some object, but that any application—or more accurately any theoretically informed and reflected analysis—is simultaneously a test whose aim is always further development.

The issue of a "subject position" raised here is a case in point. The idea seems to have originated in film theory as a means of describing the space constructed in the filmic text for the viewer, but the concept has recently been expanded to include the "subjects" of a variety of other discourses as well.[10] For literature, the notion of a "subject position" represents a significant advance over the seemingly independent and individualistic concept of the reader favored by tra-

[10]Most notably by Kaja Silverman, *The Subject of Semiotics* (New York: Oxford University Press, 1983).

ditional theories; behind any discussion of the "subject" is an implicit claim that readers are not only concrete, historical individuals but also the recipients generated at least in part by the texts they read. Of course, actual readers can always either accept or reject the subject position a given text offers them, and they can always read the text in question against the grain. In addition, no matter how circumscribed their sphere of agency might otherwise be, the same readers can also simply stop reading—at least temporarily. For no text is so compelling that we really cannot put it down, although the question of who the "we" in this sentence might be—literary critics or the compulsive consumers of Harlequin romances—complicates the issue significantly.

"Agency" is another way of raising many of the same questions generally discussed under the heading of the "subject"; in essence, the problem is the degree to which theories of subjectivity have closed off the possibility of meaningful human action. In a recent attempt to clarify the debate, Paul Smith has argued that human beings are "caught" in a dialectical process of being both *subjected to* "social formations, language, political apparatuses, and so on" and at the same time never being completely *determined by* any of those forces.[11] As a result, Smith contends: "A person is not simply the *actor* who follows ideological scripts, but is also an *agent* who reads them in order to insert him/herself into them—or not." For Smith, then, "the commonly used term 'subject' will be broken down and will be understood as . . . the series or the conglomeration of *positions*, subject positions, provisional and not necessarily indefeasible, into which a person is called momentarily by the discourses and the world that he/she inhabits."[12] How or if this process can be applied to the attempts of German immigrants to locate themselves in the discourse of German-American identity—that is, how the popular narratives published in *Die Abendschule* helped those immigrants identify themselves as German-Americans—is the real point of this study. It is important to stress, however, that I will never claim that *Die Abendschule*'s readers were provided with a single, unified identity. I prefer to view identity as a series of sometimes overlapping, sometimes adjacent, and sometimes mutually exclusive discursive spheres. For example, the positions that a person occupies

[11]Paul Smith, *Discerning the Subject* (Minneapolis: University of Minnesota Press, 1988), xxxiv.
[12]Ibid., xxxiv–xxxv.

in a family, job, church, state, and so on, are all different identities; they consist of different roles in competing though often complementary situations that can be described as narratives. But whatever description or term one accepts, it should not be understood to imply that the individual is ever located in the *one* place where his or her identities all intersect. People generally inhabit a number of different spaces simultaneously, and while they might chose to emphasize one or the other in various circumstances, they can within certain limits redefine themselves completely whenever the situation demands, by moving from one identity to another. If they are not entirely "free" agents, they nevertheless must learn who they are in order to operate in the various contexts into which their lives thrust them. At certain junctures, most notably in childhood, people are inundated with potential identities, while at other times external circumstances, like migration, force them to search out new sets of narratives that they can tell themselves and others.

One place where the readers of *Die Abendschule* obviously were offered a subject position or an identity, which they could presumably then accept or reject, was in the images of readers contained in magazine's mastheads. By showing how these mastheads suggested a certain mode of reading, I hope not only to broaden our conception of reading to include its potential as a subject position, but also to suggest that reading is often "preprogrammed," both by features formally "inside" the text and by the immediate material context in which that text appears.[13] If the argument were extended far enough, *Die Abendschule*'s masthead images could be linked to other features that are normally thought to be "outside" the text but that

---

[13] "Preprogrammed reception" is my rendering of the term *Rezeptionsvorgabe*, which was developed in the German Democratic Republic by Manfred Naumann et al. in *Gesellschaft—Literatur—Lesen: Literaturrezeption in theoretischer Sicht* (Berlin: Aufbau-Verlag, 1976). Although in need of further development, because Naumann's group does not yet include the medium in which something is published, the idea of *Rezeptionsvorgabe* is certainly more useful than Stanley Fish's "interpretative communities." Naumann and his colleagues locate readers in history at the same time that they expand the catalog of influences that might determine reading habits. I also find *Rezeptionsvorgabe* more productive than Iser's far too textually immanent and therefore dangerously ahistorical "implied reader." On the East-West debate, in which Naumann plays a crucial role, see Robert C. Holub, *Reception Theory: A Critical Introduction* (New York: Methuen, 1984), esp. 121–34. For a critique of reader-response criticism in general and of Fish in particular, see Elizabeth Freund, *The Return of the Reader: Reader-Response Criticism* (New York: Methuen, 1987).

actually serve to preprogram its reception. Take, for example, where something is published—in a book, pamphlet, or magazine. Is a novel simply a novel? Does it make no difference whether its readers are using a cheap paperback edition or a leatherbound volume? And are the texts contained in required schoolbooks equivalent to the "same" poems and narratives encountered by chance or intentionally at a later date? Of course, the words are basically the same, but everyone who has returned voluntarily to a once required text— and perhaps read it for the first time—knows how different a subsequent reading can be, solely on the basis of the altered context. So too with the location of narratives in *Die Abendschule*. To the extent that the magazine's texts were read in the manner suggested in the series of its masthead images, their textuality extended far beyond the words on the page. Understanding the context of the reading family that those images were intended to produce is therefore an important first step in coming to grips with what reading *Die Abendschule* meant to its readers.

Before finally turning to those images, it is important to step back for a moment and to make an initial attempt to locate *Die Abendschule* historically. Chapter 3 contains a fuller account of the gesture behind the journal's foundation, so we need here only a preliminary sketch to help contextualize the whole undertaking. The *Illustri[e]rte Abendschule: Ein Blatt zur Belehrung und Unterhaltung für die reifere Jugend* (The Illustrated Evening School: A Paper for the Instruction and Entertainment of Mature Young People), as it was initially called, began its existence in Buffalo, New York, in February 1854. As its name suggests, the journal's primary aim was pedagogic; the editor intended to provide parents with "a good school, in fact a better school for your small and grown children than a lot of other reading is" (I, 1). Like most other German journals of its time, *Die Abendschule* initially experienced enormous difficulties in garnering enough subscribers to make the venture profitable. When *Die Abendschule* followed its editor to St. Louis in 1856, the journal's survival was far from certain; in fact, it very nearly folded on a number of occasions. In 1859, for example, the editor absconded with what little money was left in the till (VI, 41), and it was not until 1861, when Louis Lange purchased *Die Abendschule* and its list of about 1,000 subscribers for $200,[14] that it began the long

[14]CHI, AL 648. Lange (1829–93) was born in Zennern, a village in Wesse, Germany. He emigrated to the United States at the age of seventeen and soon became an

upward climb to becoming what Karl Arndt and May Olson, the tireless bibliographers of the German-American press, termed "one of the most influential and constructive journals ever published in America."[15] At its high point in 1914, *Die Abendschule* boasted 59,631 subscribers, and there were still more than 30,000 left in 1920. Publication was not suspended until December 1940, when paid subscriptions had dropped to under 15,000.[16] Although it appeared in a variety of incarnations in the course of those eighty-seven years, such longevity is still rare enough to have been remarkable. *Die Abendschule* certainly must have struck a number of responsive chords in the course of its existence.

The journal's success was not, however, simply an accident, not just the result of Louis Lange's luck and pluck; it appeared on the scene at precisely the moment when German publishers like Ernst Keil were creating a related though not perhaps entirely new form of periodical in Lange's native Germany.[17] Certainly, the German history of the *Familienblätter*—or family journals, as those magazines came to be known—is an integral part of the history of their German-American counterparts. For example, to the extent that family journals constituted a separate genre, their origin is usually dated to

---

apprentice printer on various German- and English-language newspapers. He purchased *Die Abendschule* from his employer, the printer-publisher M. Neidner, who had himself bought whatever remained of the magazine's assets at an auction for $10, apparently in an attempt to recoup some of the printing bill left after the previous owner "fled in the course of a swindle." See Louis Lange, "Bericht an die Ehrwürdige Synode von Missouri, Ohio, und andere Staaten über die Synodaldruckerei und die 'Abendschule' " (n.d.), Concordia Historical Institute, St. Louis, Missouri, Anna and Hedwig Lange Papers doc. 1048 (hereafter cited as CHI, A & HL followed by document number).

[15]Karl J. Arndt and May E. Olson, eds., *The German-Language Press of the Americas* (New York: K. G. Sauer, 1980) 247.

[16]Ibid., 248.

[17]For a history of *Familienblätter*, see Dieter Barth, *Zeitschrift für Alle: Das Familienblatt im 19. Jahrhundert: Ein sozialhistorischer Beitrag zur Massenpresse in Deutschland* (diss., Westfälische Wilhelms-Universität, Münster, 1974), as well as Barth's "Das Familienblatt: Ein Phänomen der Unterhaltungspresse des 19. Jahrhunderts: Beispiele zur Gründungs- und Verlagsgeschichte," *Archiv für Geschichte des Buchwesens* 15 (1975): cols. 122–316. The latter publication is basically a shorter version of his dissertation. On the American tradition of family journals, see Jan Cohn, *Creating America: George Horace Lorimer and the Saturday Evening Post* (Pittsburgh: University of Pittsburgh Press, 1989). Unfortunately, Cohn wastes a great opportunity by paying too much attention to the magazine's editorials and too little to the interplay of features and fiction that were probably far more interesting and revealing.

the first appearance of *Die Gartenlaube* in January of 1853, just over a year before *Die Abendschule* made its debut.

Of course, Keil's magazine also had its precursors. One could, for example, date the idea of popular journalism to "moral weeklies" of the Enlightenment, but the eighteenth century was probably more important for the secularization and fictionalization of the norms and values represented in print than for their widespread dissemination. It was in all likelihood the mass-circulation newspapers and magazines of the early nineteenth century, most notably the so-called penny papers, that marked the real start of a truly popular press in Germany. The new genre began with *Das Pfennig-Magazin der Gesellschaft zur Verbreitung gemeinnütziger Kenntnisse* (Penny Magazine of the Society for the Dissemination of Useful Knowledge, 1833–55), a Leipzig journal whose extremely low price provided an important impetus for the circulation strategies later adopted by the publishers of the family journals. Success bred imitation, and soon there were penny papers in Berlin and Cologne too. Karl Gutzkow's *Unterhaltungen am häuslichen Herd* (Entertainment at Home by the Hearth), which began to appear in 1852, may look like a family journal, but Dieter Barth, the preeminent historian of the genre, insists that it was only with the publication of *Die Gartenlaube* that all the characteristic elements of the new medium were united for the first time.

Barth's criteria, which are in any case too rigid and not concerned enough with the dynamic aspects of the genre, are of little concern to us here, but the success these new German journals would soon enjoy is one indication of why publishers like Lange persisted in issuing *Die Abendschule* in the United States. The reward could be enormous, and the new journals' goals, which were often summarized in a subtitle as "*Belehrung und Unterhaltung*" (Instruction and Entertainment), were worthwhile, even admirable.[18] Building on the success of a weekly paper called the *Illustrirter Dorfbarbier* (The Illustrated Village Barber), in which *Die Gartenlaube* originated as a supplement, Keil managed to sell 5,000 copies a week during the first year of publication. Two years later that number was at 14,500, almost tripled but still not enough to cover the cost of production; but the fifth year, however, the magazine could boast some 60,000 subscribers. From that point onward *Die Gartenlaube* was a very profitable undertaking, and, in spite of interruptions caused by a

[18]See Barth, *Zeitschrift für Alle*, 175–77.

ban in Prussia in 1864, revenues must have soared until 1875, when the journal reached its high point of 382,000 subscriptions. By then family journals were beginning to feel the pressure of competition from illustrated newspapers, but *Die Gartenlaube* was still able to maintain the respectable number of 275,000 subscribers until 1895. In 1906, however, only 100,000 remained.[19] By contrast, Gutzkow's *Unterhaltungen*, which presumed explicitly that its readers were "well educated," was never able to attract more than 7,000 subscribers, and the average was closer to 5,000.[20] Gutzkow himself abandoned the project in 1862, and the *Unterhaltungen am häuslichen Herd* ceased to appear altogether in 1864.

Of course, other publishers quickly copied Keil's initiative, and dozens of family journals competed with *Die Gartenlaube* for the rest of the century and beyond. In a strictly literal sense, one could certainly number *Die Abendschule* among those competitors; Arndt and Olson claim that, of the journal's 30,000 subscribers, some 584 were residents of Germany.[21] In addition, as we shall see in Chapter 4, *Die Abendschule* feared competition in the other direction, and its editors were quick to admonish readers not to subscribe to various periodicals from Germany that were regularly sold in the United States (XVIII, 2).[22] Besides *Die Gartenlaube*, which remained the prototypical example of the genre and which was also the most successful German family journal throughout the nineteenth century, the ire of at least one of *Die Abendschule*'s editors was aroused by *Daheim* (At Home), a journal that began to appear in Leipzig in 1864. Since the project behind *Daheim* was similar to the expressed intentions to be discussed in connection with the founding of *Die*

[19]See ibid., 323–25. Strictly speaking, before *Familienblätter* were sent regularly through the mail—that is, when they were still sold chiefly by colporteurs (itinerant booksellers)—it is probably not correct to speak of subscribers, but because I argue that reading them was a family affair, to speak simply of readers would suggest far too small a number in that category.

[20]The quotation is from *Unterhaltungen* no. 1 (1855) and is quoted in Barth, *Zeitschrift für Alle*, 297. For the history of the magazine in general, see ibid., 286–98. Unlike Gutzkow's journal, the intended audience of pre-1850 newspapers and periodicals was often clear from their titles—e.g., the Leipzig journal *Zeitung für die elegante Welt* (Newspaper for the Elegant World) or Cotta's *Morgenblatt für gebildete Stände* (The Educated Classes' Morning Paper).

[21]Arndt and Olson, *German-Language Press*, 247.

[22]The German-American bookseller E. Steiger claims to have sold 7,500 copies of *Die Gartenlaube* in 1867; see E. Steiger, *Vertrieb deutscher Bücher und Zeitschriften in den Vereinigten Staaten* (New York, 1868), 27.

Abendschule, and since, as we shall see shortly, there was a more than coincidental relationship between their respective mastheads, *Daheim* merits a brief history here too.

Barth quotes the publisher, August Klasing, at some length, and a portion of his programmatic statement is worth repeating here because it indicates why the editors and the publisher of *Die Abendschule* seem to have regarded *Daheim* with a mixture of envy and fear: "In the course of the last several months," Klasing wrote, "I have been repeatedly implored to publish an illustrated magazine like *Die Gartenlaube*, but in contrast to it and its relatives, one based firmly on a Christian world view. This does not simply imply maintaining a morally uplifting tone and corresponding tendentiousness, but rather a literary (*belletristisch*) journal whose orientation and presuppositions are Christian."[23]

The program behind *Daheim* was close enough to the goals of its German-American counterpart for *Die Abendschule* to fear losing actual or potential subscribers to a foreign competitor, and the danger was compounded precisely because *Daheim* spoke to the very same conservative, Christian, German-immigrant families that *Die Abendschule* wanted to attract for itself. Moreover, in contrast to the struggling publication in St. Louis, *Daheim* was an immediate, if moderate, success. By the end of the first year of publication, the new journal could boast of some 24,000 subscribers, and while it was never able to match *Die Gartenlaube, Daheim* nevertheless reached the comfortably profitable figure of 44,000 subscribers by the early 1870s, a number that it was apparently able to maintain until the end of the century.[24] *Die Abendschule*, meanwhile, was barely staying afloat; in 1870, ten years after Lange had acquired the magazine, there were still only 7,000 subscribers.[25] In the United States, however, in the final third of the nineteenth century, that comparatively small number of paid subscriptions must have provided sufficient income to publish a magazine.

Besides their illustrated mastheads, one characteristic feature of the family journals was that they almost invariably contained other illustrations. It is significant that the images they published were not intended to be simply ornamentation but rather were part of these

[23]Letter from August Klasing to his son, 15 September 1862, quoted in Barth, *Zeitschrift für Alle*, 346.
[24]Barth, "Das Familienblatt," 237–40.
[25]Arndt and Olson, *German-Language Press*, 248.

journals' attempts to garner readers by providing them with easily understood texts. In other words, pictures and diagrams could often help readers comprehend an otherwise difficult concept or process. From the outset, however, the *Illustri[e]rte Abendschule* suffered from the difficulty of procuring the requisite illustrations. The first publisher had promised "26 issues a year containing approximately 80 high-quality woodcuts" (I, 3), but such illustrations were expensive, and the ready-made images available commercially were often inappropriate.[26] As a result, issues or articles were sometimes delayed for want of an illustration, and occasionally some contained no pictures at all. The high cost of woodcuts was also blamed for the journal's precarious financial situation.[27] Finally, in 1863, in the midst of the Civil War, the publisher decided to eliminate most of the illustrations rather than increase subscription rates (IX, 97). Thereafter, although it still contained the occasional illustration, *Die Illustri[e]rte Abendschule* became simply *Abendschule: Eine Zeitschrift für Belehrung und Unterhaltung* (Abendschule: A Magazine for Instruction and Entertainment). The corresponding change in the journal's masthead will be discussed below; here it is only important to note that the 1863 masthead itself continued to be illustrated, as were all subsequent mastheads until 1907. After 1881, when the magazine's fortunes improved considerably, *Die Abendschule* was once again illustrated, and it bore the subtitle *Ein illustriertes Familienblatt* (An Illustrated Family Journal) (see Figure 9).

The first issue of *Die Abendschule*, volume one, number one, appeared under the relatively complex masthead mentioned at the outset of this chapter (see Figure 1). Unfortunately, the collection of images it contains were produced as woodcuts and printed on poor-quality paper, with the result that the earliest masthead is somewhat difficult to decipher. With the aid of a magnifying glass and access to the yellowing originals, however, a fairly accurate reading is still possible. For example, as an indication of the journal's Christian orientation the left-hand image contains a triumphant Christ-figure,

---

[26]An examination of these illustrations would be an interesting topic for an article. In the volume for 1860–61, which I surveyed systematically, they ranged from "A Statue of Washington on Horseback" and "Fuad Pascha, the Turkish Grand Vizier" to "The Parrot Family" and the "Saar Castle."

[27]See, e.g., Alexander Saxer, "Gott zum Gruss dem geneigten Leser" (V,1), "Vorwort" (VI, 1), or "An die Leser" (VI, 41), where mention is made of the difficulty and expense of procuring illustrations.

while the image to the right suggests the diversity of the world's heathen population. From left to right the figures depict an American Indian, an Oriental, and an African-American, all situated for some reason in an Oriental landscape, probably because, as Edward Said would argue, the Orient was the classic location for the "other."[28] In a sense the three men represent the *objects* of Christian missionary work, which is almost by definition located elsewhere: the *other* in an-*other* place. The central image is far more interesting because it contains the clearest suggestion about how the magazine is to be read—aloud, to the familial gathering of listeners. Note, however, the cherub to the left, who seems to be peering into an opening that also permits our gaze. The view is only partial, for the frame in no way indicates that the space of the family is this limited. Aside from the two cherubs, the other of whom is reading the Bible, the central picture contains nine figures. Judging by their ages, they seem to represent an extended family seated at a table in a richly decorated parlor. The proliferation of objects in mid-century bourgeois homes was a sign of wealth and status. The oldest male (presumably the grandfather) is reading aloud to the group, while the oldest female (perhaps his wife) is knitting. The girl at her feet appears to be holding a tablet or a slate, while the rest of the figures (some mixture of sons, daughters, their spouses, and two more children) are listening intently to what is being read. Overall, the image depicts reading as a family activity with clearly defined gender—and age-specific roles.[29]

To judge by its initial masthead, *Die Abendschule* was not intended for solitary enjoyment; one of its purposes was to bond these related but nevertheless disparate individuals together by providing a common activity for the family as a whole, here defined as the extended family. No matter what texts *Die Abendschule* contained, the ideal mode of reading them is apparent from one glance at the masthead. And, to return to the perspective of the masthead as a whole for a moment, it was apparently the reading family that was to mediate between the heathens and Christ. After all, there is certainly a

[28]Edward Said, *Orientalism* (New York: Pantheon, 1978).
[29]For a recent critique of the representation of gender, see Susanne Kappeler, *The Pornography of Representation* (Minneapolis: University of Minnesota Press, 1986). In conversation, e.g., Kappeler argues (p. 193): "The speaking function is masculine, the listening function and silence are feminine."

Figure 2

wealth of biblical precedence for stressing the importance of verbal
texts (e.g., John 1:1, "In the beginning was the Word.") and the role
of narratives (parables) in teaching.

Seen in this light, the shift in 1855 from the first masthead to the
second is quite dramatic (see Figure 2). Not only is the imagery far
less elaborate, but the reader is a middle-aged man who is studying a
paper by himself. Cost-cutting and the search for a format that
would attract more subscribers shrank *Die Abendschule* from
roughly half a newspaper-size page to about a quarter sheet (quarto
to octavo) after the first year, and this change alone meant that the
paper needed a new, smaller masthead. The diminished size, complexity, and quality of the image may well have been dictated by
financial exigencies, but the results must have been disappointing,
because three years later even this meager illustration disappeared
from the masthead for the next two volumes. Whatever the underlying reason for the small and poor-quality image that graced the magazine's masthead in volumes two and three, the interesting point is
that there was a marked, and to my mind unexplainable, contradiction between the image of the lone adult male reader and the journal's subtitle. The magazine's full title remained *Illustri[e]rte Abend-
Schule: Zur Belehrung und Unterhaltung für die reifere Jugend* until
volume five, when the limiting phrase "for more mature young people" was dropped. The shortened subtitle is interesting first because
it suggests that there was always a double audience; literature intended for children or, to be precise, for somewhat more mature
youths must appeal both to the young listeners and to their parents,
who were to read it to them. Second, the truncation of the title must
be understood as a marketing ploy. Parents read the texts, but because they also controlled their children's disposable income they
were the only part of the audience that really mattered. Indeed, if the
journal was to succeed, it had to broaden its appeal and attempt to

engage the whole family with the texts it offered. Still, whether the subtitle was short or long, the fundamental contradiction remains; little entertainment is visible in the image of the solitary reader on this masthead.

One should not, however, dismiss the notion of *"Belehrung und Unterhaltung"* quite so quickly. As we have already seen, the combination was a typical feature in the programs of German family journals, the genre to which *Die Abendschule* must ultimately be reckoned. Of course, the topos is much older. The claim that poetry and other literary texts (*Dichtung*) should instruct or enlighten as well as entertain is almost as old as literature itself, and the question of whether literary texts could somehow do both, or whether they and their authors should concentrate on one or the other, for which they would then be tolerated or applauded, coursed through the debates on rhetoric and aesthetics from classical times through the eighteenth century. Horace, whose formulation was so often quoted by educated eighteenth- and nineteenth-century Europeans that his solution became a commonplace, managed to distill the essence of the controversy in his *Ars Poetica* as follows: "aut prodesse volunt aut delectare poetae." Commentators have argued about the meaning of the phrase ever since. They wonder whether Horace meant to say that "poets *either* aim to benefit, *or* to amuse," as the *Loeb Classical Library* version would have it, or whether it would be more accurate to suggest that the "aut . . . aut" construction is not to be taken as exclusionary, that it really means "both . . . and."[30] But although scholarly opinion, which is based on a reading of the whole text and the traditions on which the text built, is clearly in favor of the latter, more inclusive interpretation,[31] the phrase was probably just as often quoted out of context (it appears in Büchmann's *Geflügelte Worte* [Winged Words—i.e., Familiar Quotations] as a self-contained proverb) and was probably intended to convey the exclusive meaning. No doubt to avoid confusion and to make a strongly buttressed statement about his own art, when he used it as the motto for

[30]H. Rushton Fairclough, *Horace: Satires, Epistiles, and Ars Poetica* (1926, Cambridge: Harvard University Press, 1978), 479 (emphasis added). To be fair, Fairclough's translation of the complete sentence is "Poets aim either to benefit, or to amuse, or to utter words at once both pleasing and helpful to life."

[31]See, e.g., C. O. Brink, *Horace on Poetry*, 2: vols. *Prolegomena to the Literary Epistles* and *The Ars Poetica* (Cambridge: Cambridge University Press, 1963 and 1971) 2:352–53, 504–5. Specifically, he says Horace tells "the poet to instruct as well as delight" (1:263).

his "Neueröffnetes moralisches-politisches Puppenspiel" (Newly Opened, Moral and Political Puppet Show), Goethe rendered the phrase "*et* prodesse volunt *et* delectare poetae."[32] Significantly, Goethe's version is only intended to mean "both . . . and." Moreover, the fact that Goethe did not feel obliged to cite the source behind his version of the quotation indicates that Horace's phrase was indeed common currency among educated Germans, who would have known the source and understood the point of his modification. And there can be little doubt that *Die Abendschule*'s editors were mindful both of the tradition and of its discontents when they chose the journal's original subtitle.

For *Die Abendschule* and its potential public, however, the phrase "*Belehrung* UND *Unterhaltung*" automatically opens up a grave if only potential moral dilemma. If the two poles were understood as an opposition—that is, if the magazine provided both, while individual texts were either instructive or entertaining, then no matter how harmless the latter might be some danger still lurked there. Apparently mindful of the difficulty, Alexander Saxer, a subsequent editor who was also a pastor and professor of theology in St. Louis, informed his readers in the introduction to volume five: "Entertainment, when correctly understood, is simply whatever contains, as its heart and soul, elements of character formation or education (*Bildungselemente*)" (V, 1). His statement seems to represent a kind of fear, and it marks an attempt to distance *Die Abendschule* from purely secular journals, a goal that was in fact at the heart of the whole enterprise. Education and entertainment had to be Christian if they were to be the basis of the community *Die Abendschule* was attempting to create, but the magazine also had to be attractive enough to win over readers who might be attracted to other journals and thereby fall victim to a very different form of temptation and be lost to the Christian community. On the other hand, Saxer's interpretation was also firmly within the tradition of classical humanism.

With the shift back to quarto format in 1860, it was again time for a new masthead (Figure 3). Although this third masthead, taken as a whole, is still somewhat crude, the borders have nevertheless reacquired a certain richness, and the solitary reader is not nearly as somber as his predecessor. A bit of nature intrudes into the otherwise enclosing space defined by the capital "I." Note, however, that

---

[32]*Goethes Werke*, vol. 16 (Weimar: Herman Böhlau, 1894), p. 1 The "Neueröffnetes moralisches-politisches Puppenspiel" was originally published in 1774. (emphasis added).

Figure 3

unlike the previous, older figure, whose dress was contemporary, the young man in this masthead is dressed as a scholar from an earlier age. His contemplative pose and the assortment of books and scientific instruments at his feet are far more suggestive of "instruction" or "education" than "entertainment," even though the masthead's typography emphasizes entertainment at the expense of education. The capital "U" of "Unterhaltung" is larger and fancier. Education now seems to be defined more narrowly as the product of schooling and to be limited to the acquisition of concrete skills and knowledge rather than to indicate moral improvement (*Bildung*), which could be the result of training in the arts. Of course, this is a very narrow reading of the image of the scholar, but the contrast between the subtitle and the masthead seems to indicate a lingering confusion on the part of the editors about *Die Abendschule*'s identity and that of its intended audience. The phrase "for more mature young people" was dropped at the same time that the figure represented became markedly younger—though not under the age of sixteen, which the missing portion of the subtitle would have suggested. Moreover, even though German immigrants in this period generally came from the ranks of dispossessed peasants and artisans, this masthead appeals to the professional classes or to the males who would enter them. Or, read somewhat less restrictively in order to include the educated middle class (*Bildungsbürgertum*), the masthead's implication is that readers of *Die Abendschule* could lay claim both to the achievements of modern science and to the rewards of a classical humanist education, and enjoy themselves in the process.

The next masthead, which began to be used in 1863, oddly

Figure 4

enough in the middle of Volume IX, continued the magazine's initial uncertain appeal (see Figure 4). The entire masthead is plainer. The hard times that had befallen the journal were represented graphically; the only ornamentation the magazine, now no longer *Illustri[e]rte Abend-Schule* but rather simply *Abend-Schule*, could afford was the grouping around the letter "A." Here two women, presumably "Education and Entertainment," flank one another, though the figure on the left looks anything but amused. Again the clothing is not contemporary, but this time vaguely classical, and one could easily term the two women muses. It is significant that the two figures are subordinate to the Christian symbol of the cross, which is formed by the elaborate crossbar of the "A"; note the rays of light that stream from it. Overall, this masthead also suggests that readers of *Die Abendschule* were still heirs of classical traditions, but only to the extent that such learning was put to the service of Christianity.

Figure 5

Figure 6

Just what the figure on the right represents as a reader is nevertheless unclear; the woman's mien and pointing gesture are those of the
teacher—curiously enough for the early 1860s a female teacher and
the first female reader in *Die Abendschule*—but her audience,
whether a family or students, is missing. The overall message is confusing and ultimately unclear.

This decade of iconographic uncertainty changed abruptly in
1867, when *Die Abendschule*'s masthead returned to the family orientation of the first volume, but this time with a very different family (Figure 5). What the new subtitle, "Ein Deutsches Familienblatt"
(A German Family Journal), means is well illustrated by the figures
grouped in and around the capital "D," and it was as a family journal that *Die Abendschule* was to prosper until well into the twentieth century. It is interesting to note, however, that the whole
concept was stolen from the successful German journal—the potentially dangerous competitor from Leipzig, *Daheim*. In 1864, when
Daheim was founded, its publishers engaged the well-known illustrator Ludwig Richter to design a masthead (Figure 6).[33] Not only
are the two magazines' subtitles identical, but the image of the fam-

---

[33]For more on *Daheim*, see Dieter Barth, "Das Daheim und sein Verleger August
Klasing: Eine kultur- und zeitgeschichtliche Untersuchung über ein deutsches Fami-
lienblatt des XIX. Jahrhunderts," *Jahresbericht des Historischen Vereins für die
Grafschaft Ravensberg* 66 (1968–69): 43–110.

Figure 7

ily in *Die Abendschule*'s masthead is virtually an exact copy of the family in *Daheim*. The central group has simply been cropped to fit inside the "D," while another daughter was added to fill in the space previously occupied by the grandfather's knees. The resulting composition, whether accidental or not, has important implications. If one includes the young boy linked to the figures in the "D" by his gaze, the framed portion of the image portrays the nuclear family. The grandfather has been reversed—that is, turned away from the rest of the family—and placed outside the encircling "D." Indeed, he is but marginally connected with the remaining members of the family, not only outside their sphere but also physically outdoors, outside of the home. The servant or grandmother in *Daheim's* image has disappeared completely. The act of reading aloud now reinforces the ideal of the bourgeois nuclear family as a self-sufficient community and refuge, and the accepted, gender-specific division of labor in that developing institution extends to roles for the father as reader and for the rest of the family as listeners. Once again the assemblage of subject positions provides a clear indication of the masthead's function in preprogramming a specific mode of reception.

Judging by the rest of the masthead, prosperity seems to have returned to the journal. Not only is the space that surrounds the title and the illustration richly ornamented, but the publisher's name is featured much more prominently than before—carved in stone, no less. The engraver and the artist responsible for the theft from *Daheim* are also indicated, but the Christian motif has disappeared. The readers no longer bask in the light of a cross; an owl now occupies the "A."

Figure 8

If this all seems too neat, the next masthead, which began to appear in 1873, illustrates the danger of too facile an interpretation and of an all too linear historical trajectory (see Figure 7). Here *Die Abendschule*'s model family is once more composed of three generations, for whom reading is again a solitary occupation. What this masthead suggests is that a number of modes of reading must have existed or been advocated simultaneously. Especially for women, reading apparently could be a solitary occupation, a useful diversion like needlework or knitting, performed while the patriarch was "working." This image of women reading certainly cannot be taken to mean that they were allowed to read aloud to the rest of the family. The gender-specific division of labor continues, and the separation of labor from the home, which was so important in shrinking the economy of the entire household (*das ganze Haus*) to the more limited relationships of the nuclear family, is also apparent. Significantly, the family is now spread across a landscape at whose center is a church. Oddly, however, the two women appear to be reading in a cemetery, and while the younger woman is reading from a large bound volume, perhaps the previous year's *Abendschule*, the elderly woman seems to be holding a devotional book. Again the message is mixed. Because, as we shall see, *Die Abendschule*'s primary appeal was to conservative Lutherans, the central position of the church—the first overtly Christian element since the first masthead—is not at all surprising. What is interesting is that the images to the left (e.g., the man's clothing, particularly his hat) and to the right (the wagon train) are obviously very American. *Die Abend-*

Figure 9

schule still calls itself "A German family journal," but the German element is gradually becoming German-American.

The Americanization of the subject positions accorded *Die Abendschule*'s readers continued in the next masthead (see Figure 8). The change seems to have been prompted by a short-lived return to the quarto format in 1877, but it was retained when the journal shrunk for the next volume. Incidentally, in the larger version it is clear that the man is reading from *Die Abendschule*. The church in the background could be almost anywhere, but the rest of the landscape, particularly the family seated together on the front porch of a wooden house, is decidedly American. Although the setting is rural, the family itself is universally bourgeois. The father figure can afford to read to his wife and children at sundown while hired hands drive his livestock to the barn. The separation of home life from the world of work is nearly complete, and there is also a certain class differentiation implied in the division of labor. Not only are men divided into those who work with their hands and others who profit from that labor, but the women who are not agricultural laborers appear to be virtually confined to the house. In fact, there are no steps coming down from the porch—which if it was a mistake on the part of the illustrator is a telling one; without a few steps, the occupants of the porch are denied access to the world beyond their porch. Yet, even if they could enter it physically, the wife or older daughter in the image seems to be looking wistfully at a world that is socially and economically quite distant. The woman's assigned role is purely domestic, cut off from the "productive" world of work. Indeed, in this illustration even her "reproductive" function is limited; child care does not appear to include the transmission of familial norms and values through reading. As participants in the world of *Die Abendschule*, the two older women and the other man, perhaps an acquaintance, are passive; they are the "read-to," not the readers.

That same mode of reception for women is characteristic of the three females in *Die Abendschule*'s final illustrated masthead, which the paper bore from 1881 to 1907 (Figure 9). Here the two older women listen while carrying out tasks that are identifiably "feminine." Note too that while the younger son is reading, his considerably older sister can only watch and listen. This is not to argue that the women in any of these pictures were illiterate; women of the class of people portrayed in *Die Abendschule*'s mastheads could no doubt read and write, as well as play the piano and sew. The significant element in the iconography of three of the last four mastheads, however, is that the position assigned to the women as readers (the "read-to") is subordinate to the man's role as patriarch (reader or lector). He is once again reading what is identifiably *Die Abendschule*. The pipe-smoking gentleman in all three images is either the last remnant of an extended family or, because he seems to have become much younger in the last two mastheads, a somewhat older friend of the family and the man's wife. In this reading the ideal bourgeois family has become smaller, but it is more important to note that its relatively new function as a refuge from the world of commerce and industry is underlined by the fact that the external reality of labor has now been completely banished from the masthead. In the almost thirty years since the publication of its first masthead, *Die Abendschule*'s family of model readers first left farm work and then the farm itself behind. This final family of readers is no longer part of the so-called old middle class of artisans and independent producers, but rather members of the bourgeoisie in a thoroughly capitalist world. In fact, the men depicted here are probably supposed to represent the white-collar employees of some form of corporate capitalism, a system whose triumph was actually only beginning to be felt in 1881, while the bourgeois family itself had been developing in the direction of the nuclear family ever since the late eighteenth century.

One could also read this final image in a way that undermines the trajectory toward the bourgeois nuclear family that I have posited until now. The final masthead could once again represent an extended family. In this interpretation, it is the older couple's son or

Figure 10

son-in-law, and not the actual patriarch of an extended family, who is reading, while his wife sews and the children's grandmother entertains the youngest child. In this reading the extended family has returned as a nostalgic gesture, a nostalgia reinforced by the details in the image of the older male. In contrast to his son, the man sports a full beard and is smoking an exaggeratedly long pipe. It is, in fact, virtually the same pipe as the one favored by the elderly gentleman in the fifth masthead (Figure 5), and it could well signify both a yearning for that simpler age of large, intact families and for the ethnic component of that lost world. The reextended family in this reading exists in the same compensatory relationship to reality as the artisans and independent farmers who populate *Die Abendschule*'s narratives. Reading conceived of as a group activity provides precisely the same refuge as the one contained in the texts they read.

No matter which interpretation of the family is accurate, that this particular family idyll takes place outdoors is not surprising when we remember that the preeminent family journal in nineteenth-century Germany was *Die Gartenlaube* (see Figure 10). Indeed, the two magazines' mastheads are similar, and it is not unlikely that *Die Abendschule*'s final masthead was somehow derivative. Both are called illustrated family journals, *Die Abendschule* having dropped the word "German" from its subtitle, a change I will return to in Chapter 5. There are nonetheless a number of subtle but significant differences between the two versions of the reading family. While the vision of the outdoors represented in *Die Gartenlaube*'s masthead is that of a garden—where other, presumably unrelated people are visible in the background—*Die Abendschule*'s family is reading inside the enclosed space of a porch—that is, on the border between the security of the home and nature, where the heathens of the initial masthead might still be lurking. In addition, because *Die Gartenlaube* kept the same masthead it had at its founding in 1853, its image of the family had not kept pace with developments within the bourgeoisie. One reason for the constancy of the image might well have been the continued popularity in Germany of Riehl's version of the family, which was not really challenged until the 1890s. Then too, the magazine's immediate and lasting success no doubt mitigated against changes in its recognizable trademark. In any case, *Die Gartenlaube*'s family is clearly composed of three generations, and power within that family is still invested in the grandfatherly type, who is doing the reading. On the other hand, the German women represented there are assigned the same subordinate roles as their German-American counterparts.

The other significant difference between *Die Gartenlaube* and *Die Abendschule* can be seen in the images that surrounded the latter's central image of the family. Not only does the lack of a church in this final masthead suggest an increasing degree of secularization within the German-American community, but the two flanking pictures (perhaps a paddle wheeler on the Mississippi and a train through the American wilderness) also both point to technological triumphs associated with the journal's home in St. Louis. Curiously, it was the railroad that sounded the death knell for the steamboat, but the steamboat was apparently as much a nostalgic, idealized symbol as the extended bourgeois family. Both the steamboat and the nuclear family were products of the initial, positive phase of modernization and industrialization, but by the end of the nineteenth century the steamboat had virtually disappeared, while the extended family as a production unit was clearly threatened by the economy's continued development. For ever-increasing numbers of people in the United States during the 1880s and 1890s, although perhaps not for *Die Abendschule*'s idealized bourgeois readers, it was no longer easy for a family's women and children to lead a life of cultured leisure; working-class women and their children were increasingly being forced into the labor market. Thus *Die Abendschule*'s mastheads should be seen not as somehow reflecting reality but as depicting social roles that were as much a compensation or a refuge from reality as an accurate representation of it. They were images of what someone imagined that family should be, not what it actually was.

In 1872, for example, in the fourth section of a six-part article on the moral state of the population of the United States, *Die Abend-schule*'s editor warned of the dangers that loomed if German-American women tried to act like ladies (*Damen*) rather than house-wives—which he believed was just as dangerous as a family's decision to live in a boardinghouse rather than establish their own home. The editor contrasted those gloomy prospects with his jour-nal's ideal (specifically mentioning the masthead *Die Abendschule* bore at the time [see Figure 5]):

> some dear readers, who gather around the table with all the members of their family, large and small, after a day's hard work, approximately as is represented in our masthead illustration. Then one of them, either the father, the newly literate (*lesefertig*) son, or one of the daughters, reads from *Die Abendschule* to his or her brothers and sisters, parents and relatives, and also to the visiting friend of the household, after which they all sing a pious song and edify themselves through their shared evening prayers. Meanwhile, the peaceful mother of the house is attempting to teach the smallest member of the family in the cradle his first words in the form of a short prayer, as a companion for the night and for life. . . . (XVIII, 137–38)

The importance this quotation gives to the journal's own visual im-age of the family reading together demonstrates quite clearly that the iconography of *Die Abendschule*'s mastheads was far more than mere ornamentation. *Die Abendschule* attempted to produce readers in its own image and to reinforce their self-images, and both activ-ities were located in a social-historical moment that proffered imag-inary solutions to the very real pressures inflicted on the family in the course of the nineteenth century. Of particular interest in the series of icons contained in these mastheads is, first, the gradual shift in the image of the ideal family as it shrank from the extended to the nuclear family, perhaps to be replaced finally by a deliberately nos-talgic version of an older, idealized form of the family, and, second, the manner in which that family was integrated into the time and space of America. Furthermore, as depicted in *Die Abendschule*'s mastheads, the bourgeois family was an assemblage of age-specific and gender-specific roles for readers. It is worth noting that in the previous quotation, for example, the order of readers was first the father, then the son (if he is able to read), and only last the daugh-ters of the family, although they are presumably older and long since literate. The mother never comes into question as a reader, for what father would busy himself with an infant while his wife took over such an important, male role? Thus, as I claimed at the outset, the social act of reading and the subject positions it implied were as important as the contents of the texts published in *Die Abendschule*, although as the analysis of various texts in the chapters that follow will demonstrate, the narratives and visual images in no way contradict one another. Before turning to those verbal texts, however, the next step is to locate the men and women who actually read *Die Abendschule*.

CHAPTER TWO

Ethnicity and
Ethnic Literature

At first, the question of who read *Die Abendschule* seems easy enough to answer. Except for those who received the relatively few copies sent abroad, its readers were German-Americans. But defining just who the German-Americans were is a problem with as many solutions as there are ways of framing the inquiry. Does one speak of language loyalty, of national origin, or of a particular residual or perhaps acquired consciousness? Was whatever it meant to be a German-American transmitted to the descendants of German immigrants automatically or was it learned behavior? In other words, did German-American ethnicity, to the extent that it ever existed, persist into the second and third generations, or even to the present day? Can one even speak of *the* German-Americans, or did the German immigrants who came to the United States initially form a number of separate and distinct groups, which remained disparate for decades? And if there were German-Americans, what consequences did that identity as one or several groups have for their own lives and for the cultural, political, and social orientation of the United States? Specifically, for the purposes of this study, was there a distinctive German-American literature? If so, what were its distinguishing features? In addition, did the narratives that German-Americans read make any difference in their lives, and what can those texts tell subsequent readers?

A word of caution is in order at the outset. This chapter is not intended to answer all these questions. To the extent that they can be answered by material in *Die Abendschule*, those answers can come only in subsequent chapters from a detailed examination of the magazine's contents. What is important here is to survey the manner in which these questions have been raised in the past in an effort to decide how best to frame the analysis of *Die Abendschule* that follows.

Although German-American literature has been studied relatively little in recent years, the few scholars who have turned their attention to writings by, for, and about immigrants disagree, sometimes vehemently, about that literature's definition and significance. Since I claim that texts like those published in *Die Abendschule* are valuable as objects of inquiry, the chapter analyzes the stakes that German-American texts raise for the study of German in the United States—as well as, implicitly, for the study of other ethnic and minority literatures, which have been just as marginalized within their respective "home" disciplines.

Particularly in light of German studies' rekindled interest in its own history[1]—an interest that is, not surprisingly, connected to concern about the diminishing role German departments play within the scholarly enterprise of American universities, where German now attracts the smallest number of students among the more commonly taught languages—the fate of those German-Americans who also thought of themselves as the bearers of German culture in the United States merits some attention. This book makes it possible, for example, to assess the degree to which German-Americans share responsibility for reducing German culture in the United States either to an arid classicism or to a caricature of Bavarian village life. And because this chapter in essence locates and justifies the overall project of reading of German-American literature, especially as a potentially important part of the task of German studies in the United States, it concludes with a suggestion for a new, reader-oriented method of defining just what the study of ethnic literatures entails. It purposely avoids the question of how to read such literatures, because Chapter 3 has an extended discussion of various strands of research into popular narratives as part of an analysis of the first substantial piece of fiction published in *Die Abendschule*.

Although the bare statistics of German emigration are readily

---

[1]See Valters Nollendorfs, "History of Teaching German in America," *Monatshefte* 79 (Fall 1987): 289–91. For a survey of German studies in the late nineteenth century, see Richard Spuler, *"Germanistik" in America: The Reception of German Classicism, 1870–1905* (Stuttgart: Akademischer Verlag Hans-Dieter Heinz, 1982).

available, they nevertheless warrant a quick recapitulation.[2] In the years from 1820 to 1928, some 6 million people emigrated from the territories that were to become the German Empire. In the heaviest years of emigration, from 1840 to 1910, some 5 million left—more than 90 percent of them bound for the United States. And in spite of the unknown number who may have returned home at some point, most stayed there. But even in these years, the progress of the exodus was anything but smooth. Figures developed by Friedrich Burgdörfer in the 1920s show distinct peaks developing in the years between 1850 and 1854, when more than 654,000 Germans entered the United States, and again in the period 1880–84, which saw 797,900 Germans arrive.

Historians of immigration have long debated whether such swings were the result of the "push" of conditions in the emigrants' native lands or the "pull" of opportunity in North America, but it now seems clear that a variety of factors conditioned a multitude of individual decisions.[3] One constant of interest here is the widespread scholarly agreement that the vast majority of emigrants were part of the surplus population (*Bevölkerungsüberschuss*) that developed when the rapid increase in the population of Europe during the eighteenth and nineteenth centuries was coupled with the pressures brought on by modernization and industrialization, which exposed traditional modes of production (i.e., small-scale agriculture, and cottage industries linked to the so-called putting-out system, or, as it is now called, proto-industrialization) to foreign competition. The

[2]Friedrich Burgdörfer, "Die Wanderungen über die deutschen Reichsgrenzen im letzten Jahrhundert" (1930), in Wolfgang Köllmann and Peter Marschalk, eds., *Bevölkerungsgeschichte* (Cologne: Kiepenheuer and Witsch, 1972), 281–322. Burgdörfer's statistics are reprinted in Peter Marschalk, *Deutsche Überseewanderung im 19. Jahrhundert* (Stuttgart: Klett, 1973), 48, which is also the best modern survey of German emigration. See also Marschalk's *Bevölkerungsgeschichte Deutschlands im 19. und 20. Jahrhundert* (Frankfurt am Main: Suhrkamp, 1984), esp. 27–52; and Mack Walker, *Germany and the Emigration, 1816–1885* (Cambridge: Harvard University Press, 1964).

[3]The controversy is summarized in numerous general treatments of immigration history. See, e.g., Maldwyn Allen Jones, *American Immigration* (Chicago: University of Chicago Press, 1960); Philip Taylor, *The Distant Magnet: European Emigration to the U.S.A.* (New York: Harper and Row, 1971); and John Bodner, *The Transplanted: A History of Immigrants in Urban America* (Bloomington: Indiana University Press, 1985). For a discussion of emigration to Missouri, home of *Die Abendschule*, see Walter Kamphoefner, "Transplanted Westfalians: Persistence and Transformation of Socioeconomic and Cultural Patterns in the Northwest German Migration to Missouri" (Ph.D. diss., University of Missouri, 1979).

resultant economy left many of the still predominantly rural wage earners of Germany temporarily without adequate means of support for themselves and their families. It was only after 1871, when the pace of industrialization in Germany began to quicken, that the German economy could begin to absorb that excess population in the rapidly growing cities of Saxony, the Ruhr basin, and elsewhere. In other words, the motivation behind emigration was primarily economic; political and religious factors were important in only an extremely small number of cases.

Even after the dislocations brought on by the Revolution of 1848, it was primarily independent craftsmen and farmers who emigrated to the United States; the "real" Forty-Eighters numbered at most only a few thousand. To be sure, two of the "immediate causes" for the surge of the early 1850s were connected with the events of 1848, but they had little if anything to do with the political turmoil of that year.[4] The real culprits were the potato famine and a credit crunch. Such immediate and pressing problems made an existence that was already difficult virtually impossible, and a huge wave of emigration was set in motion. In ideological terms, one significant result of these particular pressures was that German immigrants often hoped to find new and larger farms or bigger, more prosperous groups of customers for their trades; in short, they hoped to keep their old lifestyles intact. The fundamental conservatism that motivated emigrants produced a variety of interesting precipitates in the narratives they chose to read once they established themselves in the United States.

Yet having dismissed the political and religious factors behind the bulk of German emigration, one exceptional group, which was to play an important role in the consciousness of conservative German-Americans, needs to be examined. The people in question, namely, the collection of immigrants who eventually founded the "Lutheran Church—Missouri Synod," consisted of some seven hundred Saxons

[4]The term "immediate cause" is my translation of "*Anlass*," which Marschalk differentiates from "*Grund*," "underlying motivation," in his discussion of the reasons for emigration. See Marschalk, *Deutsche Überseewanderung*, 54–55. On the number of "political" emigrants after the Revolution of 1848, Marschalk cites Marcus Lee Hansen's pioneering study, "The Revolutions of 1848 and German Emigration," *Journal of Economic and Business History* 2 (1929/30): 630–58, in which Hansen argues that the revolution was primarily an urban phenomenon, while the source of German emigration was overwhelmingly rural—i.e., however prominent the Forty-Eighters in the United States were, their actual numbers were quite small.

who left Germany in 1839 at the behest of their charismatic leader
Martin Stephan.[5] Aside from Stephan's personal feelings of persecu-
tion, the main issue motivating the so-called Saxon immigration was
theological; conservative Lutherans in Saxony feared the imposition
of a reformed and unified state church on the Prussian model. Of
course, many of the original seven hundred may have also considered social and economic factors before emigrating. One historian
who studied the group, William Forster, has argued that, at the very
least, the weavers and agricultural workers who formed the bulk of
the Saxon emigration had no economic motive to stay in Saxony and
thus had no second thoughts about Stephan's plans, while other
members of the group were quite open in admitting a desire to improve their lot economically.[6] Whatever lay behind that initial migration, it is clear that the phenomenal growth of the church they
formed in the nineteenth century could not have been the result of
an influx of people who left Germany solely to worship with their
co-religionists in the United States. Beginning in 1847, with 22 pastors in 12 congregations comprising not more than 4,000 total members, the Synod had grown to 77,832 baptized members by 1872,
and to 728,240 by 1900. And even though group migration is generally believed to be characteristic of religiously motivated emigration,
only one other group joined the Stephanites. This particular band,
which also arrived in Missouri in 1839, by way of New York, was
already linked to Stephan in Saxony, but it numbered but 140 souls.[7]
The growth of the conservative German Lutheran community in the
United States came through the recruitment of individuals and families who often first heard of the church on arriving in the New
World. The Saxons were significant not only in that they were the
founders of that church but also because they were the religious exceptions that prove the economic rule of German emigration.

The specific set of beliefs that led to the formation of what later
became the Missouri Synod in 1847 as the Saxons gradually reor-
iented themselves following Stephan's excommunication for adultery
need not concern us here. Suffice it to say that the Synod's members
based their rigorously conservative faith on what is known as the
Augsburg Confession, which was written by Martin Luther and Phi-

[5]See William O. Forster, *Zion on the Mississippi: The Settlement of the Saxon
Lutherans in Missouri, 1839–1841* (St. Louis: Concordia Publishing House, 1953).
[6]Ibid., 151–57.
[7]Ibid., 483.

lipp Melanchthon in 1530 in an effort to differentiate their own beliefs from those of their Catholic opponents.[8] That oppositional stance remained characteristic of a group that specifically renounced "all unionism and syncretism" in its founding document.[9] That constitution also specified "exclusive use of the German language in the synodical conventions": "Only guests may speak in different languages to the Synod if they cannot speak the German language."[10] The latter provision, which was originally intended to preserve the doctrinal purity of Luther's writings in his original language, was also consciously employed in the maintenance of German culture. In fact, the sect's founders saw little reason to separate their faith from its cultural background. One of their important supporters in Germany, the theologian Wilhelm Löhe, who was responsible for sending a significant number of newly trained pastors to North America, put it this way in a letter to the German-Lutheran church in America:

> You're Germans. You've rescued a beautiful language across the ocean. Indeed, in the confused mass of languages that are spoken over there, none is more beautiful. Keep what you have. . . . If you lose your language, you also lose your history, and with it the easiest means of understanding the Reformation, and thereby the easier means of understanding the true church of God. . . . Surrender neither yourselves nor your children to foreign nations![11]

The church thus provided a ready home for those whose conservatism was not just religious.

The Lutheran Church–Missouri Synod was not the only Protestant denomination that appealed to nineteenth-century German immigrants in the United States, but its theological orientation was probably closer to mainstream Protestantism than it seems in retro-

---

[8]For a documentary history of the Synod, see Carl S. Meyer, ed., *Moving Frontiers: Readings in the History of the Lutheran Church—Missouri Synod* (St. Louis: Concordia Publishing House, 1964).

[9]"The 1854 Constitution of the Missouri Synod," chap. 2, par. 3, in Meyer, *Moving Frontiers*, 150.

[10]Meyer, *Moving Frontiers*, 150.

[11]Wilhelm Löhe, *Zuruf aus der Heimat an die deutsch-lutherische Kirche Nordamerikas* (Stuttgart, 1845), 1: 29–32, quoted in Reinhard R. Doerries, *Iren und Deutsche in der Neuen Welt: Akkulturationsprozesse in der amerikanischen Gesellschaft im späten neunzehnten Jahrhundert* (Stuttgart: Franz Steiner, 1986), *Vierteljahrschrift für Sozial-und Wirtschaftsgeschichte*, suppl. 76, 236.

spect. The bewildering array of Lutheran churches that have existed in the United States over the last 150 years was more the product of separate ethnic denominations, which were based on the language preference of pastors and parishioners, than the result of doctrinal differences. The resistance of the Lutheran Church–Missouri Synod to change—in part the result of the fact that it was never linked to a European state mother-church—has left it in the conservative wing of Lutheranism today, but that position is largely the result of a leftward shift in the amalgamated products of American ecumenicism, which were willing to compromise on various doctrines in pursuit of the goal of confessional unity. Prussian and other "Union" churches, for example, eventually landed in one or another of the North American Lutheran agglomerations that culminated in 1988 in the Evangelical Lutheran Church in America, which includes virtually all Lutherans in the United States—except for the Lutheran Church–Missouri Synod, the Wisconsin Synod, and a few lesser bodies. There were, of course, German-American Baptists, Methodists, Presbyterians, and even Episcopalians, to say nothing of various smaller sects and the approximately one-third of the German immigrant population that came from Catholic areas of Germany. There was also a culturally significant number of German-American Jews, but, at least for the nineteenth century, the Lutheran Church–Missouri Synod probably constituted the Protestant mainstream for German-Americans.

The name C. F. W. Walther (1811–87) is important in connection with the history of Lutheranism in the United States, and the moral authority he lent *Die Abendschule* in its early years makes him worth mention here too. As an early and fervent supporter of Stephan, Walther was a member of the initial Saxon immigration, but he was also instrumental in having Stephan removed from office for supposed immorality. It was then Walther who justified the emigration theologically and thereby paved the way for a separate German Lutheran church in the United States. In 1847, at the founding congress of the German-Evangelical Lutheran Synod of Missouri, Ohio, and Other States (Deutsche-Evangelische Lutherische Synode von Missouri, Ohio und anderen Staaten), Walther was elected to serve as the Synod's first president, and his journal, *Der Lutheraner* (The Lutheran), founded in 1844, was the Synod's official organ. In addition, Walther was pastor of the Synod's home congregation in St. Louis, a professor of theology, and president of the Synod's main seminary, and through his voluminous and often polemical writings he became the ultimate authority on virtually every question that might trouble conservative Lutherans during his long lifetime. He was also a passionate defender of things German and apparently unable to speak or understand English.

Very early on, the Synod came to see evangelism—that is, recruitment of new members—as an essential part of its mission.[12] Pastors were enjoined to visit every new German-speaking family or individual in their parish, and the Synod supported a number of colporteurs—or itinerant booksellers who provided newcomers with Bibles, hymnals, and information about the nearest Lutheran congregation. The Synod's instructions to its first appointed colporteur, one Gustav Pfau, appointed in 1852, specified that he had "the task primarily of looking for German Lutheran settlements and families which have no pastors."[13] The church was also active in sponsoring circuit preachers (*Reiseprediger*) and visitors (*Besucher*) who traveled to those areas where there were not yet enough German Christians to form a congregation. Because the shortage of ministers was a persistent problem, the duty was sometimes taken on by regular pastors who frequently had to be defended for their activities, because congregations often felt that their pastor had more than enough to do at home. If the potentially faithful were to be reached, however, and prevented from falling into the hands of some unorthodox sect, contact with the immigrants as soon as possible after their arrival in the United States, or at their final destination was an absolute necessity.

By 1867 the problem of preventing immigrants from falling into the wrong hands, which included those of the swindlers who crowded the docks of New York and other ports of entry, led to the founding of the Synod's Immigrant Mission.[14] Its first pastor, Stephanus Keyl, not only gave arriving German immigrants advice about jobs, lodging, transportation, and finding missing family members, but also distributed church papers and various tracts, including the *Deutscher Kalender* (German Calendar), which contained a list of all the Lutheran pastors in the United States and the usual compendium of useful dates, homilies and at least one short story (*Kalen-*

---

[12]For documents relating to "visitors," "colporteurs," and "circuit preachers," see Meyer, *Moving Frontiers*, 202–8.

[13]Ibid., 203–4.

[14]See Theo. S. Keyl, "The Life and Activities of Pastor Stephanus Keyl: The First Immigrant Missionary of the Missouri Synod, June 27, 1838–Dec. 15, 1905," *Concordia Historical Institute Quarterly* 22 (July 1949): 65–77.

dergeschichte). This meant that virtually every immigrant, no matter where he or she was headed, had the name of a German Lutheran pastor in or near that destination. Eventually the Mission purchased a hostelry across from Castle Gardens, the spot where most immigrants disembarked in the years before Ellis Island was opened in 1892, and a branch was also set up in Baltimore. Both branches maintained ties to representatives in the major German ports (chiefly Hamburg and Bremen) and served as unpaid agents for those who wanted to book passage for friends and relatives still in Germany. The effect of such work is impossible to measure precisely, but Keyl reported in his 1883 annual report to the Synod that he had distributed 3,000 calenders, 33,000 tracts, and 25,000 church papers; received 5,376 letters and sent 3,971; and in the process distributed some $78,000, which included $8,645.83 given to impoverished immigrants.[15]

As the Synod's membership rolls confirm, such work was not without effect. In fact, the church's phenomenal growth could only have resulted from immigration; there were simply not enough Germans already in the United States, especially in these areas of new settlement where the church was located to have provided so many members. In short, the German Evangelical Lutheran Synod of Missouri, Ohio, and Other States was an American institution. Immigration provided the raw material, but if the institution was to survive, those German immigrants had to be shaped into a community at whose center was the church.

The notion of community again raises the question posed at the outset: Who were the German-Americans? In spite of the nationalistic fervor of the Napoleonic era and 1848, before the unification of Germany in 1871, it is difficult to argue that very many people in what became the German Empire had any sense of their German identity. People still thought of themselves as Prussians, Saxons, Bavarians, or simply as the inhabitants of this or that village, which they generally had no expectation of ever leaving. It was only in the aftermath of the Franco-Prussian War that the ruling classes began to use the idea of the German nation systematically for their own purposes, and there was resistance even then.[16] For example, even

---

[15]S. Keyl, "Unsere Emigrantenmission im Jahre 1882," *Der Lutheraner*, 39 (15 February 1883): 28–29. See also W. Sallmann, "Bericht der Emigrantenmission in Baltimore für das Jahr 1882," *Der Lutheraner*, 39 (15 February 1883): 33.

[16]For a general discussion of the phenomenon see Eric Hobsbawm and Terence

though he might have celebrated Sedan Day enthusiastically, the new emperor still preferred to think of himself as the king of Prussia. And just as emigrants often had no clear sense of what being German meant, immigrants had to learn what it meant to be German-American.[17]

In a very real sense, nationalism and ethnicity were products of the same historical moment, and they were also a general European, if not a worldwide, phenomenon. Linking the two shows that the question of national identity was a problem not just for newly isolated minorities but for majorities as well. And the debate continues. In the United States it surfaces whenever someone proposes changes in the laws governing immigration and naturalization, and in Germany the conflict used to be joined most fervently over the rights and supposed dangers posed by people seeking asylum and by the so-called foreign or guest workers (*Gastarbeiter*). At present, the issue of German unification has shifted the focus of the debate. "The German nation"—its boundaries, its economy, its place in Europe— is *the* topic of conversation, but serious discussion of the historical constructedness of the concept has all but disappeared beneath the force of political expediency.

"The German question" will not disappear with reunification, far from it. Indeed, the dispute about Berlin rather than Bonn as the capital of a unified Germany, which is certainly not Bismarck's Germany "re-unified," to choose but one example, will probably be waged with the same acrimony that characterized the recent "historians' controversy" (*Historikerstreit*), because it will never be clear which city can rightly claim the legitimizing mantle of tradition.[18] As

---

Ranger, eds., *The Invention of Tradition* (Cambridge: Cambridge University Press, 1983).

[17]Benedict Anderson, *Imagined Communities: Reflections on the Origin and Spread of Nationalism* (London: Verso, 1983), foreshortens history considerably when he claims that rise of "print languages laid the bases for national consciousness" (p. 47). It took a long time for standard languages to penetrate and then eliminate dialect boundaries—if they ever succeeded, e.g., in contemporary Germany. And although learning standard German might have been one of the real changes in the lives of ordinary immigrants to the United States, cut off as they were from their home dialects, this book's focus is the variety of contents—i.e., ethnic identities—that were acquired along with the new language.

[18]See Hans-Ulrich Wehler, *Entsorgung der deutschen Vergangenheit? Ein polemischer Essay zum "Historikerstreit"* (Munich: Beck, 1988); and Richard J. Evans, *In Hitler's Shadow: West German Historians and the Attempt to Escape from the Nazi Past* (New York: Pantheon, 1989).

self-avowed bearers of German culture in the United States, German-Americans were caught up in the same dilemma their former countrymen faced in the nineteenth century and now in the twentieth. As a result, their history shares to no small degree the peculiar legacy of German history in Europe. Just as the present-day political implications of the German "peculiar development" (*Sonderweg*) continue to trouble German historiography,[19] so too is the broad question of German-American ethnicity—and indeed of ethnicity in general—more than a minor dispute best relegated to some marginalized antiquarians with their supposedly harmless filiopietism.

Although everyone knows that in the course of the nineteenth century the once largely "open" land of the United States was gradually "filled" by immigrants from Europe, Africa, Latin America, and the Far East, Rudolph J. Vecoli could still, as late as 1970, title his important survey of immigration historiography "Ethnicity: A Neglected Dimension of American History."[20] Vecoli argues that assimilationist historians have until recently largely ignored the histories of most of the nation's ethnic groups, because those historians assumed that the Germans, Poles, Japanese, and other immigrants who settled in the United States had or would gradually cease to exist as separate groups once the "melting pot" had done its work. The immigration history that did get written was therefore largely a history of the disappearance of its object of study, a process that was equated with the success of the whole American enterprise. Interpretations differed only to the extent that they constructed a different agent responsible for "disappearing" the immigrant. For the historian Frederick Jackson Turner, the frontier made "Americans" of the disparate men and women who lived there, while for the Chicago sociologist Robert Ezra Park the city performed the amalgamating work. Both men's interpretations were followed and elaborated on by generations of their students, and the histories they produced almost invariably include a quotation from that eigh-

---

[19]See David Blackbourn and Geoff Eley, *Peculiarities of German History: Bourgeois Society and Politics in Nineteenth-Century Germany* (New York: Oxford University Press, 1984), esp. Introduction, pp. 1–35, for an analysis of the controversies involved in the reception of the German edition of their book.

[20]Rudolph J. Vecoli, "Ethnicity: A Neglected Dimension of American History," in Herbert J. Bass, ed., *The State of American History* (Chicago: Quadrangle Books, 1970), 70–88.

teenth-century French visitor to the United States, Hector St. John Crèvecoeur, and often the following passage:

> He is an American, who, leaving behind him all his ancient prejudices and manners, receives new ones from the new mode of life he has embraced, the new government he obeys, and the new rank he holds. Here individuals of all nations are melted into a new race of men, whose labours and posterity will one day cause great changes in the world.[21]

Note that although Crèvecoeur (as quoted here) uses the word "melt" the idea of the "melting pot" is usually attributed to the playwright Israel Zangwill, who wrote a play titled "The Melting Pot" in 1908. That work's significance, as Werner Sollors has recently claimed, is that "more than any social or political theory, the rhetoric of Zangwill's play shaped American discourse on immigration and ethnicity, including most notably the language of self-declared opponents of the melting-pot concept."[22] In fact, "the resurgence of American immigration history" (words Vecoli used as the title of the survey of the field he wrote a decade after his first account),[23] was largely the product of two books governed by Zangwill's metaphor: *Beyond the Melting Pot* (1963), by Nathan Glazer and Daniel Patrick Moynihan, and *The Rise of the Unmeltable Ethnics* (1972), by Michael Novak. The two books shared the central premise that ethnicity persisted as a fact of political life in the present-day United States.[24] The difficulty in terms of the present book is

[21]Hector St. John Crèvecoeur, *Letters from an American Farmer* (New York: Dutton, 1957), 39, quoted in Vecoli, "Ethnicity," 74–75.
[22]Werner Sollors, *Beyond Ethnicity: Consent and Descent in American Culture* (New York: Oxford University Press, 1986), 66.
[23]Rudolph J. Vecoli, "The Resurgence of American Immigration History," *American Studies International* 17 (Winter 1979): 46–66. See also Vecoli's "Return to the Melting Pot: Ethnicity in the United States in the Eighties," *Journal of American Ethnic History* 5 (Fall 1985): 7–20.
[24]Nathan Glazer and Daniel Patrick Moynihan, *Beyond the Melting Pot: The Negroes, Puerto Ricans, Jews, Italians, and Irish of New York City* (Cambridge: M.I.T. Press, 1963); and Michael Novak, *The Rise of the Unmeltable Ethnics: Politics and Culture in the Seventies* (New York: Macmillan, 1975). Stephen Steinberg disputes these interpretations in his *The Ethnic Myth: Race, Ethnicity, and Class in America* (Boston: Beacon Press, 1981) by claiming that the discussion of ethnicity has generally been an attempt to mask the class divisions in American society. It is worth noting that Novak's discussion was conditioned both by the rise of black power in the 1960s and by the first inklings of a neoconservative debate on the shape of an

that the debate sparked by Glazer, Moynihan, and Novak has continued to center on the degree to which ethnicity survives as a relevant variable in people's lives today. While it is understandable that the scholars who are again turning to the history of immigration are motivated, at least in part, by contemporary concerns like "cultural pluralism," the question raised by *Die Abendschule* is not the survival of ethnicity but its origins and trajectory through the nineteenth and early twentieth centuries.

In a sense, the consolidation of the American republic in the 1780s, and the national identity the new nation offered its citizens, implied the existence of an "other," the noncitizen or foreigner. (Etymologically the word "ethnic" is directly linked to "otherness." Its root originally designated non-Jews or heathens in Greek translations of the Bible.) But because it was soon obvious that the United States would continue to depend on an influx of settlers, laws governing their acceptance into that developing body politic were already part of the legislative agenda of the first Congress that met under the federal Constitution. It is not surprising that the dispute over how and when someone—that is, a white male, because in the eighteenth and nineteenth centuries race and gender differences meant permanent, unalterable otherness—might become a citizen was intimately connected with the ruling party's perception of whom he would vote for. But even when a long waiting period limited voters for the "wrong" candidate, the historian Philip Gleason concludes, "the ease with which these standards could be met and the absence of adequate machinery to check the applicant's statements testified to confidence that a free, white person could become an American no matter what his national background or language."[25] Noncitizenship, which was essentially equal to the category of a person's unrenounced membership in an ethnic group, was simply a period of limbo before acquisition of an identity that was

emerging coalition in American elections—i.e., by Kevin Phillips, *The Emerging Republican Majority* (New Rochelle, N.Y.: Arlington House, 1969). On a related note, there is ample evidence that ethnicity is a global phenomenon; see Anthony D. Smith, *The Ethnic Revival* (Cambridge: Cambridge University Press, 1981). As will be demonstrated, the "postmodern" discussion of ethnicity is also resolutely present-minded.

[25]Philip Gleason, "American Identity and Americanization," *Harvard Encyclopedia of American Ethnic Groups* (1980), reprinted in William Peterson, Michael Novak, and Philip Gleason, *Concepts of Ethnicity* (Cambridge: Harvard University Press, 1982), 67.

primarily ideological in nature. Of course, in 1790, when eight out of ten white males in the territory of the United States were of British origin, it was easy to ignore the question of national origins. There had been strong outbreaks of nativist sentiment in the colonial period which were directed against Roman Catholics and against German enclaves in Pennsylvania, but it was not necessary to attempt to classify the white male "other" until the resumption of immigration following the end of the Napoleonic wars in 1815. In subsequent decades new modes of classification emerged, especially as immigration began to accelerate in the 1840s, when the newcomers were increasingly seen as a threat to the supposedly homogeneous citizenry already there.

Aside from the basic statistics of how many people arrived, much of what we know of immigrants in the United States is based on census data, which has included the category "foreign-born" ever since 1850. General information about the residence patterns, occupations, and living conditions of various ethnic groups exists only to the extent that census-takers were instructed to ask the right questions. For those registered as Germans before 1871, one difficulty is immediately apparent: Germany did not yet exist as a political entity, so the statistics must include a number of people who spoke German but who were not born within the borders of what would become the German Empire. And for some of the people who were born there—for example, Saxons, Bavarians, and Prussians—the question of national origin may have been puzzling, or it may have produced an answer that the census-takers were unequipped to deal with. In any case, in measurements based on the category "German" some slippage was inevitable. More important, the census data omits all subsequent generations, because it usually lists separately only those who were born abroad and does not include the children of immigrants, who were arguably as much part of an ethnic group as their foreign-born siblings.

Whether subsequent generations, and especially the third generation, were part of the group is a hotly debated issue.[26] For my purposes, however, what is interesting here is the Census Bureau's implicit belief that a person's country of origin defined a category of people who then were assumed to have exhibited various behaviors, both publicly and privately. For example, the interpreters of census

[26]For the classic statement on this issue, see Marcus Lee Hanson, "The Third Generation in America," *Commentary* 14 (November 1952): 492–500.

data report that in the nineteenth century German-born immigrants were concentrated in the triangle formed by Milwaukee, Cincinnati, and St. Louis; that they dominated the trade of brewing; and that they either did or did not vote for Lincoln in numbers large enough to have affected the outcome of the election of 1860[27]—as if those facts demonstrated something of a particular population's "Germanness." In short, although we know a good deal about what that category meant in terms of certain types of public behavior, particularly within the narrower confines of the political behavior of German-Americans, something significant is missing when German-American ethnicity is reduced to activities in the public sphere.

A typical example of the political studies of ethnicity is Frederick C. Luebke's *Immigrants and Politics: The Germans of Nebraska, 1880-1900*, but the list of similar studies from this particular genre could be lengthened almost at will.[28] Luebke basically analyzes voting behavior and concludes that for German-Americans in Nebraska "electoral decisions appear to have been largely influenced by ethnic considerations even though the corporate decision lacked distinctiveness."[29] The final caution is interesting because it suggests that Luebke's data could not really provide any content for the notion of German-American consciousness. National origin was one factor among the many variables that apparently could be correlated with voting patterns, but the whole undertaking hinges theoretically on the preexistent category of ethnic identity, which is present only in the statistics gathered by the census. At this point in his analysis, and apparently sensing the difficulty, Luebke not atypically provides a largely anecdotal account of the one significant variable in his study:

> In his heart . . . the acculturating immigrant *often* remained a German, an Italian, or a Swede. His accommodation *usually* did not involve his

[27]Andreas Dorpalen, "The German Element and the Issues of the Civil War," *Mississippi Valley Historical Review* 29 (June 1942): 55–76, was the first to test the popular belief that Germans were generally opposed to slavery and thus supported Lincoln. One of the earliest doubters was Hildegard Binder Johnson, "The Election of 1860 and the Germans in Minnesota," *Minnesota History* 28 (March 1947): 20–36. For a summary of the controversy, see Frederick Luebke, ed., *Ethnic Voters and the Election of Lincoln* (Lincoln: University of Nebraska Press, 1973).
[28]Luebke, *Immigrants and Politics* (Lincoln: University of Nebraska Press, 1969). Doerries (*Iren und Deutsche*, 319–51) provides the most comprehensive and most recent bibliography, but for the latest work the annual bibliographies in the *Yearbook of German-American Studies* are essential.
[29]Luebke, *Immigrants and Politics*, 185.

family relationships, his circle of close friends, or his church. The *typi-cal* German immigrant continued to speak German in his home and among his friends. He continued to read German-language publications, to worship his German God in his German church, and to send his children to a German school. He had his reservations about American ways, but *usually* he was discreet enough to voice them only in his family circle or among his close friends. His self-image was that of a German in America, a German-American, a hyphenate.[30] (Emphasis added)

Note how the qualifiers (*italicized*) allow for the inevitable statistical deviations that then appear in a chapter entitled "The Germans of Nebraska: A Collective Portrait," which is essentially a narrative version of the census records.[31] But when Luebke eventually concludes that the decisive correlations were actually "ethnoreligious" in nature[32]—that is, that German Catholics and "high-church" Protestants (essentially the members of the Lutheran Church–Missouri Synod) tended to vote Democratic, while "low-church" Protestants voted Republican, unless they were all united in their opposition to women's suffrage and dry Sundays—he renders his own notion of "Germanness" moot. While it is perhaps true that the "Germans" of Nebraska did vote in a distinguishable pattern, ethnicity has in the course of Luebke's analysis turned into an essentially empty category. One is left wondering whether there is any justification for the broad framework of "The Germans of X" when voting behavior and other statistically verifiable activities seem to demand the a priori acceptance of categories whose discursive content is both so minimal and so differentiated that "the Germans" disappear as a unit of measurement. To borrow a metaphor from physics, analysis of the empirical data of ethnicity almost always produces an ethnic "uncertainty principle": to the extent that ethnicity can be defined statistically, it lacks all content, but when content is supplied, the real historical object of inquiry seems to disappear from view.

Although the "new social history," at least of the type practiced by Luebke, now appears to have gone out of fashion in favor of a return to "narrative history,"[33] the point of exploring the generic

---

[30]Ibid., 34. The other disturbing and unreflected bias, which would require a different set of italics, is the exclusively male orientation of the passage.
[31]Ibid., 53–70.
[32]Ibid., 180.
[33]See Lawrence Stone, "The Revival of Narrative: Reflections on a New Old His-

difficulties in this mode of immigration history is simply to show how difficult it has been for historians to come to terms with the concept of ethnicity. There is a long tradition of works written in the hope of describing the culture of the German-Americans. Albert B. Faust, for example, produced a two-volume survey titled *The German Element in the United States* in 1909, while the culture was still thought to be flourishing, whereas a generation later—after the debacle of World War I, when German-language theater, periodicals, and schooling were all but completely forbidden—John Hawgood's volume was titled *The Tragedy of German-America*.[34] A complete survey of the genre would also include the German-language publications that appeared throughout the period, including those written in Germany during the Nazi era, but the task of commenting on them all would far exceed the purposes of this account. More interesting in terms of the implicit concept of German-American ethnicity they contain is the recent turn to local or regional histories and to accounts of specific institutions. Examples of useful studies include Kathleen Conzen's work on Milwaukee, that of Guido Dobbert on Cincinnati, and that of Audrey Louise Olson on St. Louis, to name but a few works whose orientation is local history.[35] Among the institutional approaches, Harmut Keil's Chicago project, which focuses on the city's industrial workers, and Kathleen Conzen's attempts to spur research into rural ethnicity warrant particular attention.[36]

---

tory," in his *The Past and the Present Revisited* (London: Routledge and Kegan Paul, 1987), 74–96.

[34] Albert Bernhard Faust, *The German Element in the United States* (Boston: Houghton Mifflin, 1909); and John A. Hawgood, *The Tragedy of German-America: The Germans in the United States of America during the Nineteenth Century—and After* (New York: G. P. Putnam's Sons, 1940). For a recent example of this curious genre, see La Vern J. Rippley, *The German-Americans* (Boston: G. K. Hall, 1976).

[35] Kathleen Niels Conzen, *Immigrant Milwaukee, 1836–1860* (Cambridge: Harvard University Press, 1976); Guido Dobbert, "The Disintegration of an Immigrant Community: The Cincinnati Germans, 1870–1920" (Ph.D. diss., University of Chicago, 1965), Audrey Louise Olson, "The St. Louis Germans, 1850–1920: The Nature of an Immigrant Community and Its Relation to the Assimilation Process" (Ph.D. diss., University of Kansas, 1970). Although centered on the decline of the Deutsch-Amerikanischer National-Bund, David W. Detjen's, *The Germans in Missouri, 1900–1918: Prohibition, Neutrality, and Assimilation* (Columbia: University of Missouri Press, 1985) is a useful supplement to Olson. See also George K. Kellner, "The German Element on the Urban Frontier: St. Louis Germans, 1830–1869" (Ph.D. diss., University of Missouri, 1973).

[36] See, e.g., Hartmut Keil and John B. Jentz, eds., *German Workers in Industrial*

All these studies help round out the picture of the complex and vibrant infrastructure produced by German-Americans in the latter half of the nineteenth century, but the question any limited approach must address, at least implicitly, is whether there was such a category as *the* German-Americans. Doerries's recent comparative account of German and Irish acculturation strikes at the heart of the problem when it speaks of the supposedly unifying force of the Germans' common language:

> Introducing standard German to the children of immigrants who spoke Low German, Bavarian, or Swabian was not instruction in the native language of a minority as much as an attempt by outsiders to impose a new medium of communication on each of those minorities. It is therefore not irrelevant to ask whether standard German really was the *ethnic language* of German immigrants, or whether nineteenth-century Germans did not actually bring various dialects, i.e., numerous *spoken ethnic languages* into the United States.[37]

One obvious solution to the question Doerries raises is to conceptualize ethnicity as a form of subjectivity with multiple centers, with allowances made for a whole range of religious, social, economic, political, and other factors, all of which need to be examined as they varied over time. In short, the answer to the question of ethnicity must be that, like so many other categories, the best solution is for the analyst to differentiate and to historicize—relentlessly.

Although he would ultimately like to rescue some virtually universal sense of "Germanness" among German immigrants in the United States, Richard Albares's recent work on the "structural ambivalence" of the German-Americans of Chicago provides a sociological method of framing a more productive and multivariant analysis of

Chicago, 1850–1910: A Comparative Perspective (DeKalb: Northern Illinois University Press, 1983); Hartmut Keil, ed., German Workers' Culture in the United States, 1850 to 1920 (Washington, D.C.: Smithsonian Institution Press, 1988); and, among the many articles she has produced on the subject, Kathleen Niels Conzen, "Historical Approaches to the Study of Rural Ethnic Communities," in Frederick Luebke, ed., Ethnicity on the Great Plains (Lincoln: University of Nebraska Press, 1980), 1–18, as well as her "Peasant Pioneers: Generational Succession among German Farmers in Frontier Minnesota," in Steven Hahn and Jonathan Prude, eds., The Countryside in the Age of Capitalist Transformation: Essays in the Social History of Rural America (Chapel Hill: University of North Carolina Press, 1985), 259–92.
[37]Doerries, Iren und Deutsche, 205.

ethnicity.[38] To begin, Albares insists on "the production of ethnicity": "Ethnicity is not something inherited, but rather it is something produced out of the raw material of Old World heritage and New World experience."[39] And Albares identifies two interconnected modes of production. First, he claims that the day-to-day experience of discrimination at the hands of representatives of the dominant culture tends to produce either rapid assimilation as members of the minority attempt to pass themselves off as "natives," or ethnic unity in the face of adversity. Second, whenever an ethnic community starts to form, at least among some immigrants at some time, their sense of unity is the result of institutions such as clubs, political parties, churches, and the ethnic press, all of which help immigrants find and articulate feelings of commonality that transcend the boundaries of family and neighborhood.

After having located these multiple sources of ethnic consciousness, however, Albares seems to shift gears; he casts his inquiry as a search for the factors that constituted "pan-Germanic ethnic solidarity," and he thereby reduces whatever it meant to be "German" in Chicago in the nineteenth and early twentieth century to its lowest common denominator—that is, to the *single* factor that all Chicago German-Americans apparently shared, namely, their identity as Germans.[40] For example, in a chapter titled "The Social Construction of a German Ethnic 'Center' in the City of Chicago," which essentially details the composition of a parade staged in 1871 for the *entire* German community, Albares overlooks the variety of more or less highly developed but still widely differentiated German-American content that he claims was subsumed under that single, unitary identity. But it is precisely because he examines ethnicity from the top down that his search locates one identity in the very places where he claims multiple German ethnicities were produced: in the city's German clubs, parishes, and newspapers. By concentrating on an overarching event like the celebration at the German victory in 1871—that is, by looking for what Edward Shils has identified as a given society's "center"—Albares is forced to mimic the homogenizing gesture that the parade's organizers enforced on the religious,

---

[38]Richard Paul Albares, "The Structural Ambivalence of German Ethnicity in Chicago" (Ph.D. diss., University of Chicago, 1981).

[39]Ibid., 5.

[40]Ibid., 2.

political, and class diversity of their German-American constituency.[41]
In essence, Albares seems to have forgotten the advantages of his
own central principle:

> The concept of structural ambivalence makes it unnecessary to
> choose between these two competing models of ethnic German social
> structure ["several ethno-religious groups" vs. a single, albeit "highly
> differentiated" ethnic group], and instead it allows one to visualize the
> organization of this ethnic community through time as an oscillation
> between segmental disunity and centralized cohesion.[42]

As tempting as it is to concentrate on the "center" around which
"pan-Germanic ethnic solidarity" was organized, that strategy ignores the production and specific content of the various fragments
of whole cloth (particular times, places, groups, and activities) from
which the crazy-quilt of German-American ethnicity was eventually
constructed in favor of the few bits and pieces that overlap. At the
very least, one should remember that those unifying characteristics
were embedded in a whole range of individual discourses, not all of
which were connected with an emerging German-American ethnicity. As the history of their emigration recounted above shows, to
the extent that German-Americans forged a distinctive identity they
did so in the midst of the same pressures and changes that were
affecting virtually all the world's inhabitants, including "nonethnic"
Americans. The fate of prospective German-Americans was tied,
first and foremost, to industrialization and modernization, twin
processes that overlay the diverse cultural, religious, and political
traditions immigrants brought with them to the United States. Despite its faults, Albares's concept of structural ambivalence does provide a practical framework for a "microanalysis" of the interaction
between literature and a single developing ethnic community.

In the midst of the multitude of German-American centers, the
readers of *Die Abendschule* can be regarded as a group constituted
by its members' choice of reading material. Of course, they were

---

[41]At sixty-five pages (pp. 82–146) the chapter on the 1871 parade seems overlong.
I wonder whether the spectators were eventually as bored as I was by the seemingly
endless procession of floats. For the discussion of Shils, see pp. 133–40. According
to Detjen, *The Germans in Missouri*, 31–43, the Deutsch-Amerikanischer National-
Bund, which is Albares's other example of pan-Germanic ethnic solidarity ("Structural Ambivalence," 11–13), was composed largely of paper members, who may not
have even realized that their clubs had joined the national organization.

[42]Albares, "Structural Ambivalence," 15.

also members of numerous other, overlapping groups, but I maintain that these particular readers used *Die Abendschule* as a source in their acquisition of the narratives that helped them explain who they were and what made them distinct both from rest of the citizenry of the United States and from the other immigrants who were flooding into the same new homeland. Reading affected the lives of readers whose inherited culture was no longer adequate for the situation in which they found themselves, but how to decipher their search for identity is a problem from the realm of literary history rather than from history per se. Narratives, especially the particular group of narratives published in *Die Abendschule*, whose constant and underlying theme was the search for a shared identity, contributed to the formation of an acquired consciousness—and specifically one variety of German-American consciousness. That identity, which gradually overlay the culture the immigrants brought with them, was not limited to the unifying notion of Germanness, and it did not spring into existence full-blown and then remain constant over the forty-seven years covered by this book. In fact, the hope of documenting a change led me to *Die Abendschule*. My "reading" is an attempt to understand the magazine's readers' own experience with these texts.

It would be useful at this juncture to know just who *Die Abendschule*'s subscribers really were, but aside from the subject positions or potential identities created for them by the texts the magazine published (which are discussed beginning in Chapter 3), we know little about those who actually read the journal. The surviving archives contain almost no information about the first subscribers, and nothing but the number and geographical distribution of later readers. The only listing of early subscribers is contained in the fiftieth anniversary issue (Vol. L), where the sixty-three people who had received every issue were pictured in a golden crown of laurels. Those sixty-three included fifteen women, and sixteen pastors were among the males. All but two of the pastors were affiliated with the Missouri Synod; one was a member of the equally if not more conservative Wisconsin Synod, which was also German-speaking. Fourteen of the loyal subscribers were from Missouri, and twelve were from Illinois, eleven were from Indiana, seven from Michigan, and six from Wisconsin—all states where the Missouri Synod was strongly represented and where there was a large population of German immigrants. Given *Die Abendschule*'s openly Christian tone, the preponderance of pastors is hardly surprising, because clergymen seem to have had a personal interest in the journal's success. Pastors

were the obvious recipients of Walther's supportive missives, and
they also appear to have acted as agents in *Die Abendschule*'s early
years. Early issues generally contained a list of those who had sent in
money, which was their receipt and assurance that their check or
money order had actually arrived in St. Louis. A startlingly large
number of the people in such lists were pastors or teachers—respectively, twenty and five of the thirty-three people listed in a typical
issue from the period (XIV/24 [1868]), but because two are credited
with two subscriptions each, they must either have sold subscriptions ("Agents receive every seventh copy free") or have taken care
of correspondence for at least some members of their congregations.
The fact that several pastors' names appear again in subsequent lists
in the same volume confirms this hypothesis.

The connection with some church, at least for many of the subscribers to early issues, is therefore quite certain, but aside from
guesses on basis of the magazine's decidedly Christian tone, little can
be deduced about the character of its subscribers. Anecdotal evidence seems to confirm their conservative religious orientation, but
such evidence is scarce, of questionable validity, and difficult to find
except by accident. For example, Jürnjakob Swehn, a pious farm
laborer who left Mecklenburg for Iowa in 1868 and whose letters to
the village teacher were ordered, edited, augmented, "improved,"
and then published by the teacher's son in 1917, reported subscribing to *Die Abendschule*.[43] But even if subscribers like Swehn were
still predominantly members of conservative Lutheran denominations, what that characterization meant vis-à-vis the rest of society—
and compared to their forebears, is clearly worth investigating. The
only other evidence about subsequent subscribers is an English-language advertising prospectus issued in 1895, which it may well have
been slanted to sell space in the journal. In answering the rhetorical
question of who its readers were, the editors of the journal claimed
"the high class and prosperous Germans to whom it [*Die Abendschule*] is, what the Century, Harper, and Lippincott magazines are
to the reading and thoughtful, well-to-do Americans."[44] It remains to
be seen whether such characterizations matched the subject positions
offered readers by the texts published in *Die Abendschule*.

Data about these subscribers are equally scarce. When Louis

[43]Johannes Gillhoff, *Jürnjakob Swehn der Amerikafahrer* (Munich: DTV, 1978).
On the process and justification for his editing ("sorgfältige Schonung der Origi-
nalbriefe"), see Gillhof's foreword, pp. 7–8; *Die Abendschule* is mentioned on 173.
[44]CHI, AL 648.

Lange purchased *Die Abendschule* in 1861, there were reportedly about 1,000 subscribers.[45] Arndt and Olson report a circulation of 7,000 for 1870–74, some 28,700 for 1895, and 43,833 for 1901.[46] Although it is beyond the time frame for this study, which follows *Die Abendschule* only up to 1900, the high point of 59,631 subscribers was reached in 1914, only to fall to 23,127 by the end of World War I. Circulation climbed back to 31,920 in 1920 but declined steadily thereafter. At the time of its demise in 1940, *Die Abendschule* counted fewer than 15,000 subscribers. Apart from ramifications that resulted from various thematic changes, which will be discussed below, my guess is that by the 1930s the journal's readership was simply dying off. The end of the mass immigration of Germans into the United States around the turn of the century meant that the size of potential audience for German-American publications had reached a high point that it would never regain. Thus, at least in a strictly numerical sense, the decline of German-American journalism had begun long before World War I.

Information about the geographical distribution of readers is just as sketchy. A circular distributed to prospective advertisers in 1910 claimed 51,539 subscribers, of whom 1926 resided outside the United States, mainly in Australia and Canada, while Arndt and Olson number 584 Germans among some 30,000 subscribers at a date that is unfortunately unspecified, presumably around 1930, but perhaps as early as 1895. In 1910 there were subscribers in all forty-eight states, but they were concentrated in the Midwest. Illinois was in first place with 8,883 subscribers, followed by Wisconsin with 5,875, Missouri with 4,693, Michigan with 3,772, Minnesota with 3,388, New York with 3,327, and Ohio with 3,197. Pennsylvania, the center of German Pietist immigration in the colonial period, only had 1,708 subscribers. As a glance at the addresses of the sixty-three long-term subscribers mentioned earlier above shows, the distribution had changed somewhat in the intervening years. One can only speculate about the reason for the differences between the two rankings, but the fact that Wisconsin was still mainly wilderness in 1854, whereas Missouri already was much more densely settled, might well explain the relatively small number of long-term readers from a number of states that later attracted a large German population.

This summary exhausts the available statistical evidence about

[45]Ibid.
[46]Arndt and Olson, *The German-Language Press of the Americas*, 3:247–48.

Die Abendschule's readers. The data are much too limited to suggest anything concrete about the magazine itself, and even if one could locate more material the result would only be the kind of collective biography that would necessarily leave out the interaction between readers and texts. In any case, the question here is what the texts published in *Die Abendschule* can tell us about its readers and their mode of reading. To frame that inquiry, the next step is to examine the large body of scholarship that deals with ethnic literature, first in more general terms and then paying particular attention to the work done on German-American literature.

Any discussion of ethnic literature begins perforce with a question: Who is an ethnic writer, or, slightly restated, who produces ethnic literature? For some scholars, convinced as they are that ethnicity is the central experience of American life, that question ultimately becomes: Who isn't an ethnic writer? Unfortunately, their answers permute alarmingly as one group is included only to exclude another. For example, speaking very broadly, one could identify an ethnic writer as anyone writing about ethnic characters—say, Jews in New York City or the Germans and Poles in Milwaukee, or one could limit the category to include only those who write about the experience of ethnicity or immigration. The next step would be to restrict the designation of ethnic writer even further—for example, to those who write about that experience on the basis of their own extended stays in the United States. At this point it is interesting to note that until very recently this type of definition was applied almost exclusively to experiences associated with emigration to the United States, rather than to the experience of ethnicity by German *Gastarbeiter* or by any of the host of "others" writing from within a dominant culture.[47] In any case, the point of this particular category is that the writer's formative cultural experience, often referred to as his or her "cultural baggage," would be from somewhere other than North America.

Another group, related in a way to the previous category, consists of those who came to the United States and wrote something—that

---

[47]For a more enlightened approach, see Arlene A. Teraoka, "*Gastarbeiterliteratur*: The Other Speaks Back," *Cultural Critique* 7 (Fall 1987), Special Issue: "The Nature and Context of Minority Discourse II," 77–101. The real parallel, however, is not to the *Gastarbeiter* who write German but to those who continue to write in Turkish, Spanish, etc., while in the Federal Republic of Germany.

is, a text not necessarily about the experience of ethnicity, at least not overtly—and who stayed here, as well as a subgroup that includes those who eventually returned to their native land but nevertheless wrote about their experiences while in the United States. Within the field of German studies in the United States, the so-called exile literature comes to mind here, but the category is by no means limited to the twentieth century. Another still-narrower circle contains only those who emigrated to the United States before beginning a career as a writer, and who then began writing in their new homeland. Their initial orientation is thus more likely to be American, although in all likelihood within the confines of an established ethnic community. Here too one could differentiate between those who were lifelong residents of the United States and those who eventually returned "home." Finally, one could speculate about the status of the writing members of the second and succeeding generations of virtually all the above categories. In short, as will be even clearer shortly, the category "ethnic writer" is scarcely amenable to delimitation in any one fashion; there are simply too many legitimate variables that enter into any definition.

But if the rhetorical question is revised to "What is ethnic literature?" the difficulties actually multiply. Most important, at least for immigrants who hailed from countries other than England, Scotland, and Ireland, is the question of language. Is ethnic literature limited to texts produced in a language other than English? And if English-language works are included, do non-English works have a special status based on their virtual inaccessibility to members of the dominant culture? In addition, the language question can also be addressed thematically. English-language works by ethnic authors might have attempted to explain a given ethnic culture to members of the majority, while at least some of the works written in another language can be read as explanations—intended for immigrants—of the workings of a "foreign" society. The difficulty is not only that there are vast numbers of texts that refuse to be forced into these categories; there are also examples to validate every conceivable variation.

Lest these distinctions appear to be nothing more than the workings of an idle mind, consider the case of George Condoyannis's encyclopedic dissertation titled "German American Prose Fiction from 1850 to 1914." Not only does Condoyannis restrict his study to works published in book form, he also accepts G. A. Zimmermann's definition of German-American literature: "the total of the *literary* products *in the German language* by Germans *permanently* settled in the United States."⁴⁸ The italicized portions of the quotation suggest where the category of German-American literature could easily be broadened, and Condoyannis does indeed include "the few immigrants who later left their adopted country to return to their homeland, provided their works were written while they were still in America." He thus excludes "those authors who merely spent some time in America as travelers or adventurers and who subsequently wrote prose fiction based on their American experiences *after they had returned home to Europe.*"⁴⁹ Because, even with the fairly restrictive boundaries that Condoyannis set for himself, his project turned out to be 634 pages long, one suspects that most such limitations are to no small degree pragmatic in nature. For example, had it been necessary for Condoyannis to include the "Amerika books" of authors like Charles Sealsfield, Friedrich Gerstäcker, and their imitators, his task might have become virtually endless. So long as it is clear that the decision to include or exclude particular works is merely practical rather than principled, in large part because the literature produced by, for, and about any one ethnic group presents an unmanageable richness of material, the selection is much easier to justify. Yet it is precisely the problem of agreeing on an object of inquiry that clouds much of the theoretical work done on ethnic literature.

If it is still necessary to discuss the scholarship of ethnic literature, the reason is simply that, in spite of the ambiguities involved in specifying the object of any given analysis, such categorizing has traditionally defined the discipline. Given the nature of the beast—a host of "literatures" generally kept separate by the sheer number of languages involved and the paucity of translations—it is not surprising that there are relatively few general treatments of ethnic literature. Not only are comprehensive surveys of literary history no longer fashionable, but there also seems to be a radical disjunction at the point where practitioners of the theory of ethnic literature encounter scholars working within any one literary or linguistic tradition. In point of fact, in the United States the former are often housed in

⁴⁸Gustav Adolf Zimmermann, *Deutsch in Amerika: Beiträge zur Geschichte der Deutsch-amerikanischen Literatur* (Chicago, 1892), xvi, quoted in George Condoyannis, "German-American Prose Fiction from 1850 to 1914" (Ph.D. diss., Columbia University, 1954), 9 (emphasis added).
⁴⁹Condoyannis, "German-American Prose Fiction," 9–10.

departments of English or American studies, while the latter are generally (marginalized) members of foreign-language departments. By looking first at the issues involved in the study of ethnic literature in general and then turning to works on German-American literature in particular, however, it should be possible to explore the unspoken gaps and unreflected assumptions of previous analyses.

One place to begin the analysis is to turn again to the question of what constitutes ethnic literature. Unlike most of the scholars who are interested only in German-American literature, who usually operate with some version of Condoyannis's definition, the theorists of ethnic literature as such almost always attempt to stake out an extremely broad territory for themselves. For example, in his article on "Literature and Ethnicity" in the *Harvard Encyclopedia of American Ethnic Groups*, the standard reference work in the field of ethnic studies, Werner Sollors claims: "Ethnicity is a pervasive theme in all American literature."[50] And in a recent book-length treatment of the same subject, Sollors includes in ethnic literature: "works written by, about, or for persons who perceived themselves, or were perceived by others, as members of ethnic groups, including even nationally and internationally popular writings by 'major' authors and formally intricate and modernist texts."[51] Sollors' gesture is ultimately intended to expand the canon of American literature (and to insert himself into the center of the discipline), but he gets caught up in all the difficulties associated with such lists, starting with the necessity of establishing some transcendent notion of literary value. His criteria are basically very traditional. Sollors would simply like to argue that ethnic writers, who were more familiar with developments in European literature than their American counterparts, brought high modernism to the United States. While it is true that certain modernist writers have been defined out of the category of ethnic literature because the genre was generally assumed to contain only the quaint trash that appealed to mass audiences, claiming eth-

[50]Werner Sollors, "Literature and Ethnicity," *Harvard Encyclopedia of American Ethnic Groups*, ed. Stephen Thernstrom (Cambridge: Harvard University Press, 1980), 649.

[51]Werner Sollors, *Beyond Ethnicity: Consent and Descent in American Culture* (New York: Oxford University Press, 1986), 243. Berndt Ostendorf's term "ghetto literature" is unfortunate in that it seems to reinforce the mistaken impression that ethnic neighborhoods were the real birthplace of ethnicity. See his "Einleitung" to Berndt Ostendorf, ed., *Amerikanische Gettoliteratur: Zur Literatur ethnischer, marginaler und unterdrückter Gruppen in Amerika* (Darmstadt: Wissenschaftliche Buchgesellschaft, 1983), 1–26.

nic status for writers of recognized "quality" (to take Sollors's example, Carl Sandburg, but the list is easily expanded) is a fundamentally self-defeating tactic in that it still leaves most ethnic writing outside the canon.[52]

The difficulty arises in part because Sollors's horizon is not just ethnic literature but American literature, and the audience he addresses is composed of English literature teachers who are supposed to enrich their own and their students' reading lists, but the issue of quality also impinges drastically on the kind of readings that the underlying structure of any canon allows. Speaking of a Polish-American play that was later rewritten for black characters, Sollors writes: "The literary interest [sic] lies less in the specific cultural emanation of one ethnic group than in the relationship of a minority to a majority—which makes it ethnically interchangeable."[53] But if the characters and themes of ethnic literature really are "ethnically interchangeable," if ethnic writings deal primarily with transcendent themes from world literature or even from the more limited experience of ethnicity in the United States, they are thereby robbed of any historical specificity on the part of writers or readers. Indeed, despite protestations to the contrary, much of the theoretical work done by scholars like Sollors conveys nothing so much as a sense of fairly primitive, generic structuralism.[54] Paradoxically, the result of making the master narratives that structure "the immigrant novel" and "the immigrant autobiography" quintessentially American is once again

[52]Sollors, *Beyond Ethnicity*, 241–47; his specific target is Dorothy Burton Skårdal, discussed below. William Boelhower's *Through a Glass Darkly: Ethnic Semiosis in American Literature* (New York: Oxford University Press, 1987) is similarly inclusive. The book's list of ethnic writers, which includes Mark Twain, William Faulkner, Willa Cather, and Ralph Ellison, is an attempt to show not only "how ubiquitous the ethnic sign is in American literature but also how hopelessly American ethnic fiction is" (p. 36).

[53]Sollors, "Literature and Ethnicity," 664.

[54]Boelhower again provides an extreme example of the difficulty. In "The Immigrant Novel as Genre," *MELUS* 8 (Spring 1981): 10, he writes: "Unless the immigrant novel genre is considered an ideal abstraction, one cannot account for its peculiar elements (fabula, characters/actants, stock frames, microstructural sequences), its structural coherence, by remaining at the descriptive and immanent level alone." Even though he then grants world-views social and historical status, for Boelhower their realization is possible only within the narrow confines of one Greimasian square. For more of the same, see Boelhower's *Immigrant Autobiography in the United States (Four Versions of the Italian American Self)* (Verona, Italy: Essedue edizioni, 1982). See also Berndt Ostendorf, "Literary Acculturation: What Makes Ethnic Literature 'Ethnic,'" in Monique Lecomte and Claudine Thomas, eds., *Le facteur ethnique aux Etats-Unis et au Canada* (Lille: Université de Lille III, 1983), 149–61.

to reduce ethnicity to an empty category. The claim that all American literature is ethnic, especially if it is true, ultimately says nothing at all, for there is no nonethnic literature, no opposition from which to derive a meaning. The whole gesture collapses under the weight of its success.

It is certainly worth investigating whether ethnic and "nonethnic" writings share various structures or thematic concerns at specific times and places, and ethnic writings often do provide weapons in the battle against the strictures of the canon that are every bit as useful as texts by women or blacks or homosexuals, as long as none of these categories is itself reified and then canonized. Still the historicity of such texts raises another difficult issue: the question of audience. Sollors once again provides a useful target for analyzing the difficulties raised by this type of approach:

> The point of departure of classic ethnic literature, and especially of writings in English, often was to blur ethnic stereotypes by presenting an inside view of ethnicity which could make "otherness" understandable to American readers. Consciously or unconsciously, ethnic writers often assumed the roles of pleaders, mediators, or translators who explained ethnic traits, annotated ethnic jokes and phrases, or provided glossaries for the benefit of the reader.[55]

To begin, "classic ethnic literature" is apparently a reference to the writings of the earliest immigrants—those who wrote before ethnic writers were able to produce works of "literary interest" with a more universal appeal. Note, however, that despite their lack of quality, in fact because they were useless as anything other than guidebooks to foreign cultures and idioms, these "writings in English" were "understandable to an American reader," who in the next sentence is elevated to the generic "reader." While it is no doubt true that some of the texts written by hyphenate Americans did serve to mediate between cultures, it is patently absurd to suggest that "writings in English" for the "American reader" somehow constituted the norm, or that either the texts or the experience of these readers was similar to what happened when immigrants read works written in their native languages. First, although there appear to be no statistics available on the subject, there is no reason to believe that the majority of writings by immigrants were in English, especially in the case of immigrants from so literate a culture as Germany. The existence

---

[55]Sollors, "Literature and Ethnicity," 658.

of thousands of non-English newspapers, magazines, and book publishers in the latter half of the nineteenth century suggests that just
the opposite was the case, that immigrants tended to publish in their
own languages—for fellow members of their linguistic community.
Second, as my analysis of the texts published in *Die Abendschule*
demonstrates, writings intended for the immigrants themselves
clearly cannot be equated with writings for linguistic outsiders. Even
the relatively limited number of works that attempted to translate
the culture of the United States into an immigrant's idiom were
marked by a reversal in the direction of mediation that Sollors
posits.

Sollors does address "the problem of audience" by suggesting that
non-English writings, like the writings of some African-Americans,
may have had a "double audience," but the analogy works only to
the extent that both English and non-English works were translated
for that half of the audience to whom the original was inaccessible.[56]
He also assumes the equivalence of original and translation, although for works written by African-Americans the difference is not
located in the part of the text that is circumscribed by the printed
page, but in those aspects of textuality that depend on the experiences of concrete and therefore different readers—black and white.
Moreover, audience and translation also play a more subtle role in
any analysis made from the perspective of American literature, because the attempt to broaden the canon demands translations that
can be put in the hands of those who normally read something
else—in English. Here transcendence has come full circle not only to
embrace the work's literary quality and thematic content but also to
include the unmarked "other" of the "American reader."

Quite a different set of issues arises when the "ultimate"—nonethnic—reader approaches these works from the standpoint of history rather than literature, and few books are better suited to the
purpose of exploring the kind of questions that historians raise than
Dorothy Burton Skårdal's *Divided Heart: Scandinavian Immigrant
Experience through Literature*, one of the most widely read studies
of ethnic literature in the United States and a prototypical example
of a very different mode of reading what immigrants wrote.[57] Skårdal sets out "to use literary works as historical documents, in an

[56]Ibid., 661.

[57]Dorothy Burton Skårdal, *The Divided Heart: Scandinavian Immigrant Experience through Literature* (Lincoln: University of Nebraska Press, 1974). Subsequent
page references to Skårdal are given in the text.

attempt to preserve the depth, vividness, and complexity of individual human lives within the broad generalizations of history" (p. 15). Without denying the possibility of approaching these works as literature, even though her notion of what literary studies is about is unreflected and extremely narrow ("I have made no attempt to write evaluative literary history," p. 22)—Skårdal locates her project elsewhere. Her aim is "to put together a composite picture of Scandinavian-American experience from imaginative literature which immigrants wrote about their own lives" (pp. 15–16), and she actually produced nearly three hundred pages of her brand of social history drawn from Scandinavian-American narratives. It is no doubt true that one reason for reading ethnic literature is to explore the represented world of its writers, but a number of serious difficulties arise from Skårdal's use of traditional narrative history as a horizon. First, one should remember that, like literature, history is a socially constructed signifying practice; its truth is just as suspect as literature's.[58] Second, employing literature as evidence necessarily invokes some model of reflection, with all its well-known pitfalls.[59] Skårdal seems to be aware of the danger, though just barely, for as she puts it: "I limited my reading to stories which, so far as I could judge, portrayed immigrant life contemporaneous with the author" (pp. 17–18). Not only did she eliminate works about temporally distant grandparents and the like, choosing instead "to rely solely on authors writing out of their own experience" (p. 18), but she also subjected the remaining evidence to a variety of tests. The fact that the majority of her sources agreed with one another is for her an important indication of their veracity, but to claim that the reading public's taste for "naive realism" (p. 23) also mitigated against representations that were less than authentic puts far too heavy a burden on the conventions of the genre, which demanded only unobtrusive narration and a degree of plausibility—rather than empirical "truth."

[58]See, e.g., Hayden White, *Metahistory: The Historical Imagination in Nineteenth-Century Europe* (Baltimore: Johns Hopkins University Press, 1973); and Dominick LaCapra, *History and Criticism* (Ithaca, N.Y.: Cornell University Press, 1985).

[59]Without rehashing the realism debates along their whole trajectory from the Weimar Republic to the German Democratic Republic, Toril Moi presents a perceptive critique of what she labels "the crypto-Lukácsian perspective" in her *Sexual/Textual Politics: Feminist Literary Theory* (London: Methuen, 1985), 8. In such accounts—and Skårdal's certainly fits the pattern—"truth" becomes an a priori category that Moi describes as "the right content being represented in the correct realist form," whereby narration is invisible and unproblematized.

Moreover, to suggest that these writers are to be believed because "most were too unskilled to be inventive" (p. 23) is to fall back to criteria that she has already disavowed as "evaluative literary history." Raising evidentiary questions may seem like nitpicking, but asking what ethnic literature actually represents is absolutely critical to the present undertaking.

At this point I shall defer a number of specific arguments to the next chapter, where I can discuss the more general issue of reading popular literature with the help of the first such narrative published in *Die Abendschule*, but even a cursory analysis reveals a much more serious difficulty with Skårdal's approach. The text in question, a story titled *Die hölzernen Teller* (The Wooden Plates), which is set in the eighteenth century instead of the year 1855, when it was published, would fall outside what she considers useful. Overtly, the novel is not about the lives of immigrants, nor is it written on the basis of their actual experiences. But if reality is both discursive and material—that is, if reality is not only *in* but also necessarily dealt with *through* narration, then "Die hölzernen Teller" may indeed contain some version of what it meant to be a German immigrant in the United States. If nothing else, its presence in *Die Abendschule* meant that it spoke to the magazine's immigrant readers at some level. In addition, even "realistic" depictions of immigrant life were no doubt tainted by the writer's or the culture industry's notion of what should have been, as well as by the readers' search for compensation for what was. Yet none of the anxieties and aspirations inscribed into texts like "Die hölzernen Teller" was in any sense "unreal." If ethnicity was anything, if it existed anywhere, then whatever it was certainly was located in the hearts and minds of immigrants—and not just when they were reading or writing about a narrowly circumscribed set of circumstances. Thus, although Skårdal's readings are not completely false, the foundation on which she bases them is too limited and too shaky to sustain even her own project. More important, by insisting on the documentary value of ethnic literature, Skårdal eliminates a whole realm of texts that spoke from, to, and of the ethnic experience.

One might expect that poststructuralism, with its "central" concepts of "difference" and "marginality," would be ideally suited to a more productive rethinking of ethnicity, and indeed poststructuralists are beginning to turn their attention in that direction. As a result of a recent conference titled "The Nature and Context of Minority

Discourse," we can now expect sustained discussion of "objective non-identity."[60] In other words, in addition to its fruitful exchanges with Marxism and feminism, poststructuralism is now confronting race, culture, and ethnicity, all of which raise the epistemological critique of structuralism to the level of real political choices. Unfortunately, however, the anchor for most of the discussion so far, even by those who ultimately reject their conclusions, has been Gilles Deleuze and Félix Guattari's *Kafka: Toward a Minor Literature*,[61] a work that appears to be singularly unsuited to the task of providing a framework for the whole question of ethnicity, including what I would like to call "historical ethnicity." Its inclusion here therefore represents their book's central role in the contemporary discussion of ethnicity, rather than its usefulness or appropriateness for the study of German-American popular narratives. Pointing out the inadequacy of current debates from the standpoint of nineteenth-century immigrants could, however, serve as an important corrective.

Deleuze and Guattari do raise the issue of minority status, which perhaps unintentionally implies a consciousness of inferiority or at least threatened otherness, not for its own sake but as a possible means of locating and grounding a theory of agency. From my perspective, the difficulty with their argument, especially as it has been appropriated, is that it overlooks both the history and the historicity of ethnicity—how, when, where, and why ethnic consciousness developed—in order to concentrate on its present-day incarnations. Deleuze and Guattari's move may have had some tactical or even strategic advantages, particularly in a French context, where large-scale immigration is a relatively recent though increasingly sensitive "problem," but as should become clear below, their perspective is simply too narrow to be so widely applied. In what follows, therefore, I use the example of nineteenth-century German-Americans to broaden a discussion of ethnicity that is already under way.

[60]See *Cultural Critique* 6–7 (Spring and Winter 1987), ed. Abdul R. JanMohamed and David Lloyd, for the published versions of papers presented in Berkeley from May 24 to May 27, 1986. The phrase "objective *non-identity*" is from JanMohamed and Lloyd's introduction to the second volume, "Minority Discourse—What Is to Be Done?" 16.

[61]Gilles Deleuze and Félix Guattari, *Kafka: Toward a Minor Literature*, trans., Dana Polan, Theory and History of Literature 30 (Minneapolis: University of Minnesota Press, 1986). In addition to the texts in *Cultural Critique* 6–7, to be discussed below, see also Heidrun Suhr, "*Ausländerliteratur*: Minority Literature in the Federal Republic of Germany," *New German Critique* 46 (Winter 1989): 71–103.

We begin with a look at what Deleuze and Guattari mean by the category "minor literature." Essentially, they say, minority discourse, of which literature is the most salient example, is characterized by three features: the deterritorialization of language, an emphasis on politics, and an adherence to collective values. While all three notions present problems for an analysis of historical ethnicity and will be discussed in turn, the role assigned to language is the most problematical. As Deleuze and Guattari see it, a special relationship to language is the enabling condition for minority status: "A minor literature doesn't come from a minor language; it is rather that which a minority constructs within a major language."[62] Their referent here is Franz Kafka, a Jewish author writing in German in Czechoslovakia—that is, a member of a minority in a minority in a minority (all defined numerically rather than in terms of cultural prestige), but the claim is extended to include Joyce, Beckett, and everyone living "in a language that is not their own. . . This is the problem of immigrants, and especially of their children, the problem of minorities, the problem of a minor literature."[63] But given the fact that nineteenth-century German immigrants in the United States continued to read, write, and speak German until well into the twentieth century, their behavior and the multiplicity of discourses thereby produced present an immediate difficulty for theorists of minor literature. It is true that one could view German-American literature as a minor literature if the referent were all of German-language literature—that is, if one were to include the literature produced in the German-speaking areas of Europe, but that would be a problem quite different from the question of its status in the United States. Moreover, if the first, relatively small contingent of German-Americans was still dominated by English-speakers in the 1850s and 1860s, was that still the case once they had begun to achieve some semblance of collective identity in the 1870s, or once the new waves

[62]Deleuze and Guattari, *Kafka*, 16.

[63]Ibid., 19. At this point the argument is already muddied, because a page earlier Deleuze and Guattari left themselves a tantalizing, albeit undefined, escape hatch. They claim that it is only "the possibility of setting up a minor practice of major language from within [that] allows one to define popular literature, marginal literature, and so on" (p. 17). If some ethnic literature might legitimately be called "popular" or "marginal" rather than minor, and if it were also clear what those two terms meant, then such texts would not have to sustain the comparison with recognized "classics" like Kafka, Joyce, and Beckett, but no one, at least neither Deleuze and Guattari nor the authors of the texts published in *Cultural Critique*, seems to have worked out the distinctions.

of eastern and southern European immigrants began to appear in the United States in the 1880s, giving the majority culture another and even more different "other"? And what is to be made of the gradual acceptance of the majority ideological position by at least some sectors of the minority population, which shaped that particular minority's form of resistance from the start? And what was the effect of the German-Americans' continued connection to a dominant culture in Europe?

The difficulty here arises not only as a result of the rigorous present-mindedness of Deleuze and Guattari's analysis, which recent poststructuralist work on ethnicity unfortunately shares, but also because of their peculiarly narrow notion of the "political" content of minor literatures. When the claim is made, for example, that an important "characteristic of minor literatures is that everything in them is political," the observation would be utterly trivial except for the fact that Deleuze and Guattari essentially limit their notion of what is "political" to a minor literature's ability to "challenge the language" thus "making it follow a sober revolutionary path."[64] Not only is politics reduced here to the particular goals that Deleuze and Guattari find most palatable, but they valorize one particular mode of resistance, namely, the transformation of language rather than other, more direct forms of struggle, and at the same time privilege a specific set of agents whose ability to intervene is apparently the automatic result of their oppression at the hands of a majority. As admirable—and, one would hope, as true—as their analysis is when applied to Kafka or what is now labeled "emergent literature," it overlooks the overwhelmingly conservative nature of much of what has traditionally been thought of as ethnic literature.

The political hopes and fears inscribed in the narratives read by nineteenth-century immigrants—that is, by people who left Europe under the threat of an industrial transformation of what had been a largely rural society—consist largely of the longing for a return to an imaginary, precapitalist utopia, where small producers flourished in the midst of an intact, organic community.[65] Moreover, the narra-

[64]Deleuze and Guattari, *Kafka*, 17–19. Oddly enough, their argument here mirrors that of Sollors.

[65]See my article "The 'Political' and the German-American Press," *Yearbook of German-American Studies* 23 (1988): 41–48, where I argue that a major failing in previous studies of German-language newspapers in the United States has been the assumption that their "political" content was limited to the editorial page. I show that the narratives such papers published were intensely political, albeit obliquely, as well as implicitly in the service of conservative anti-modernism.

tive strategies these texts employed was just as conservative; they adhered to the realist strictures shared by German and American literature, high and low, for most of the nineteenth century. This is not to say that nineteenth-century ethnic literature was all written by and for reactionaries, but a great deal of it was, and the resistance contained in such texts must be differentiated, both from working-class ethnic literature of the same period and from present-day ethnic literature, as well as from the "minor" masterpieces apparently lurking about, waiting to be discovered by some careful reader schooled in Deleuze and Guattari. After all, they write: "There is nothing major or revolutionary except the minor."[66] But even if their evaluative criteria are political rather than aesthetic—that is, even if the discovery does not have to be of another Kafka, this mode of reading minor literatures is too narrow to be sustainable for historical ethnicity.

In fact, it is precisely this assumption of political radicalism on the part of ethnic writers that makes much of the poststructuralist discussion of ethnicity sound more than slightly skewed, especially when considering ethnic minorities in other times and places. Consider, for example, R. Radhakrishnan's injunction: "The task for radical ethnicity is to thematize and subsequently problematize its entrapment within these binary elaborations with the intention of 'stepping beyond' to find its own adequate language."[67] No matter how deeply one looks into what was merely implied or left unsaid, or, to use more fashionable terminology, into the cracks and aporia of *Die Abendschule*, that particular kind of resistance is simply not there, and it would be unfair to fault its editors and readers for the absence. In addition, to limit the task of investigating ethnicity to its radical component, no matter how broadly this radicalism might be defined, is to miss much of what ethnicity, especially nineteenth-century ethnicity, was about. As will become abundantly clear below, a century ago a significant proportion of ethnic Americans were extremely conservative, both culturally and politically.

One would also search in vain for the kind of collective enunciation that, according to Abdul R. JanMohamed and David Lloyd, characterizes "*all* minority discourse."[68] It is simply impossible to insert most of the experience of historical ethnicity into statements

[66]Deleuze and Guattari, *Kafka*, 26.
[67]R. Radhakrishnan, "Ethnic Identity and Post-Structuralist Differance," *Cultural Critique* 6 (Spring 1987): 216.
[68]JanMohamed and Lloyd, "Minority Discourse," 10.

like the following: "Out of the damage inflicted upon minority cultures, which, as Fanon so clearly recognized, prevents their 'development' according to the Western model of individual and racial identity, emerges the possibility of a collective subjectivity formed in
practice rather than contemplation."[69] Moreover, given the regional,
linguistic, political, cultural, and particularly the religious diversity
of an ethnic group like the German-Americans, it is clearly not the
case "that minority individuals are always treated and forced to experience themselves generically."[70] Coupled with the failure to take a
more differentiated view of individual ethnic groups, as well as of
the collective actions that created ethnicity in the first place, there is
also a disturbing tendency here to treat whites as an undifferentiated
mass. At the present time that may not be so far off the mark, but
for the Germans, Poles, and Italians—to say nothing of the Jews—
who along with the then far less visible African-Americans were the
nineteenth-century's "others," this kind of analysis is startlingly
ahistorical. I shall demonstrate, for example, that a major tension in
German-American literature was its unambiguous desire to shape a
particular community—composed of Lutherans or Catholics or socialists, but never realistically of all Germans, except in those rare
instances, like 1871, when religious and political differences were
pointedly but then only temporarily overlooked in the brief celebration of some greater whole. By contrast, a real sense of community
within any one subgroup could exist only at the expense of the pan-
Germanic solidarity implicit in every celebration of Germanness. Indeed, some sense of what it meant to be German in the United States
was paradoxically both the enabling ideology of the German-American community and the principle threat to its existence. A multivariant analysis of German-American ethnicity—or any other ethnicity, for that matter—must include the search for community
inscribed in most ethnic writing, without overlooking the fact that

[69]Ibid., 9, 16. The denigration of "contemplation" here might seem like nothing
more than a curious aside, odd only that it comes from two literary critics. It has to
be understood, however, as an oblique reference to the once hotly debated issue of
the intellectual's uncertain role in socialist parties and the subsequent status of *the
party* in Eastern Europe. The question was whether the proletariat could ever
achieve anything more than "trade union consciousness" without the *guiding* intervention of the party, i.e., of intellectuals. The party's most successful supporter was
Lenin, particularly in his famous pamphlet "What is to be done?" (1902), where he
argued precisely the opposite position from the one that JanMohamed and Lloyd
attribute to him with the unacknowledged quotation of his title in their own.
[70]Ibid., 10.

what particular subgroups understood when they imagined that community was not always and everywhere the same.

Even if German-American literature cannot be characterized by its linguistic deterritorialization, the necessarily "radical" politics of language, and this unproblematized view of collectivity, I nevertheless do not believe that the challenge of poststructuralism can be completely dismissed. For while the specific claims made for present-day ethnics contradict much of the experience of nineteenth-century German-Americans, Germans in the United States were nevertheless troubled by the dangers that emigration and the lure of assimilation posed to their language and culture. They were also intensely (albeit often unconsciously) political, and their resistance to the dominant culture revolved around the question of what it meant to be German in America. If one takes "minor" to be, among other things, a contested evaluative category, it is certainly true that German-American literature has been subjected to the same process of institutional forgetting that has characterized the hegemonic culture's treatment of the cultural practices of other minority groups. As we shall see, this has certainly been the case within the discipline of *Germanistik*, especially and most problematically in the United States. In short, instead of rejecting the notion of minor literature, a more productive approach might be to admit minority status as one of many possible trajectories for ethnic literature and to ask, perhaps using the notion of a minor literature as an ideal type, why some ethnic literatures become "minor" and others fail to do so. Of course, an answer to that question can only be attempted in the course of a detailed analysis of specific texts, but it should be clear from the foregoing discussion that previous attempts to frame the inquiry in poststructuralist terms have been woefully inadequate. As the rich textures of historical ethnicity can show, any search for "objective nonidentity" can ignore difference only at its own peril.

It is unfortunate that the label "minor literature" cannot be affixed without reservation to the texts associated with nineteenth-century German-Americans. Being able to lay claim to the moral and political high ground implicit in Deleuze and Guattari's use of the term would make it far easier to justify the study of German-American literature within the discipline of *Germanistik*. Yet ever since World War I the field of German-American literature has been so completely neglected that it can now just barely aspire to that other, dubious honorific of recent critical theory: an existence on the "margins" of a dominant discourse, where its presence might provide the space necessary to launch a critique of the hegemonic center—although in practice it seldom does. As it is, German-American literature is either little more than a hobby for otherwise serious scholars or, worse, the purview of amateurs, antiquarians, and the politically suspect. And it is especially the latter—those who are themselves still tainted by the same unsavory signs of excessive Germanness (*Teutschtümelei*) that infest so much of the literature and culture that they study—who make it difficult to reconstitute German-American studies as part of the study of German in the United States. A "minor" German-American literature would no doubt have produced a whole host of other problems—and opportunities—but it could never have been implicated in the disciplinary history I survey in the remainder of this chapter.

Perhaps the most common motif in that history is best exemplified by the apology with which Albert Faust began his survey of German-American literature—significantly enough as the first entry in a chapter titled "Non-English Writings" in the *Cambridge History of American Literature* published in 1921: "The memoirs, poems, and essays, the books of travel, fiction, and science that have been written in the German language in the United States are of greater historical than literary interest."[71] Over fifty years later, Robert Ward would attempt to make "The Case for German-American Literature," as his 1977 article is titled, by faulting previous scholars: "Their preference is thus for the genius of the great masters such as Goethe and Schiller, rather than works which perhaps have more cultural significance for the study of social, political, religious, and economic phenomena than to art for its own sake."[72] Not only are

[71]Albert Bernhardt Faust, "Non-English Writings I: German, French, Yiddish," in William Peterfield Trent et al., eds., *A History of American Literature*, supplement to *The Cambridge History of English Literature* (New York: G. P. Putnam's Sons, 1921), 572. Faust was responsible only for the German portion of the chapter, and he was no doubt chosen to write about German-American literature on the basis of his massive, earlier study, *The German Element in the United States: With Special Reference to Its Political, Moral, Social, and Educational Influence* (Boston: Houghton Mifflin, 1909), where the chapter on literature begins with his estimation that "its chief value consists in its historical interest, as it is descriptive of the weal and woe of the German immigrants in this country and furnishes a record of their outer and inner life," 2:338.

[72]Robert E. Ward, "The Case for German-American Literature," in Gerhard K. Friesen and Walter Schatzberg, eds., *The German Contribution to the Building of the Americas: Studies in Honor of Karl J. R. Arndt* (Hanover, N.H.: Clark University Press, 1977), 373. One could extend the list of similar examples almost at will.

both these gestures essentially defensive in that they ask for the reader's attention in spite of the shortcomings of their subject, but theirs is also a curious defense, for the case rests on two unequal and even contradictory pillars. To begin, when Faust and Ward speak of "historical" or "cultural" interest, their referent is apparently literature's ability to *reflect* reality. Thus, according to Faust, Friedrich Gerstäcker "draws with a realistic pen, and does not fail to emphasize the hardships and disappointments of frontier life," while Otto Ruppius's works "give a just view of the German immigrant and refugee in America."[73] And Ward compares, albeit unfavorably, "the concern of German-American fiction writers of the nineteenth century for minute details of physical appearance and landscape" with the German masters of "poetic realism."[74] Writing in a similar vein, Robert Bishoff, whose work appears in a volume published and therefore sanctioned by the Modern Language Association, claims that a novel titled *Die Auswanderer nach Texas* (Emigrants to Texas) "has special interest historically because it relates incidents in the lives of several prominent figures of the time."[75] The list of examples could go on and on, but the essential point is that by reducing the value of German-American literature to its overtly documentary aspects, Faust and scholars who have followed in his footsteps are simply but misguidedly attempting to exempt the German-language literature written in the United States from the apparently timeless category of "literary interest" that constitute the second line of his original argument.

The difficulties that arise with the addition of the aesthetic portion of the argument are threefold. First, much of the German-language literature produced in the United States is not overtly concerned

[73]Faust, "Non-English Writings," 580.
[74]Ward, "Case for German-American Literature," 381.
[75]Robert Bishoff, "German-American Literature," in Robert J. Di Pietro and Edward Ifkovic, eds., *Ethnic Perspectives in American Literature: Selected Essays on the European Perspective* (New York: Modern Language Association of America, 1983), 55. An earlier and not unrelated undertaking is the collection edited by Wolodymyr T. Zyla and Wendell M. Aycock, *Ethnic Literatures since 1776: The Many Voices of America*, Proceedings of the Comparative Literature Symposium, No. 9, 1976 (Lubbock: Texas Tech University Press, 1978), which contains an article by Carl Hammer, Jr., "A Glance at Three Centuries of German-American Writing," 217–32. In fact, surveys of this sort—"rounding up the usual suspects"—are relatively common; see also the chapter titled "German-Language Newspapers and Belles-Lettres in the United States," in Rippley, *The German-Americans*, 144–60; and Robert Spiller and Willard Thorp, "German-American Literature," in Don Heinrich Tolzman, ed., *German-American Literature* (Metuchen, N.J.: Scarecrow Press, 1977), 2–6.

with the immigrant experience. That literature also contains historical novels, lyric poetry, and all the other forms and contents that
were common to the last three hundred years of both German and
American literary production. Yet without these "nonhistorical"
works, which supposedly fail to live up to various aesthetic norms,
scholars of German-American literature would either have very little
to write about or would be forced to do nothing but catalog varying
degrees of failure. Both alternatives present relatively dismal prospects, but not, unfortunately, uncommon research projects. Bishoff,
for example, concludes, "The German-American literature of the latter part of the nineteenth century is often marred by implausible
plots or poor characterization."[76] Indeed, no account is complete
without some reference to the poor quality of the author's style,
tone, or subject matter. The second difficulty is that because none of
these critics can really sustain such relentless condemnation, their
work is actually filled with references to what they nevertheless
think of as positive literary qualities. Faust, for example, who might
be considered a typical representative of turn-of-the-century German
studies, praises Charles Sealsfield's ability to paint "nature pictures
in wonderful colours" and complains that the translation of Hermann von Holst's history of the United States "by no means does
justice to the virile [sic] style of the original."[77] By extending his own
unarticulated categories only slightly, Ward can write: "Although
generally written in a journalistic fashion, many travel books and
sketches of the late eighteenth and early nineteenth centuries contain
beautifully written passages which border on creative literature."[78]
In short, the "interest" in German-American texts is not just historical after all; it is also literary. That admission raises the third and
most problematical aspect of the aesthetic argument, for the values
represented here not only are largely unarticulated and unreflected,
but also reflect a lingering conservative consensus about literary
value that has virtually disappeared from serious scholarship during
the last two decades. Ever since the demise of New Criticism in the
United States—and of its counterpart, *werkimmanente Interpretation*, in the German-speaking world—it is simply no longer possible
to pretend that notions as "literary interest" have anything but a
purely conventional and therefore largely arbitrary content. It was at

---

[76]Bishoff, "German-American Literature," 63.
[77]Faust, "Non-English Writings," 579, 586.
[78]Ward, "Case for German-American Literature," 379–80.

least partially the discussion of popular literature that fractured the canon and its timeless values,[79] but the shock has yet to be felt either in the field of German-American literature or in most studies of ethnic literature.

One reason for its absence is the fact that Condoyannis's 1954 dissertation is still universally cited as the major work of scholarship on German-American literature. To Condoyannis's credit, it must be acknowledged at the outset that he actually performed the herculean task of finding, reading, and dealing with virtually all the extant German-language prose fiction published in book form in the United States, and he provides an extensive bibliography of nineteenth-century German-American authors and their writings, as well as 117 pages of plot summaries [!] from the works he consulted. One can, of course, quibble with his selection process. As already mentioned, Condoyannis limited his research (again one must assume that his decision was to no small degree pragmatic) to works published as books, but as a result he overlooked a good deal of what German immigrants actually wrote and read—namely, the short stories, sketches, and serialized novels that appeared in the German-American press.[80] One can only speculate about the amount of literature and also about the specific texts that he missed with this procedure, but the omission of newspaper and other periodical sources could well explain the paucity of socialist writings in Condoyannis's sample.[81] And although he mentions *Die Abendschule* at one point, Condoyannis neglects virtually all the authors published there.[82] Yet the problem with Condoyannis's approach is clearly not that he failed to live up to some chimerical ideal of completeness, but rather that he

---

[79]See Jochen Schulte-Sasse, *Literarische Wertung*, 2d ed. (Stuttgart: Metzler, 1976).

[80]For a discussion of the problem, see Peter C. Merrill, "The Serial Novel in the German-American Press of the Nineteenth Century," *Journal of German-American Studies* 13.1 (1978): 16–22. Merrill cataloged several volumes of two Milwaukee papers, *Banner und Volksfreund* and *Freie Presse*, in an attempt to show how the gaps in Condoyannis's research might be filled. The difficulty with this approach is that researchers (and here the plural is almost an understatement, because the task of surveying all the estimated 5,000 German-language periodicals published in the United States is indeed immense) would have to search through hundreds of journals, rather than being able to rely on library catalogs as Condoyannis did.

[81]See Condoyannis's chapter "The 'Social Tendency' up to the First World War," 327–95.

[82]Ibid., 326.

relies on largely unstated, and unreflected categories of literary evaluation:

> In the present study we shall adhere as closely as possible to the crite-
> rion of literary evaluation without, on the one hand . . . maintaining
> unrealistically high standards—we cannot expect to find any Goethes
> or Schillers among these writers . . . Attention will be focused on the
> presence or absence of continuity and interrelationships, on an analysis
> of subject matter and of the author's attitude toward life and toward
> his fellow man, and insofar as possible on a fairminded evaluation of
> the entire output as literature.[83]

Condoyannis is obviously a product of that perhaps largely mythical and happy age when critics seemed to agree on "the criterion of
literary evaluation" (note the surprisingly singular noun at the head
of this phrase) and were therefore actually able to convince themselves that they were evaluating these texts "as literature." Almost
by definition no subsequent writer would ever again match Goethe
and Schiller, but authors could still be judged according to the degree to which they approached that high ideal. For example, on at
least eight occasions Condoyannis faults works that he believed were
incorrectly labeled "Novellen,"[84] and he registers numerous complaints about implausible plots, poorly drawn characters, and unconscious Anglicisms. Of far greater importance, however, is the political agenda concealed behind the supposedly objective "criterion
of literary evaluation." Speaking of Karl Adolf Douai's *Fata Morgana*, Condoyannis complains that the author was "far more interested in his 'progressive' ideas and their dissemination than in actual
German American life. There is not even a hint in the story of his
awareness of the approaching Civil War and of the part Germans
would play in it." For a novel published in 1858, the latter criticism
seems silly indeed, and the whole category of the "historical" rather
than "literary" interest of German-American literature has again become an almost self-fulfilling prophecy. Works either document "actual German American life" or are faulted for failing to do so.

The circularity of the argument would not be so problematical if it

[83]Ibid., 14–18.
[84]Ibid., 55–58, 62–63, 81, 127, 131, 167, 189, 192. Condoyannis's criticism of
Georg Asmus's *Camp Paradise, Novelle*, is a revealing case in point: "The story is
not technically a *Novelle*, and one suspects that Asmus was quite unaware of exactly
what constitutes a *Novelle*, much less of Goethe's or any other German writer's
definition" (Condoyannis, "German-American Prose Fiction," 167).

were not for the implicitly narrow range of acceptable depictions and the extent to which Condoyannis attempts to mask his own political prejudices with the "objective" status of literary criticism. Samuel Ludvigh's portrayal of religious intolerance in the United States is supposedly atypical. According to Condoyannis, most Germans apparently found the United States quite agreeable in religious matters and are to be praised for their powers of observation: "Lexow strives at all times to be objective while giving us sensational reading matter; . . . he is in this country as an immigrant and regards it as his second home."[85] On the other hand, in Condoyannis's eyes it is probably not accidental that Ludvigh's political sins have artistic repercussions: "In view of the story's ["Der Doktor und der Teufel"] obvious tendentiousness, we are not surprised to find that it lacks unity and consistency."[86] It short, it sounds as though criticism of the United States (*Nestbeschmutzung*) was the most heinous crime a German-American author could commit, particularly if the criticism came from beyond the pale of what was politically acceptable in 1954: "The author shows fair talent as a belletristic writer, although his left-wing bias is obvious at every point and considerably weakens his characters."[87] This mode of analysis, which mixes unspecified formal criteria with an unreflected political agenda, is unfortunately typical of Condoyannis's whole enterprise. And not only is Condoyannis's dissertation frequently praised and cited as one of the major works in German-American literature, but almost everyone in the field continues to follow his lead—generally with disastrous results.[88]

[85]Ibid., 54, 123.

[86]Ibid., 100.

[87]Ibid., 339; the criticism is directed against A. Otto-Walster. To be fair, it should be noted that Condoyannis occasionally tries to rise above the contemporary political categories he otherwise parrots: "Our conclusion with regard to Arlberg's novel is that in spite of its tendentiousness and obvious bias it can still lay claim to literary recognition of the basis of its skillful structure, its subtle characterizations and its essential realism." This particular appraisal seems to have come easier because "there may be some doubt as to whether Max Arlberg can be called a socialist in the strict sense" (ibid., 347–48).

[88]Robert E. Ward's review of Barbara Lang, *The Process of Immigration in German-American Literature from 1850 to 1900* (Munich: Fink, 1988), *Yearbook of German-American Studies* 24 (1989): 172, demonstrates Condoyannis's continuing presence as *the* standard of comparison: "Aside from George F. Condoyannis's dissertation on German-American prose fiction (1953), Lang's study is the only work to consider a wide scope of German-American novelists." A brief quotation from Lang will have to suffice as proof of just how bleak the field is: "The aspect that distin-

In fact, because much of the recent research into German-American literature essentially follows Condoyannis's cataloging mode, a major problem is that it seems to have no real raison d'être; aside from recording the hitherto unremarked existence of some newspaper, novel, or poem, there is really nothing at stake. The authors of works on German-American literature almost invariably proceed without problematizing either their own political position or their status within the discipline they are addressing, and they are seldom even aware of the kind of theoretical questions Deleuze and Guattari raise, however unsuccessfully. The reviews and biographical sketches that constitute much of what gets published mostly read like obituaries, brief accounts in which the author's writings are little more than an aspect of his or her exemplary life. My favorite title is "Konrad Nies, German-American Literary Knight," by Robert E. Ward, but "The Last Cincinnati German Poet: Heinrich H. Fick," by Don Heinrich Tolzmann, runs a close second.[89] Both articles claim to rescue their objects from an undeserved obscurity, but neither attempts to justify the choice by actually analyzing the author's writings. In both cases the subject's chief distinction was his service in the cause of German-American letters, and it is for that reason alone that their lives are examined. Such unreconstructed positivism means that we are left with little more than the explanation of why some people choose to climb Mount Everest: "Because it's there."

---

guished the multitude of novels written between 1850 and 1900 most proved to be literary form and subject-matter rather than the authors' respective ethno-political position" (p. 28). Whatever might be hidden behind the notion of "literary form," which German-American authors apparently either did or did not have in common, I am puzzled by the opposition between "subject-matter" and "ethno-political position." Is ethnicity not subject matter?

[89]The articles, originally written in 1971 and 1976, respectively, are part of a collection Tolzmann edited, entitled German-American Literature, pp. 245–51, 273–84. These particular articles were chosen in part because they represent the work of two of the best-known scholars in the field, men who are tireless campaigners for German-American causes ranging from observance of an annual German-American day in the United States, officially in place by presidential proclamation since 1987, to the Society for German-American Studies, of which Ward was a founder and Tolzmann is the perennial president. There is, however, an agenda behind Tolzmann's book. It seems to be part of the call "to implement German Americana into the curriculum on all levels," as outlined in the report of an "Educational Task Force Meeting," Society for German-American Studies Newsletter 8 (September 1987): 18. According to the "Foreword": p. iii, "The purpose of this work is to present for the first time an introductory history of German-American literature." The difficulty is that the works it presents represent exactly the kind of sentimental, filiopietistic scholarship that is unfortunately so common in German-American studies.

There is something to be said for simply recording the literary experiences of the German-Americans, but the goal of completeness ("A bibliography of *all* German books printed in the U.S. since 1830. . . . An anthology of the German writings of *all* American-born authors)"[90] is by itself an insufficient research agenda. And the danger of objective marginality is all the more acute if the selection process ("books" and "American-born authors") means that both the popular narratives read by much of the middle class and most of the texts addressed to the German-American working class are still left out of the augmented canon. The real danger is that the study of German-American literature will remain little more than antiquarianism, a *Liebhaberwissenschaft* nostalgically collating traces of a "German" spirit that is now so irrevocably lost.[91] For it is precisely in the realm of unstated premises and unreflected assumptions that the political, ideological, and theoretical stakes are actually the highest. Behind the goal of uncovering one more unknown text or yet another unappreciated author, "historical interest" and "literary quality" return as the arbiters of an avowedly depoliticized ethnic universe, where bourgeois values—like common sense and objectivity before their deconstruction—reign supreme. Predictably enough, the result is that it is precisely the middle-class values and the writers who represented them that come to exemplify a thoroughly sanitized version of German-American literary history. As Carol Poore argues in one of the few attempts to rescue a different, namely a socialist, literary tradition, "the writers in the area of German-American studies after 1945 have continued these trends of emphasizing the most assimilable or conservative sides of the ethnic group, of portraying it as an essentially homogeneous block, and of downplaying conflicts within the group itself or between its less conformist members."[92]

The difficulty is easily explained in institutional terms. As Patricia Herminghouse has suggested, one reason for the relative paucity of

---

[90]Tolzmann, *German-American Literature*, iii (emphasis added).

[91]See, e.g., Robert Elmer Ward, *Dictionary of German-American Creative Writers: From the Seventeenth Century to the Present* (Cleveland, Ohio: German-American Publishing Co., 1978), which contains an exhaustive bibliography of secondary source material as well as a listing of the "creative literature" written by German-Americans. The biographical data is superseded by Ward's *A Bio-Bibliography of German-American Writers, 1670–1970* (White Plains, N.Y.: Kraus International Publications, 1985).

[92]Carol J. Poore, *German-American Socialist Literature, 1865–1900* (Bern: Peter Lang, 1982), 16.

more serious scholarship "may be our own discomfort at dealing with most of the existing scholarship on the topic. Much of what has been written grew out of fears of a decline of Germandom in the United States, and history has taught us, more than the students of most ethnic groups, a justifiable apprehensiveness towards such thinking."[93] And once a field has been marked by a particularly problematical scholarly tradition, other researchers are understandably wary of risking their reputations in face of the danger of guilt by association.

One tangible result is that German departments were left almost completely untouched by the resurgence of ethnicity and ethnic studies in the 1970s. Since 1970, of the hundreds of Ph.D. dissertations written in the field of German, the number concerned with German-American topics is less than three dozen.[94] If one then looks at those actually concerned with German-American literature, rather than with the survival of various dialects, with the reception of "authentically" German literature in various American journals or on the American stage, or with the accounts of Germans traveling through the United States, the total is under ten. Not only is German-American literature apparently still "of greater historical than literary interest," but those interested in German-American topics are virtually all historians, or at least from disciplines other than German.[95] Judging from the *Yearbook of German-American Studies*—which came into existence in 1981 to replace the considerably less serious-looking *Journal of German-American Studies: A Journal of History, Literature, Biography, and Genealogy*, with its mixture of scholarly articles, genealogies, and poetry by German-American writers—interdisciplinarity has been achieved largely without Germanists. As far as the *Yearbook* is concerned, except for the occa-

---

[93]Patricia Herminghouse, "German-American Studies in a New Vein: Resources and Possibilities," *Die Unterrichtspraxis* 9, no. 2 (1976): 4. It seems, however, that Herminghouse is mistaken when, except for certain textbooks, she locates so much of the problem in the past.

[94]The figures are based on a survey of the annual listing of doctoral degrees printed in *Monatshefte*. Because they are indexed not by topic but simply by title, I might have missed several of them, but the overall thrust of the analysis is certainly true.

[95]See Peter Merrill, "Recent Doctoral Dissertations in German-American Studies," *Society for German-American Studies Newsletter* 8 (March 1987): 6. The ten dissertations listed include Klaus Heinrich Metzendorf, "Viability of the Wine Industries in New York State and West Germany," as well as histories of Hutterite architecture and the Americanization of Weimar culture through the movies—but not a single "literary" topic, at least not on German-American literature.

sional article on Sealsfield, who can, for professional reasons, be safely labeled Austrian or even German, rather than strictly German-American, there are scarcely any treatments of German-American literature at all. In short, to judge by the production of new scholars by German departments in the United States and by the contents of the leading journal of German-American studies, German-American literature barely exists as a legitimate field of study within the discipline of German. Those who nevertheless practice it are often forced to construct elaborate defenses for their efforts—an argument that could easily be directed at this chapter.

One could also paint a brighter picture, especially if one concentrated on literature rather than on the broader notion of popular narratives used in this book. For example, although mainly concerned with the image of America in German literature, the 1975 collection *Amerika in der deutschen Literatur* (America in German Literature) does contain a number of interesting pieces on German-American literature by Frank Trommler, Horst Denkler, and Christoph Hering, and the two volumes edited by Trommler and Joseph McVeigh to commemorate the tricentennial of German immigration to the United States in 1983 also contain a number of articles on literature.[96] But I shall concentrate here on Carol Poore's treatment of German-American socialist literature because its strengths and weaknesses are apparently shared by all the works just cited.

Poore's work is a good example of an alternative research agenda that shares a sense of purpose with the poststructuralist accounts of ethnicity discussed above: "The struggle which continues over the preservation and dissemination of the radical tradition, over the reinterpretation of the forgotten part of the German-American legacy, is in fact a struggle for the power of a sense of historical development and progress which we can win from the past."[97] In fact, this is the same past that can provide the shining examples of early German-American feminists and the virtually ubiquitous Forty-Eighters,

---

[96]Sigrid Bauschinger, Horst Denkler, and Wilfried Malsch, eds., *Amerika in der deutschen Literatur: Neue Welt—Nordamerika—U.S.A.* (Stuttgart: Reclam, 1975), which includes Frank Trommler, "Vom Vormärz zum Bürgerkrieg: Die Achtundvierziger und ihre Lyrik," 93–107; Horst Denkler, "Die Schule des Kapitalismus: Reinhold Solgers deutsch-amerikanisches 'Seitenstück' zu Gustav Freytags 'Soll und Haben,'" 108–23; and Christoph Hering, "Otto Ruppius, der Amerikafahrer, Flüchtling, Exilschriftsteller, Rückwanderer," 124–34. The other volume is Trommler and Joseph McVeigh, eds., *America and the Germans: An Assessment of a Three-Hundred-Year History* (Philadelphia: University of Pennsylvania Press, 1985).

[97]Poore, *German-American Socialist Literature*, 164.

who figure almost too prominently in works about the German immigrants in the United States.[98] Like the feminists and the Forty-Eighters, German-American socialists were fiercely literate, and like their bourgeois counterparts the socialist journals they produced were filled with a mixture of poems, short stories, and serialized novels that reveal a great deal about the experience of German immigrants in the United States: "As a means of articulating their situation in the present and their visions of the future, this literature constituted a vital part of the socialist subculture."[99]

There are, however, two dangers lurking in every valorization of heroic figures from the past. First, one must apologize for whatever shortcomings those figures may have had, in part to explain why—despite their obvious virtues—they failed to bring about anything other than the unsatisfactory present we all still occupy. Thus Poore admits that, in addition to their revolutionary texts, the socialist journals she studied also had to offer their readers some of the same sentimental fare common to bourgeois literature "to satisfy a need for entertainment and diversion."[100] Yet, while she argues that such texts induced people (women) to buy a particular paper so that they (men) would also read its editorial content, she leaves the sentimental literature and the tension it must have produced within those papers unexamined. For Poore, German-American literature is more important for its overt content—that is, for a stance we either accept or reject on the basis of our own preconceived political position—than for the related question of how these texts worked and whether they can still be read with profit.

Second, and even more serious, is her tendency to overlook, or even to denigrate, what was written by the valorized object's opponents. Poore appears to accept the notion that nonsocialist literature

[98]On the feminists, particularly Mathilde Franziska Anneke, see Dorothea Diver Stuecher, *Double Jeopardy: Nineteenth-Century German American Women Writers*, (Ph.D. diss., University of Minnesota, 1981). Publications about the Forty-Eighters are so numerous that they would require another chapter, but Trommler's article in the Bauschinger volume is a good place to start. See also Carl Wittke, *Refugees of Revolution: The Forty-eighters in America* (Philadelphia: University of Pennsylvania Press, 1952); and Eitel Wolf Dobert, *Deutsche Demokraten in Amerika: Die Achtundvierziger und ihre Schriften* (Göttingen: Vandenhoeck and Ruprecht, 1958).

[99]Poore, *German-American Socialist Literature*, 76.

[100]Ibid., 96. In a similar vein, Trommler ("Vom Vormärz zum Bürgerkrieg," in Bauschinger et al., eds., *Amerika in der deutschen Literatur*, 100) writes: "The profusion of similar, often quite clumsy verse corresponded to the demand from social and political gatherings."

was of universally inferior quality and, worse yet in her estimation, that it was written as "l'art pour l'art," without political content.[101] It is interesting that Poore here makes use of the same categories of literary evaluation she decries when they are applied to socialist literature. In addition, she denies bourgeois literature a similar role in the formation of German-American identities. In her view, socialist literature "is really the only portion of German-American literature which went beyond internalization and affirmation to grasp and enter into the real social conflicts German working-class immigrants experienced in America."[102] Not only is it unclear just what "real social conflicts" might be, but it is simply untrue to maintain that other German-American literatures did not speak to the problems that both working-class immigrants and their bourgeois counterparts regarded as very real indeed, however dubious their solutions may have been. Moreover, understanding just how the process of "internalization and affirmation" functioned, if that is what actually went on in periodicals like *Die Abendschule*, is no less important than surveying the literature produced and read by German socialists in the United States. Indeed, at some level internalization and affirmation may have been at work there too. Of course, this is not to deny the value of Poore's work, or of any serious work done on marginalized groups of German-Americans, and Poore is also certainly correct in arguing that unstated ideologies have played a large role in these groups' absence as objects of study. Yet Herminghouse was no doubt just as correct in wondering about "the legitimacy of any study of German-Americana which limits itself to dealing with the more appealing and adventuresome elite radicals and intellectuals or the quaint German settlements without confronting the basic issues of ethnicity in America."[103]

When the pendulum swings from literary quality to political sympathy, it also describes a fairly large arc of intermediate positions. Readers of *Die Abendschule*, at least to judge by the representations of them in the journal's mastheads and as we shall see later by what they read, were neither socialists nor the Bavarian caricatures we now associate with German-American ethnicity. One of the chief reasons that a periodical like *Die Abendschule* is so interesting is that its readers were apparently so average; they were right square in

---

[101]Poore, *German-American Socialist Literature*, 80.
[102]Ibid., 85.
[103]Herminghouse, "German-American Studies," 8.

the middle—between the socialists Poore lionizes and the quaint remnants she rejects. What they read was neither "high" literature nor the overtly tendentious tracts and engaged texts of any particular political orientation. *Die Abendschule*'s subscribers probably represented the normal—that is, fundamentally conservative— readers of German-language newspapers and magazines published in the United States, and this book examines what those ordinary readers read and how they read it.

Virtually everyone who works with the German-Americans would side with Poore against Condoyannis and say that newspapers and journals provide almost unmatched access to the everyday experiences of German immigrants. And even if scholars are, perhaps understandably, reluctant to delve into those largely uncharted depths, there is widespread agreement that the German-language periodicals published in the United States are also an important source of German-American literature. In part, both the problem and the opportunity presented by the German-language press in the United States is an embarrassment of riches. There were literally thousands of German papers published in North America—ranging from daily and weekly newspapers of every conceivable political stripe to the organs of various religious and fraternal organizations, and also to avowedly highbrow literary journals and crime sheets (sometimes, as in the case of the intriguingly titled *New Yorker Kriminalzeitung und Belletristisches Journal* [The New York Crime Reporter and Belletristic Journal], combined into one paper[104]). And nearly all these periodicals also published literature in some form.[105] But when one turns from studies of German-American literature to research concerned specifically with the German-American press, a curious omission immediately becomes apparent: the literature contained in those journals simply disappears.

In his history of *The German-Language Press in America*, Carl

[104]See Edmund E. Miller, "Das New Yorker Belletristische Journal, 1851–1911," *American-German Review* 8, no. 2 (1941): 24–27.
[105]Luckily, the German-American press has been well served by bibliographers, most notably by Karl J. Arndt, *German-American Newspapers and Periodicals, 1732–1955* (Heidelberg: Quelle and Meyer, 1961), as well as two additional volumes by Arndt and May E. Olson, *The German-Language Press of the Americas, 1732–1968: History and Bibliography* (Munich: Verlag Dokumentation, 1973); and *German-American Press Research from the American Revolution to the Bicentennial* (Munich: K. G. Sauer, 1980).

Wittke, still regarded as the preeminent scholar in the field, characterizes nineteenth-century German-American newspapers as follows: "The only distinctive feature of the German press, compared with typical American dailies, was the serial story and the section devoted to belles-lettres, known as the *feuilleton*."[106] Although Wittke overlooks the fact that German-American newspapers were printed in German and therefore provided their readers with a linguistic link to their European homeland, his remark is still significant in that it should pave the way for an exhaustive analysis of the novels, stories, and poems published in the German-American press. Instead, Wittke treats literature as an extraneous filler whose sole purpose was to persuade readers to buy a paper in the hope that they would also read its editorial content, or at least browse through the advertisements for patent medicines and steamship tickets that were the real reason for the existence of a commercial press. Here Wittke carries on the tradition begun more than a generation earlier by the Chicago sociologist Robert Park, whose pioneering book, *The Immigrant Press and Its Control*, contains but a single reference to the literature published in the foreign-language press in the United States: "The peasants [who in Park's view comprised the majority of immigrants] are sentimental; the editor prints poetry for them in the vernacular. He fills the paper with cheap fiction and writes loud-sounding editorials, double-leaded, so they will be easily read."[107] For both Wittke and Park the real content of the immigrant press is reduced to what is overtly political, and politics' relationship to the rest of the paper, particularly to the literature contained there, is merely coincidental, except when advertisers attempted to intrude.[108]

By examining the political positions espoused by various papers, both Wittke and Park hoped to explain how readers were influenced by specific editorial content. For example, after a lengthy discussion of various election issues seen through the eyes of the German-American press, Wittke concludes: "In Wisconsin the Germans voted for Hayes in 1876 largely because their newspapers had con-

[106]Carl Wittke, *The German-Language Press in America* (Lexington: University of Kentucky Press, 1957), 217.

[107]Robert E. Park, *The Immigrant Press and Its Control* (New York: Harper, 1922), 72.

[108]The "control" in Park's title refers to pressure exerted by Louis N. Hammerling in his efforts to manipulate advertising revenue through the American Association of Foreign Language Newspapers. See ibid., 377–99.

vinced them that he was sound on financial matters."[109] Just why German immigrants may have been troubled by fiscal questions in 1876 remains unclear in Wittke's analysis, but the larger problem with his model is that it posits autonomous individuals, unfettered by ideology, rationally weighing alternatives and deciding freely on the merits of the arguments set before them. There is, however, little reason to believe that anyone, including nineteenth-century German-Americans, actually makes decisions on this basis. All behavior, even or especially political behavior, occurs in a historically specific, discursive framework that sets the boundaries for what is believed to be legitimate or true. People's beliefs about how their world operates cannot therefore be reduced to a series of rationally articulated beliefs; the planks in a party's platform, the issues of war and peace, and the problems of economic survival resonate as much in people's hearts as in their minds. And it is precisely by speaking to those emotional needs that literature helped readers make sense of the world in which they lived. Thus, if literature provided immigrants with an interpretive orientation, even if only to compensate for the problems they experienced in the new environment of the United States, the implicit model of what is interesting about the German-American press is revealed to be so narrow that it breaks down irreparably. Moreover, the inadequacy of Wittke's paradigm should call into question the activities of those scholars who are merely cataloging the German-American press, just as the act of collecting more and more examples of German-American literature is an inadequate research agenda for scholars in that particular subfield.

Again, this is not to argue that it is unimportant for researchers to determine what papers were published where, when, and by whom, or that their editorial stance is of no concern. On the other hand, to suggest (as one recent assessment did) that "[s]urplus space was filled with serialized fiction or abstruse scientific discussion"[110] and then to relegate the narratives contained in these spaces to the academic margins, where a footnote or a passing reference suffices to affirm the texts' essentially inessential nature, is to miss something extraordinarily significant not only about the German-American press but also about German-Americans in general and about the

[109]Wittke, *The German-Language Press in America*, 161.

[110]James M. Bergquist, "The German-American Press," in Sally M. Miller, ed., *The Ethnic Press in the United States: A Historical Analysis and Handbook* (Westport, Conn.: Greenwood Press, 1987), 141.

role popular narratives played in their culture.[111] If Wittke is right in claiming that the literature published there was "the only distinctive feature of the German press," and he is certainly correct about its prominence, then popular narratives should be central to any consideration of the German-American experience. Even the supposedly "political" decision to support Hayes in 1876 was conditioned by the voters' reaction to the financial panic of 1873 and the ensuing depression, both of which coursed through the novels and stories subsequently published in "apolitical" sections of the German-American press.[112]

The counterargument is curiously like an analysis of television in the United States, because while it is true that the major reason for the existence of the programs that appear on commercial stations is to keep people in their seats for the advertisements, it would be preposterous to reduce the message of television to these ads alone, just as it would be difficult to assess the full impact of advertising without reference to the context of the programming that surrounds it and to the interconnections between the two. But as far as I can determine, there have only been two attempts to deal with literature in the German-American press. The first, a study written by Erich Hofacker in 1946, limits itself to the "works of famous German poets and novelists found in the newspapers" of St. Louis, apparently in an effort to determine how well editors fulfilled the task of trying "to improve the literary taste of their readers."[113] Not surprisingly, they failed, in part because their "readers were of the

[111]Most studies seem to stop short of this point—i.e., their contributions, while valuable, appear to be too limited. See, e.g., Steven Rowan and James Neal Primm, *Germans for a Free Missouri: Translations from the St. Louis Press, 1857–1862* (Columbia: University of Missouri Press, 1983); Paul Schach, "German-Language Newspapers in Nebraska, 1860–1890," *Nebraska History* 65 (1984): 84–107; and John Kulas, "*Der Wanderer* of Saint Paul: An Overview of the First Years," and Gerhard H. Weiss, "The German Language Press in Minnesota," in *A Heritage Fulfilled: German-Americans*, ed. Clarence A. Glasrud, (Moorhead, Minn.: Concordia College, 1984), 64–93, 47–63.

The one previous account of *Die Abendschule*, which was a kind of popular obituary published two years after the magazine's demise, is clearly written in this mode. See A. E. Zucker, "Die Abendschule, 1853–1940: A Pioneer Weekly," *American-German Review* 8 (February 1942): 14–17.

[112]See the analysis of "Der Schlosser von Philadelphia," *Die Abendschule* 26 (1880) in Chapter 5, below.

[113]Erich P. Hofacker, *German Literature as Reflected in the German-Language Press of St. Louis Prior to 1898*, Washington University Studies, New Series: Language and Literature 16 (St. Louis: Washington University, 1946), 2.

lower middle class" and in part because, astonishing as it may seem, "the daily newspaper is not the place where we would ordinarily look for information on such a specialized field of interest as Old German literature and the history of German words."[114] By way of contrast, the second study concludes that Robert Reitzel, a sometime pastor and popular lecturer, who edited his own idiosyncratic journal, *Der arme Teufel* (The Poor Devil), from 1884 to 1898, was fairly successful in his attempts at "transmitting fine literature to his German-American audience."[115] Yet, as strange as the orientation of these two studies may be, it is even more remarkable that in both cases the literature itself is given relatively short shrift.

This book is a different type of project, one that contributes to an understanding of how at least one periodical and the narratives it published were read. And while it should be clear from the discussion of previous research in the field of German-American literature that this line of inquiry that has not been pursued by Germanists in the United States, German scholars in Germany have done significant work in this direction. Aside from the debates surrounding popular narratives, which will be dealt with more fully in the next chapter, a number of nineteenth-century publications have also attracted a good deal of scholarly attention, much of which is concerned with the journals' literary content. The most notable example is *Die Gartenlaube*,[116] but as we saw in the previous chapter, there are also more general accounts of the family journals as a genre—including the Christian family journal *Daheim*, which is of particular interest as a point of reference for *Die Abendschule*.[117] In order to be clear about what has been missing in previous accounts of the German-American press, it is important to note what Bodo Rollka concluded in his book on the literature published in newspapers in Berlin during the nineteenth century:

[114]Ibid., 1, 9.

[115]Randall Paul Donaldson, "Robert Reitzel (1849–1898) and his German American Periodical *Der arme Teufel*," Ph.D., diss. Johns Hopkins University, 1976, 149.

[116]E.g., Heidemarie Gruppe, *"Volk" zwischen Politik und Idylle in der Gartenlaube, 1853–1914* (Bern: Lang, 1976); Günter Häntzschel, "Lyrik-Vermittlung in Familienblättern am Beispiel der 'Gartenlaube' 1885 bis 1895," *Literaturwissenschaftliches Jahrbuch*, N.F. 22 (1981): 155–85; Anne-Susanne Rischke, *Die Lyrik in der "Gartenlaube" 1853–1903: Untersuchungen zu Thematik, Form und Funktion* (Frankfurt: Peter Lang, 1982); and Hazel E. Rosenstrauch, "Zum Beispiel *Die Gartenlaube*," in Annamaria Rucktäschel and Hans Dieter Zimmermann, eds., *Trivialliteratur* (Munich: Wilhelm Fink, 1976), 169–89.

[117]See Barth, "Das Daheim und sein Verleger August Klasing," 43–111.

In the realm of the daily newspaper there developed a type of journalistic belletrist in whose work literature renounced its function as a
potential form of opposition; indeed, the development of the popular
novel could become the saga of Wilhelmine Germany. Subject as it was
to the laws of the marketplace, the popular novel's tendency toward
apology for and glorification of national achievements became absolute.[118]

At this point in the analysis it is too early to know the degree to
which the narratives published in *Die Abendschule* were similar or
different, but the fundamental question to be posed here is precisely
the one raised in Rollka's subtitle, namely, what was the "socializing
function of entertainment" in *Die Abendschule*? My basic premise is
not only that popular narratives were connected with the process of
socialization, especially as German immigrants were forced to adapt
to various historically specific circumstances over the course of the
four and a half decades to be covered here, but also that the notion
of a relationship between literature and community provides an interesting perspective from which to investigate the narratives read
by German-Americans. Furthermore, because of the fact that *Die
Abendschule*'s readers were engaged in the process of inserting
themselves into a new culture—that is because they were attempting
to create new identities by somehow combining remnants of their
Old World selves with lives shaped by the demands of a rapidly
changing new world, their search for community, including the portion of the search carried out in and through literature, was all the
more intense. Therefore the question of how German-American popular narratives spoke to the needs of immigrant readers is a necessary addition to any inquiry into German-American literature, and
that is why the more general problems of ethnic identity and ethnic
literature discussed above are so important to my effort to provide a
framework for the analysis of texts from *Die Abendschule*.

What now remains is to use the previous discussion to define, very
briefly, just what it was that *Die Abendschule* published. In other
words, the final question is whether we can meaningfully speak of
ethnic or of German-American literature when reading the often
anonymous popular narratives to be found there, knowing full well

---

[118]Bodo Rollka, *Die Belletristik in der Berliner Presse des 19. Jahrhunderts: Untersuchungen zur Sozialisationsfunktion unterhaltender Beiträge in der Nachrichten-
presse* (Berlin: Colloquium Verlag, 1985), 433.

that some were actually written by Germans in Germany. The question is even more intractable than one might expect. Aside from the enormous theoretical difficulties involved in ever really delimiting either ethnic literature in general or German-American literature in particular, practical considerations from the history of the nineteenth-century publishing industry intrude at every turn. The answer outlined below is therefore not simply a rejection of the conventional wisdom, which has already been discussed at such great length, but an attempt to solve a reformulated question: What role did popular narratives play in the discourse of German-American identity? In short, my emphasis is not on the ultimately unresolvable and in my view relatively trivial question of textual authenticity but on the far more interesting problem of what reading *Die Abendschule* meant to the magazine's subscribers and their families. As a result, this book is inclusive rather than exclusive; it deals with the broad range of texts the magazine actually published without limiting the selection for some predetermined theoretical reason.

Until the advent of international copyright agreements in 1891, pirating texts was a normal if not quite acceptable business practice—and not just among the publishers of popular literature. Unauthorized editions were commonplace, for example, among English-language dime novels published in the United States, as publishers often stole stories from their British counterparts or procured unauthorized translations from French or German sources.[119] Similarly, German-American publications regularly stole (or perhaps paid for) material from authors living in Germany.[120] Not only did this reduce costs, but established foreign popular authors were also

---

[119]Michael Denning, *Mechanic Accents: Dime Novels and Working-Class Culture in America* (London: Verso, 1987), 37, speaks of "a kind of 'world literature' as sensational novels were translated back and forth from English, French, German and Yiddish, translated not to be faithful to the 'original', but . . . to be adapted to local names, geography and customs."

[120]There is no direct evidence available about *Die Abendschule*'s policies in this question, but circumstantial evidence suggests that they were no more honest than anyone else's. In 1878 the editor decided to publish a bowdlerized version of Wilhelm Raabe's novel, *Unseres Herrgotts Kanzlei*, and it is unlikely that Raabe would have agreed to the resultant bowdlerization. For a full account, see Chapter 5, below. We also should remember that complaints about unauthorized reprints were common in the history of German literature, especially in the eighteenth century, when unscrupulous publishers in the "foreign" jurisdictions of southern Germany got rich printing versions of Goethe or Campe without the expense of royalties for the author.

less of a gamble than unproven German-American writers. Initially, of course, there were also few of the latter, and publishers sometimes staged elaborate competitions to draw out immigrant writers, often with little success.[121] To add to the researcher's difficulties, a great deal of material was published anonymously, and many of the acknowledged authors were so obscure that they left few traces of their lives behind.

More important, however, was the notion of "Belehrung und Unterhaltung" that was characteristic of periodicals like *Die Abendschule*, which implied a sense of mission on the part of their editors and publishers. Among other things, transmitting German culture meant that they felt obligated to provide their readers with some sense of recent developments in literature. And there was no better means of educating the German-American public's taste in literature than reprinting the best works of contemporary authors. Of course, in retrospect, the works that these (male) members of the educated middle class (*Bildungsbürger*) chose to print might well be viewed as nothing short of appalling, but their tastes, which ran strongly toward the historical novels of Louise Mühlbach, were certainly no worse than their German counterparts in the publishing industry, to say nothing of the critics. Heinrich Börnstein, editor of the influential St. Louis daily *Anzeiger des Westens* (The Western Advocate), who was certainly no fool, numbered Mühlbach's novels among the "better works of modern German literature." Börnstein reprinted them in his paper's Sunday supplement in part because historical novels enjoyed an "eager and active readership," but he also claimed that by publishing them "historical knowledge was disseminated to the masses."[122]

---

[121]Adolph Douai's *Fata Morgana* (St. Louis: Verlag des Anzeiger des Westens, 1858) was the product of one such competition, which produced just six entries. In her foreword to the book version, Bertha Behrens, one of the judges, reports, "A number of years ago [I] was one of the judges in a similar undertaking sponsored by the N.Y. Staats-Zeitung. We had so much mediocre, superficial stuff (*Zeug*) to judge that we tried to get out of this Danaidian task and took no part in the decision (if one was ever made)." In his memoirs, the *Anzeiger*'s publisher, Heinrich Börnstein reports of a second contest, which produced F. X. Arming's *General Kalb* (Börnstein, *Fünfundsiebzig Jahre in der Alten und Neuen Welt: Memoiren eines Unbedeutenden*, ed. Patricia A. Herminghouse [1881; reprint Bern: Peter Lang, 1984], 2:221).

[122]Börnstein, *Fünfundsiebzig Jahre*, 2:221. Steiger (*Vertrieb deutscher Bücher*, 18–20) quotes from a flyer for Appleton's Illustri[e]rte Romanbibliothek, which included Mühlbach, her husband Theodor Mundt, and Friedrich Gerstäcker—i.e.,

The role of German history in the discourse of German-American identity is a topic that will be explored more thoroughly in Chapters 4 and 5, but to the extent that Mühlbach and others partook of that discussion through their texts, the mere fact of their German birth and residence cannot exclude them from consideration here. Even if the works of German authors were printed without alterations, their appearance in German-American periodicals was essentially a reinscription in a different cultural context; in fact, depending on how loosely or narrowly one defines the "text," the German-American incarnations of these works might well be regarded as new and therefore "authentic."

Practically speaking, it might help to think of *Die Abendschule* as an institution with a certain historical continuity in which an audience's needs were addressed by whoever wrote there. An editor's decision to publish a German author rather than a German-American author was significant in that it constituted an implicit statement about and from within the discursive universe of nineteenth-century German immigrants in the United States, but there is no reason to believe that readers shunned the texts of foreign authors or that they compartmentalized what they were able to garner from them. My plan is therefore basically to ignore the national origin of *Die Abendschule*'s writers. This pragmatic solution obviates the problem of an author's status as an ethnic writer; one simply must assume that, whatever their nationality, and however obliquely, writers who spoke to the critical issues of the day were printed. Although many if not most of the authors published in *Die Abendschule* were identifiably German-American, for my purposes it seems more useful to identify their texts not as ethnic literature but as narratives for ethnic readers. While this distinction does not clear up either the terminological or the more intractable theoretical difficulties discussed at such great length in this chapter, it does help. At least for a study of the connection between literature and community in *Die Abendschule*, the single most important question is how the texts German immigrants read functioned, not who wrote them. At any rate, with the distinction between ethnic writing and ethnic reading in mind, it is time to turn to the magazine itself and to the texts published there.

---

mainly historical novels, in its selection of the "best and most famous of recent German novels."

CHAPTER THREE

The Founding Gesture: Popular
Narratives for German-Americans

By 1854, when *Die Abendschule* was founded, German journalism in the United States was a far cry from the sleepy provincialism that had characterized it only a decade earlier.[1] Intellectuals fleeing the Revolution of 1848 are generally credited with improving the style and tone of the newspapers and magazines they took over or founded, with vastly increasing the number of journals available to the exploding population of German-speakers in North America, and with shifting their papers' political positions decidedly to the left. Forty-Eighter papers were typically antislavery, and they generally opposed temperance and organized religion as well. Many of these papers supported the new Republican party, and the German-Americans they "influenced" are thought to have pushed Lincoln over the top in the election of 1860.[2] Yet even without touching on the problematical notion of influence for the moment, the identification of the Forty-Eighters with German-American journalism in this era breaks down as soon as one looks more closely. *Die Abendschule* was not only conservative but also above all a Christian family journal that flourished in spite of—indeed, expressly in opposition to—the Forty-Eighters and their press. Inasmuch as the few thousand democrats, free-thinkers, and socialists who fled the conservative backlash in their homelands were a tiny minority among the millions of German immigrants who streamed into the United States in the second half of the nineteenth century, political radicalism may well have been the exception to the rule. In any case, the

[1] See Wittke, *The German-Language Press in America*.
[2] See above, pp. 52ff.

existence and success of *Die Abendschule* indicates that the German-American press was far more differentiated than has generally been assumed. This chapter therefore examines that diversity as it related to *Die Abendschule* and sketches the interplay between the various interests, communities, and beliefs that produced this particular journal in the specific historical circumstances of its birth.

This chapter discusses the relatively long and difficult childhood and adolescence of *Die Abendschule*—roughly the period from 1854 to 1867, when the series of crises and reorientations we have already seen in the journal's changing mastheads finally ended. In fact, as early as 1861, a new editor and a new publisher had already begun the gradual process of stabilizing the mixture of serialized fiction, short stories, popular science, brief biographies, and historical accounts that allowed *Die Abendschule* to become one of the most widely read periodicals in the United States during the nineteenth century. The editorials and mastheads that culminated in the purloined version of 1867 are evidence that the journal's editors and publishers spent more than a dozen years trying first to decide just what *Die Abendschule* should become and then justifying the project to their potential readers.

When *Die Abendschule* first appeared the editor was aware that the new magazine was something of an anomaly. In fact, his initial appeal to the journal's potential readers included the following statement:

> We ask that the Christian fathers and mothers of families (*die christlichen Hausväter und Hausmütter*) subject this magazine to a leisurely but thorough examination to see whether it is not a good and better school for their smaller and grown children than much other reading matter. We are convinced that a magazine like this will prove to be extremely useful in your family, and its low price allows every father to purchase it.[3]

Not only is the editor aware of a difference between his magazine and "other reading matter," but he is also attempting to distance his undertaking from much of the rest of German-American journalism.

---

[3]*Illustri[e]rte Abendschule*, I.1 (1 February 1854): 1. Because volume one of *Die Abendschule* is unpaginated, the issue number is also included here; the page numbers are simply my counting within each issue. Beginning with volume two there is continuous pagination.

Because the statement is addressed specifically to "the Christian fathers and mothers of families" and promises them that the new journal will be welcome in their families, one obvious conclusion is that *Die Abendschule*'s own identity as a Christian family journal was the result of its opposition to a world that its writers and editors regarded as increasingly secular and individualistic. The magazine's mission, which was defined in pedagogic terms, was nothing less than to counter the influence of the rest of the German-language press. To achieve that end, it offered families "a good and better school": *Die Abendschule*. As the name suggests, "classes" were scheduled for the evening, when the entire family could gather, and instruction was open to all—even to the poorest family: "its low price allows every father [though, conspicuously, not every mother] to purchase it."

Even before this first number appeared, a prospectus announcing the *Illustri[e]rte Abendschule: Ein Blatt zur Belehrung und Unterhaltung für die reifere Jugend* was issued in Buffalo, New York.[4] The name *Abendschule* refers to the evening schools established for artisans and workers beginning in the first half of the nineteenth century,[5] and although the primary audience named in the subtitle was "more mature young people," *Die Abendschule* appears to have been constituted as a magazine for the entire family from the very beginning of its existence. While other periodicals, particularly newspapers, concentrated on political and economic events and thereby excluded younger readers, *Die Abendschule* intended to include both young and old in a single group of readers. In fact, as analysis of the mastheads has demonstrated, the journal advocated an inclusive mode of group reading; the claim that the magazine would nevertheless address "more mature young people" seems to indicate a certain confusion in *Die Abendschule*'s orientation which may have adversely affected subscriptions. Moreover, as we shall see, the magazine soon began to include items like the news and market reports, which could scarcely have been of interest to its avowed audience. Nor were prices for flour and hogs likely to be read aloud to the assembled family. Thus, by July 1858, probably in

[4]"Prospectus der Illustri[e]rten Abendschule," CHI, A & HL 1052. The prospectus was a two-page document, and there are two columns of newsprint on both sides of a standard-format (c. 8.5 x 11 inches) page. Quotations from the "Prospectus" will be identified in the text with a "P."

[5]See Mary Jo Maynes, *Schooling in Western Europe: A Social History* (Albany: State University of New York Press, 1985), 109–12.

an effort to reflect its actual orientation more closely, volume five was renamed; the title on the masthead was pared down to *Illustrir[e]te Abendschule: Eine Zeitschrift für Belehrung und Unterhaltung*. The limiting qualifier, "für die reifere Jugend," was simply eliminated. Then, in 1863, economic pressures stemming from the Civil War forced the publisher to omit most of the illustrations rather than raise subscription prices, and the journal became simply *Die Abendschule*. Its subtitle remained *Eine Zeitschrift für Belehrung und Unterhaltung* until 1867, when the publisher finally hit on the name with which *Die Abendschule* was to prosper until well into the twentieth century—*Die Abendschule: Ein Deutsches Familienblatt*. But although both the concept and the masthead were stolen, the magazine's orientation was actually already implicit at the outset; *Die Abendschule* apparently just needed a dozen years before its title corresponded to the image projected by the first masthead, namely, to the icon of the family—including its younger members—as a single, united group of readers.

The image of an entire family reading together in an *Abendschule* provides a key to the editor's and publisher's initial conception of what their magazine was to be. As they wrote in the first sentence of the prospectus that came with the first number, "A glance at the situation in America has to convince everyone who is able to make a judgment that the education of the populace, particularly of young people, leaves a lot to be desired" (P). For the men behind *Die Abendschule*, however, education was not simply a blessing in and of itself, nor was it a luxury; universal education was a prerequisite for the American form of self-government, and education was also a precondition for participation of German immigrants in the affairs of their "adoptive fatherland" (P). Unfortunately, unsettled conditions on the frontier made schooling difficult, and the trials and opportunities posed by immigration and life in America made formal education a low priority for the country's millions of new residents. In addition, the lack of history in the United States meant that its institutions were not automatically legitimated by the weight of tradition—there were, for example, no cathedrals or castles whose very existence bore witness to the continuity of American freedoms: "The people who have constituted themselves as a state through migration have to invent everything for themselves" (P). Under these conditions some new form of education would have to lay a foundation, and it was here that *Die Abendschule* saw its mission: "Where the elementary school stopped or left something out is where we would like to proceed further, where we would like to fill in what is missing" (P). And it is worth noting that the editor's view of what might have been "missing" was extremely broad:

> The whole world, what and how it was and is, including its inhabitants and products, people, animals, plants, and minerals; including all its elements, colossal and microscopic in size; including its hidden and visible forms of energy, etc., namely, world and religious history, the history of culture and inventions, ethnography, geography, physics, mechanics, prose and poetry (English and German), music, painting, architecture. . . . That which is beyond the world and time, God and eternity, should not be forgotten; they are rather the foundation and goal of our magazine, where the world and time are included, where they begin and end. (P)

Before turning to the question of how well *Die Abendschule* met those goals, two other elements in the prospectus merit some attention. They are, first, the journal's editorial stance and, second, its sense of mission vis-à-vis German immigrants in the United States.

The editorial stance was quite explicit: "We do not intend to produce a religious, confessional magazine, but neither should it be un-Christian or anti-Christian" (P). The question of confessionalism concerns the connection, or lack of connection, between *Die Abendschule* and Walther's Synod, while the characterization not "un-Christian or anti-Christian" is the editor's attempt to distance his undertaking from the rest of the press in the United States, particularly from the rest of the German-American press. Both topoi were central to the founding gesture of *Die Abendschule*, and they were repeatedly stressed, internally and by outside supporters, as long as the journal was still struggling to define and attract its own particular audience. The danger was that *Die Abendschule* would either lose its conservative Lutheran audience if it were perceived as being too liberal or, in gaining them, lose the potentially much larger audience that included German Lutherans hostile to or in areas not yet served by Walther's synod, as well as German Methodists, Baptists, Catholics, and so on. Thus, in one of its early reconstitutions, marked by the change of format in 1860, the editor again explained "why *Die Abendschule* does not have a confessional character": . . . "It does not take sides for this or that Protestant denomination, but rather, standing on the foundation of belief, it wants to serve all the Germans of this country by attempting to promote Christian education in general (VII, 1)." How successful this ploy was is unclear;

again the lack of a comprehensive list of subscribers means that there is no hard evidence on the subject. But because the author of this particular missive was Pastor C. J. H. Fick, one of Walther's closest associates, it seems clear that the primary appeal of *Die Abendschule* was still within the Lutheran Church–Missouri Synod.

Walther's enthusiasm for a project like *Die Abendschule* can be seen not only in the fact that the Synod's official theological organ, *Der Lutheraner*, reprinted *Die Abendschule*'s prospectus in full, but also that Walther himself endorsed the paper and urged his readers to subscribe.[6] Because one of the Synod's pastors, C. Diehlmann, was the magazine's first editor, Walther thought he could guarantee "that, in contrast to so many other secular journals that claim to be written for Christians, [the reader of] *Die Abendschule* will not be presented with items steeped in the unbelief and frivolity of our age." A year later Walther repeated his endorsement, apparently with this hope:

> The summaries of political and other important contemporary events, which have been included in the magazine for some time now, have made every other political journal superfluous for most readers, and they have thereby brought about the great blessing of, in part, displacing bad newspapers written in the spirit of irreligion and immorality, in part, preventing their appearance.[7]

By 1860 Walther was promoting *Die Abendschule* as a means of forcing "godless German newspaper prose (*Zeitungsliteratur*) out of the home," and he cautioned parents against the "frivolity" of subscribing to such papers. The whole family would inevitably read them, with the result "that their children's souls would be poisoned by wicked scandal sheets and the foundation for their future fall [into sin and eternal damnation] would be laid."[8]

The escalation in his argument and the fact that it was repeated so often reflects the importance Walther accorded the press in shaping his church as a community of German Lutherans whose interests

[6] "Anmerkung der Red. des 'Lutheraner,'" *Der Lutheraner* 10 (14 February 1854): 103–4.

[7] "Illustri[e]rte Abendschule," *Der Lutheraner* 11 (13 March 1855):119.

[8] "Die Abendschule," *Der Lutheraner* 17 (21 August 1860): 7. Walther and the other writers of *Der Lutheraner* periodically repeated endorsements of this type— i.e., they always emphasized the dangers involved in reading other papers. See, e.g., *Der Lutheraner* 15 (14 June 1859): 175, 21 (1 September 1864): 7, 31 (1 January 1875): 4.

were not limited to the theological matters discussed in the Synod's official publications. And the tone, while vintage Walther, also conveys a feeling for the high stakes involved in the battle for the hearts and minds of German-Americans. It was for this reason that Walther did not limit himself to promoting *Die Abendschule*; he encouraged the publishers of other Christian newspapers, and he also campaigned for the foundation of more of them. In 1854, for example, he welcomed the appearance of the *Saint Louiser Volksblatt* (Saint Louis People's Paper), mainly because of the editor's promise that it would be "purely political but still never irreligious, never unchristian." According to Walther, that stance represented a significant change from the previous state of affairs:

> The local German secular newspapers were either edited by atheists, the morally indifferent, and crazy revolutionaries, and were so filled with mockery at all that is holy, with filth, and with declarations that ridiculed every system that it sickened every German with any moral or religious feelings to have one of them in his hands; or they were so obviously in the service of papists and Jesuits seeking political influence that Protestants at least should have hesitated to support them and be instructed by them about what they need to know as citizens of the world and their country.[9]

Despite of the vigor of his attacks, Walther seems to have lost most of these battles. Three years later *Der Lutheraner* reluctantly informed its readers that there had been a change in editors at the *Volksblatt*, which meant "there is no more Christian spirit to be found in this newspaper."[10]

One of the chief culprits and the most popular German paper in St. Louis, where *Die Abendschule* had relocated in 1856, was the *Anzeiger des Westens* (Western Advocate), edited by the notorious free-thinker Heinrich Börnstein. Although, as we shall see below, his own literary production and the belletristic offerings of the *Anzeiger* were relatively conservative, Börnstein himself had impressive radical credentials. In 1844 in Paris he had edited *Vorwärts*, the successor to the *Deutsch-Französische Jahrbücher*, where his contributors included Karl Marx, Friedrich Engels, Heinrich Heine, Georg

---

[9]Christian Fr. Schneider, quoted in "'Saint Louiser Volksblatt,'" *Der Lutheraner* 11 (22 May 1854): 158.

[10]"'Saint Louiser Volksblatt,'" *Der Lutheraner* 14 (22 September 1857): 22.

Herwegh, Georg Weerth, and Michail Bakunin.[11] And Börnstein was not just an atheist; he also promoted such dangerous frivolity as a German-language theater and opera, and he owned a brewery and several saloons.[12] *Der Lutheraner*'s defense of the *Saint Louiser Volksblatt* was directed specifically "against attacks . . . that come from the atheistic editor of the local 'Anzeiger des Westens.'"[13] In essence, the collective opposition to Börnstein and others like him, as evidenced by the prospectus, by Walther's endorsements, and by the contents of *Die Abendschule*, itself constituted an attempt at self-definition carried out in large part through repeated acts of negation. In proclaiming that it would not be "unchristian or anti-Christian," *Die Abendschule* and its supporters staked out a specific territory for their subsequent efforts.

In addition to the attempt to characterize the new magazine's contents and editorial stance, the second element addressed at some length in the prospectus was the plight of German immigrants in the United States. According to the founders of *Die Abendschule*, immigration from diverse parts of the world was potentially a two-edged sword. On the one hand, the country's mixed population might be counted as a blessing: "Contact, exchange, and communication between peoples encourages and increases their intelligence" (P). On the other hand, "any given people either takes up, works through, [or] adopts existing foreign or new elements of culture in its own peculiar manner, or it has to abandon its own peculiar character and accommodate itself to one that is foreign (*fremd*) and be assimilated. We *Germans* are in danger of the latter" (P; emphasis in the original).

In a very real sense, *Die Abendschule*'s editor was already aware of the complex set of issues raised by the question of ethnic identity—that is, by the nature and content of ethnic consciousness. The choice for assimilation was fraught with danger, because it implies both abandoning one's own real or essential character and accommodating oneself to a mode of being that is foreign, which could easily mean simply "different" or, in current jargon, the far more distant and disturbing "other." The difficulty Germans had in the

[11]Heinrich Börnstein, *Fünfundsiebzig Jahre*, 1:351–54.
[12]In addition to Börnstein's own account, see Steven Rowan, "The Cultural Program of Heinrich Börnstein in St. Louis, 1851–1861," *In Their Own Words* 3.2 (1986): 187–206.
[13]*Der Lutheraner* 11 (22 March 1854): 158.

United States was compounded by the fact that "the dominant element is English and if we are not aided or English is not stopped, it will swallow up our noble German language, including all of our other invaluable treasures" (P). There follows an extensive list of German virtues, ranging from "German openness and rectitude, German loyalty and honesty" to "German genius and intellectual depth (*Geistestiefe*), German erudition, German sociability (*Gemütlichkeit*)," which suggest nothing so much as an embarrassing cliché of what "German" must have suggested to the rest of the population in the middle of the nineteenth century. (German modesty, admittedly an almost oxymoronic construction in this context, is conspicuously absent.) Nineteenth-century Germans seem to have been absolutely convinced of the superiority of their own culture, but rather than a demand that the United States become German, the prospectus announced: "We do not want to be American Germans (*amerikanische Deutsche*), but rather Americans, German Americans (*deutsche Amerikaner*)." Whatever it might have meant for "Germans" to become "German-Americans," whatever the specific content of the narratives they would have to acquire, whatever processes they would have to undergo, the key element to note in the whole prospectus is that in the opinion of *Die Abendschule*'s editors some form of education was necessary. By educating its readers, *Die Abendschule* proposed to unite and shape a specific German-American community, and at the same time combat the free-thinking anticlericalism that was characteristic of another, competing group of German-Americans. The question of how its writers and editors addressed those goals brings us back to the contents of the first issue.

That issue, dated 1 February 1854, was just four quarto pages long—one newspaper-size sheet folded in half—but it contained nearly all the features that were eventually to make *Die Abendschule* a success. Item number one, as was appropriate for a magazine that called itself *Illustri[e]rte Abendschule*, was a woodcut entitled "The Blind Fiddler." The main figure, an older man, was shown in the midst of two peasant families with all their children. The picture's extended caption reminded readers that it was possible to be happy while suffering adversity, and it also explained the rationale behind the illustrations: "Children love pictures, and so do grownups. Who doesn't enjoy it when he reads something nice and can see it illustrated at the same time" (I.1, 1). Such images were thus both illustrations and inducements to read the texts with which they were coupled. *Die Abendschule* tried to avoid gratuitous illustrations, and its pictorial images were always supposed to be subordinate to some form of written text. As we have already seen, there were often problems connected with the illustrations, but, as promised, the first issue actually contained two other pictures. One was the complex set of images that made up the masthead, while the other served to illustrate the well-known proverb "What little Hans doesn't know, Hans will never know" (I.1, 3).[14] In other words, children must learn or be taught everything they need to know in later life or else they will grow up ignorant and stay that way. The moral is both a denial of the more optimistic theories that had dominated pedagogy since Rousseau and an obvious bit of propaganda for the new publication. In fact, that proverb was one of the justifications for *Die Abend-schule* that was mentioned specifically in the prospectus. No doubt, pictures were also one means of selling the magazine.

In addition to the illustrated texts and the editorial introduction discussed above, the first issue of *Die Abendschule* contained a short poem, a riddle, and three somewhat longer prose texts. The poem, "Three Pairs and One," is simply an exhortation to see, listen, and work—that is to use both eyes, both ears, and both hands—rather than to complain, talk, and eat, which are all activities connected with the solitary mouth. The riddle was also a poem, twenty-four lines in length, whose solution was "N D," two letters that when pronounced yield the German word "*Ende*" (end): "A goal that ev-eryone will achieve sometime" (I.1, 3). Both the poem and the riddle are examples of straightforward moral imperatives; the prose is more complex and, as a result, more interesting. The first of the three texts, an article entitled simply "The Earth" (I.1, 3), was the opening installment in a long series of articles on physical geogra-phy, knowledge of which, if we are to believe the list of topics con-tained in the "Prospectus," was apparently an important aspect of a person's general education.[15] The first issue also contained the first episode of a biography of Christopher Columbus (I.1, 4). His life story seems to have been so popular that it was continued until Vol-ume two, number 11, when it was replaced by an equally long biog-

---

[14]For some reason, which is particularly odd in the context of an *Abendschule*, the caption is not the conventional "What little Hans doesn't learn, Hans will never learn."

[15]The series really got under way only in issue number eighteen with an article on water, but it continued until volume two, number ten.

raphy of Cortés, which was then followed by a life of Pizarro.[16] New Americans were apparently supposed to be interested in, and supposed to need to know something of, the history of their adopted homeland, but, as the prospectus argued, they also had to maintain their German heritage. To that end, the third prose text in the first issue of *Die Abendschule* dealt with German history. Although Germany was far from democratic at the time, the first number's text, entitled "A Public Meeting of the Ancient Germans," tried to prove that even in the murky past the German people had been "full of noble energies but still raw and unrefined" (p. 2) In short, the first issue contained almost exactly the mixture of education and entertainment that the Prospectus had promised, and it reminded the magazine's immigrant readers that they could be proud of their German heritage.

One nevertheless senses that the editor and publisher were still groping for a successful formula. Issue number five, for example, contained the first installment of what were soon to become regular reports on current events. The initial *Geschichte des Tages* (History of the Day) occupied one column on the last page and contained three items: First, there was an assessment of the political situation in Europe, which concentrated on the dangers of war breaking out between Russia and Turkey. This report, perhaps not coincidentally, complemented a new seventeen-part series on Turkey (I.5, 1), and once the Crimean War broke out, *Die Abendschule* went so far as to publish a two-page map of Sevastopol so readers could follow the course of the siege there (I.22, 3–4). Second came an account of events in China, where a revolution seems to have just begun. And third, a discussion of political questions in the immigrants' new homeland. As might be expected, the latter revolved around the events that eventually led to the Civil War. Here the issue was whether, in spite of the Missouri Compromise, Nebraska would become a slave state, to which the editor commented: "It is almost incomprehensible how, in a country based on free principles, the most enormous servitude, slavery, not only exists but even finds defenders!" (I.5, 4).[17]

[16]"Christoph Columbus oder Die Entdeckung Amerikas," *Die Abendschule* I.1–26 and II.1–11; "Cortes" was taken from a biography written by the popular German author of children's books, Joachim Heinrich Campe (II, 12–26 and III, 1–11); "Pisarro" appeared in III.12–26 and IV.1–13.

[17]Issue number nine (10 June 1854) opens with a half-page picture titled "The

The importance of the news for the emerging character of *Die Abendschule* was twofold. First, it marked the beginning of a gradual attempt to attract adults—that is, to add them to the magazine's primary audience—for if fathers were to read *Die Abendschule* to their assembled families, there could certainly be sections constructed to interest them alone, for example, a section that addressed the males in their role within the family as those individuals who dealt with the outside world. The implicit tension between simplified stories from the history of the United States and Germany, for instance, and the news of the Crimean War can partially be explained away by the fact that the *pater familias* might well have chosen not to read everything aloud. Second, the news, and the reports from the commodity markets that were later also added as a regular feature of *Die Abendschule*, were clearly intended to obviate the need for Christian readers to subscribe to another paper. Again it was Walther who was most open about the stakes involved in the inclusion of the news: parents who leave "godless German newspaper prose" lying about merely to satisfy "their curiosity about current political events" unnecessarily endanger their children's souls:

> *Die Abendschule* can also satisfy this need because it provides a condensed survey of the most important events in the world every two weeks. So long as we do not have a political paper edited according to Christian principles, the current events in *Die Abendschule* are certainly enough for the moderate (*genügsamen*) reader.[18]

This defensive stance is one way that the readers of *Die Abendschule* crystallized into a specific subgroup among the German-Americans in the United States. Drawing boundaries around what was dangerous was not enough, however. Readers also had to be provided with positive images, which brings me to the literature and to the other narrative texts published in *Die Abendschule*.

It was not until the sixteenth number of the first volume that *Die Abendschule* began to print what was to become one of its standard features: serialized fiction, in this case a short anonymous novel

---

Branding of Black Slaves"; the accompanying commentary reads, in part, as follows: "Imagine, dear reader, you have black skin rather than white, and your homeland is not Europe or America but Africa—you would still be a human being like any other, a living soul, created at the beginning of time in God's image . . . only your dark skin and your curly, woolen hair would differentiate you from other human beings."
[18] "*Die Abendschule*," *Der Lutheraner* 17 (21 August 1860): 7.

titled *Die hölzernen Teller* (The Wooden Plates), which was continued in six subsequent issues.[19] After the phenomenal success of Eugène Sue's *Les Mystères de Paris* (*The Mysteries of Paris*), which began appearing in the Parisian newspaper *Journal des Débats* in 1842, serialized fiction became one of the mainstays of the nineteenth-century popular press.[20] Here *Die Abendschule* was only following a well-established lead, particularly for the German-American press. Such narratives were an important means of enticing readers to buy or to subscribe to a particular journal, and papers' advertisements often contained the promise of future exciting reading.

Sated as we are by the experience of weekly television programs and daily soap operas, it is hard to imagine that one hundred years ago people waited impatiently for the next issue of the newspaper or magazine in order to find out what had happened to their favorite hero or heroine. Just as television displaced serialized radio drama and the cliffhangers shown before most feature films a generation ago, so too did the lure of serialized popular fiction fall victim to technological and commercial advances. Still, we have to remember that the interest aroused by serialized fiction—ranging from what most people consider the high art of Charles Dickens and Theodor Fontane to the "suspect" but far more popular romances of E. Marlitt and Philipp Galen—was every bit as intense as our contemporaries' feelings about "Dallas," "thirtysomething," or "General Hospital." Although *Die hölzernen Teller* may not be quite as thrilling or as technically sophisticated as its modern counterparts, once one makes allowances for the different set of historical circumstances in which it appeared it becomes clear that its purpose in *Die Abendschule* was virtually identical. How *Die hölzernen Teller* functioned for the magazine's readers, and what it meant to them, are questions that can be addressed only after a brief summary of that short novel's salient elements.[21]

At the outset *Die hölzernen Teller* reads like a satirical attack on

[19]*Die Abendschule* I, 16–21, 23.

[20]For a discussion of Sue, see Umberto Eco, "Rhetoric and Ideology in Sue's *Les Mystères de Paris*," in Eco, *The Role of the Reader: Explorations in the Semiotics of Texts* (Bloomington: Indiana University Press, 1979), 125–43.

[21]Because almost all the works discussed in this book are completely unknown, even to specialists, summarizing them has proved unavoidable. I have tried to keep these accounts to an absolute minimum, and I have also attempted to integrate the elements of plot that I do relate into the analysis.

European courtly life, whose oppressive excesses were no doubt familiar to every former resident of a German principaly. The narrator begins by reminding readers that certain people sometimes behave coarsely but on other occasions are subservient, that their behavior depends on their surroundings: ′

> One such crumb, who crawled before his superiors, only to be all the coarser to those beneath him, was the royal Polish and electoral Saxon court kitchen-and-utensils clerk, Mr. Daniel Benjamin Wippermann. Since he also supervised the court's drum and bugle corps, he permitted himself to be called the Court Drum and Bugle Inspector, because these instruments sounded better than kitchen utensils when they are banged together or thrown about. (I.16, 2)

This quotation, although from a narrative that is popular in the negative sense of the word, is actually quite sophisticated. It contains what the Russian literary theorist M. M. Bakhtin would call a "hybrid construction," "an utterance that belongs by its grammatical (syntactic) and compositional markers to a single speaker, but that actually contains mixed within it two utterances, two speech manners, two styles, two 'languages,' two semantic and axiological belief systems."[22] Thus the parody that makes the passage work depends on its stylized quotation of official discourse. The phrase "royal Polish, and electoral Saxon court kitchen-and-utensils Clerk" ("Court Drum and Bugle Inspector") is a faithful rendering of the elaborate but ultimately ridiculous titles actually accorded the officials of German principalities. Because it is here borne by a lower-echelon clerk, the title serves to denigrate the whole undertaking of absolutism as it was still practiced in the middle of the nineteenth century in Germany. Furthermore, by revealing the social conditions behind the luxury of the court, Wippermann's actions continue the indictment. But the plot is so disjointed that the initial episodes actually seem to be introducing a story very different from the one that subsequently unfolds, and Wippermann disappears for good in the fifth installment.

While traveling to a remote village in the Harz Mountains on a secret mission in the service of the supreme ruler, Wippermann very nearly duels with an insolent student, who is unwilling to cower before this more than slightly ridiculous representative of distant au-

[22]M. M. Bakhtin "Discourse in the Novel," in *The Dialogic Imagination*, trans. Caryl Emerson and Michael Holquist (Austin: University of Texas Press, 1981), 304.

thority. The local schoolteacher is similarly unimpressed, in part because he mistakenly believes that he has finally found someone to share the burden of dealing with one hundred noisy pupils, which he had done all by himself. Besides, the teacher is deaf. In the next episode, Wippermann tries to impress a local merchant by placing an order for 30,000 wooden plates. At first, he seems to be simply trying to shame the man into admitting that such a large number of plates is far more than the yokels living in the village could possibly produce in the next few days, but Wippermann actually signs a contract for 28,000 plates; he hopes to cash in on the difference between the order and the number of plates he plans to bill the state for. Then, at the end of the second episode, the scene shifts abruptly to the house of a poor widow whose entire family, including a six-year-old daughter, is busily manufacturing wooden trinkets in order to stay just barely alive. Episode three introduces the widow's honest, upright son Lukas, the town's overworked substitute teacher, who also operates a lathe in the evening. By this time everyone, including the merchant's daughter Gertrud, is busy making plates for the king-elector; even Max, the insolent student, is burning the royal coat of arms into the freshly turned plates, mainly to be near Gertrud. As his idea of a joke Max brands Lukas on the hand, and poor Lukas, who also loves Gertrud, is pained particularly by the smile he thinks he sees on Gertrud's face. At this point the plot is reminiscent of Samuel Richardson; the question is whether Gertrud will eventually find happiness with Lukas (*Pamela*) or whether her smile, which might reveal her complicity with Lukas's competitor, will eventually doom her (*Clarissa*). Later the whole party then travels to Dresden to deliver the plates, and there the simple villagers are able to witness the excessive richness of the capital city for the first time. When the officer in charge of this round of court festivities inspects their shipment, he finds it 4,076 plates short. Lukas is blamed for the mess and ends up being drafted into the army, while Max and Gertrud illicitly join the celebration. In the final episode, all 25,924 wooden plates are thrown into the river, apparently to cover the surface with the royal coat of arms, but in spite of the court's wasteful extravagance some good comes of the affair. An honest major discharges Lukas and replaces him in the army with Max, which eventually turns the rowdy student into a decent human being. Gertrud meanwhile marries a rich miller, but ends unhappily; her husband is a drunk and mistreats her. And Lukas returns to the village, where he relieves the old schoolmaster, marries, and has children. In short, virtue is rewarded, evil is punished, and life continues as before.

As the first example of literature in *Die Abendschule*, this seems like an unremarkable story. In fact, if the central question in this book did not revolve around the relationship between literature and community, one might expect me to dismiss *Die hölzernen Teller* as a bit of harmless entertainment. But to ignore texts like *Die hölzernen Teller* is to presume either that the real content of the journals where they were published is contained in explicit statements about politics or the immigrant experience, or that popular narratives lack the aesthetic qualities that would merit further attention. Rather than ignore *Die hölzernen Teller* on the basis of either of these often unreflected assumptions, one can also ask whether this particular text was simply an extraneous filler or whether it performed some function for its readers. To answer those questions, we must return to the narrative to see how it works, and follow that answer with a discussion of what the way a text works means in the context of the scholarship of popular literature.

The plot of *Die hölzernen Teller* is structured by the opposition between the villainous Wippermann, who is aided and eventually replaced in his role by Max, and the protagonist, Lukas. Gertrud is initially located in the middle, and much of the story's tension revolves around the question of her loyalties, which are initially unclear. This primary opposition propels the narrative forward because the semantic markers that define the two major sets of characters create an unavoidable conflict between two antagonistic worldviews. To be sure, both Wippermann and Max represent an odd mixture, conditioned in part by the fact that the narrative was both set and written in periods of social and economic transition.

The text's own time and space—or to use Bakhtin's term, its "chronotope"[23]—is a middle-size state in Germany in the 1730s, a period that witnessed the onset of the conflict between absolutism and the developing bourgeoisie, a group that was then only beginning to demand economic autonomy and a political voice. The novel then appeared in the United States in 1854, long before the Civil War accelerated that country's industrial takeoff.[24] It is not surpris-

[23]See Bakhtin, "Forms of Time and Chronotope in the Novel," in *The Dialogic Imagination*, 84–258.
[24]If the text was actually written in Germany, the economic argument is just as solid; Germany's takeoff came only after the foundation of the Empire in 1871.

ing, therefore, that both Wippermann and Max have a foot in each of two camps; they are neither solely creatures of the still largely feudal society nor simply representatives of bourgeois capitalism, but both simultaneously in an uneasy alliance. Wippermann sets the plot's main action in motion in his role as a merchant, but he is a merchant caught up in the mechanisms of an absolutist state. The money he earns comes from supplying its need for (mindless) representation. Max is the son of a village pastor, but by studying he too hopes to enter into court service. He carries a dagger and nearly duels with Wippermann, which is a clear indication that both of them subscribe to an aristocratic code of honor. In fact, both believe that their social position entitles them to be treated with a certain amount of deference, and neither shows much real interest either in his profession or in his family. Lukas, by contrast, is extremely hardworking, and his primary occupation is that of a traditional artisan. He is willing to substitute for the local teacher not for the honor of the position but out of a sense of personal loyalty to a fellow member of the community. Lukas recognizes the importance of getting ahead, but his dreams are all played out within the confines of the village. He is repeatedly shown with his mother and his brothers and sisters, who are actively engaged in artisan production within their home, and he reproduces that life when he marries and has children of his own. Gertrud, the third point in the triangle of relationships, is initially defined by her indecision. Unsure whether to chose Max or Lukas, and the differing views of the world that they represent, she at first shares some of the characteristics of the two rivals. She works in her father's shop but eventually falls victim to the allures of the court in Dresden. She marries, but her choice is for money rather than love, and the union ends unhappily. She dooms herself and becomes unworthy of Lukas by choosing the values represented by Max, whereas Lukas's triumph is preprogrammed by the fact that all his determining characteristics are positive.

Even more important than the mechanical triumph of the positive characters over their negative counterparts is the specific content of their opposition. In order to understand the readers of the first volume of *Die Abendschule*, it is important to note that when virtue is rewarded it is a particular form of virtue, one defined by the values of the family, traditional vocational patterns, and the intact life of the village. Evil, on the other hand, is embodied in characters who scorn their families, reject the idea of a profession, and trespass against the limits of an artisan or agrarian community.

It should be obvious that the categories of good and evil represented in *Die hölzernen Teller* corresponded to the experiences of
mid-century Germans and German-Americans. Emigration, as was
pointed out previously, was not primarily a search for political or
religious freedom but an attempt to escape the collapse of a traditional economy. Wooden plates, which might be taken as a typical
example of "proto-industrial" production,"[25] are the type of commodities that would increasingly be produced in England by machines. Thus, as the nineteenth century progressed the artisan producers of the Harz Mountains, where *Die hölzernen Teller* is set,
found the economic base of their existence disappearing for reasons
over which they had no control. As the experience of the Silesian
weavers in the 1840s had already demonstrated, the economy of
Saxony was particularly vulnerable, in part because it was also home
to some of the earliest industrialization in the German states and in
part because the Saxon monarchy, which had been involved in min-
ing and related developments for centuries, offered no shelter to its
subjects. In fact, as we shall see in Chapter 5, it was not until the
1880s that princes and kings began to appear in popular literature in
a positive light, namely, as the guarantors of the old order. Moreover, against their fondest hopes, the New World proved no more
hospitable to traditional producers. Even the letters sent back home
by those who "succeeded" in the United States were generally from
immigrants who were able to make the transition to a new occupation and to a new way of life.[26] What is particularly interesting about
Die hölzernen Teller is therefore that a character as traditional as
Lukas succeeds in a text published in 1854.

The manner in which the characters and the plot of *Die hölzernen
Teller* are structured represents a view of the world that was indeed
located in a particular time and space. For the moment, and for
want of a better term, such a world-view might be termed an ideology, whereby ideology is defined as a historically specific discursive
framework that sets the boundaries for what is believed to be legiti-

[25]See Kriedke, Medick, and Schlumbohm, *Industrialization before Industrialization*, and, more specifically for the present text, Jean H. Quataert, "Teamwork in
Saxon Homeweaving Families in the Nineteenth Century: A Preliminary Investigation into the Issue of Gender Work Roles," in Ruth-Ellen B. Joeres and Mary Jo
Maynes, eds., *German Women in the Eighteenth and Nineteenth Centuries: A Social
and Literary History* (Bloomington: Indiana University Press, 1986), 3–23.
[26]See Wolfgang Helbich, ed., *"Amerika ist ein freies Land . . ." Auswanderer
schreiben nach Deutschland* (Darmstadt: Luchterhand, 1985), esp. 72–107.

mate or true. This definition is not meant to imply that any particular ideology or system of beliefs is false or somehow irrational, just that people's actions and their notions of how the world operates often cannot be reduced to a set of rationally articulated beliefs. The planks in a party's platform, the issues of war and peace, the problems of economic survival, and (of particular concern to the readers of *Die Abendschule*) religious beliefs resonate in people's hearts as much as in their minds. By speaking principally to their emotional needs, literature helps readers make sense of the world they live in, and it sometimes offers them models of how to act in their own particular corner of the world. Thus, even if the narratives published in *Die Abendschule* were entertaining, if they helped readers escape, or if they offered compensation for problems that immigrants experienced in their new environment, narratives like *Die hölzernen Teller* nevertheless provided or reinforced a specific interpretative framework. Their importance therefore lies not in whether or to what extent they embody certain timeless literary values, or in whether they accurately mirror conditions in the United States, but in the insight they provide into the ideology of German-Americans, especially as their interpretive frameworks changed over time.

Note that I do not argue that popular narratives simply transmit ideology.[27] Literature is seldom successful when plot merely serves as the occasion for a series of lectures or sermons; its preferred mode of operation is to represent norms and values indirectly. The characters employed in *Die hölzernen Teller* were constructed to embody particular traits, either positively or negatively, and to reveal these traits through their actions. Moreover, once the reader has invested a certain amount of emotional energy in a character and begins to care what happens to him or her, what that character says or does is far more meaningful than any narrator's asides. When *Die hölzernen Teller* finally gets on track—that is, once Lukas is finally allowed to assume his rightful place at the text's center—the process of identification is set in motion.[28] Not only do readers share an interest in the hero's fate, but the text also attempts to heighten their concern by the way in which it is presented from week to week. Episode two closes as an already tired Lukas returns from the schoolroom to start

---

[27]In this connection, see Jochen Schulte-Sasse, "Toward a 'Culture' for the Masses: The Socio-Psychological Function of Popular Literature in Germany and the U.S., 1880–1920," *New German Critique*, 29 (Spring–Summer 1983): 85–105.

[28] For more on the process, see below.

turning out plates, and there is a sense of doom hanging over him and the rest of his family. At the very end of episode three, Lukas thinks he has discovered Gertrud's mocking glance, which would align her with Max. As episode five ends, Lukas is threatened by the draft, and so on. Every episode ends with an unresolved conflict, in which it seems that some misfortune is about to befall the hero or heroine. Of course, leaving the reader hanging is the familiar tactic used to persuade soap opera fans to tune in again the next day; it works, in part, because of the viewer's or reader's involvement with the characters. Readers have invested enough of themselves to care what happens next, particularly what happens next to a sympathetic character. (The hypothetical reader of *Die hölzernen Teller* is better off as a male; there are positive female characters—Lukas's mother and a sister—but their roles are so subordinate as to be almost nonexistent. At least at this relatively early stage in the history of the serialized novel, female readers were often forced to accept a male perspective.)

Because both characters and plot are constructed with oppositions that define a particular world-view, the act of identification also involves an implicit acceptance of that character's ideological stance. Readers can take that step because of the parallels between their own extraliterary world and the world of the text. For contemporary readers, the norms and values of *Die hölzernen Teller* were to a large extent already present and internalized. Having faced the same problems that confronted Lukas in their own lives, namely, the oppression of an absolutist prince, the difficulties of maintaining an artisan or agrarian existence in the face of industrialization and changes in the agricultural economy of Germany, and the deceptions employed by middlemen and merchants, such literature gave the readers of *Die Abendschule* the chance to succeed vicariously. The protagonists are successful in doing what those readers, against increasing odds, would like to believe possible in their own lives, and although there is nothing in *Die hölzernen Teller* that refers to the specific situation of German immigrants in the United States, it is worth noting that Lukas succeeds fictionally with the very same norms and values that were increasingly threatened in the world that the readers of *Die Abendschule* actually occupied in 1854.

This rather negative reading of *Die hölzernen Teller* has so far been a mixture of semiotics and ideological criticism (*Ideologiekritik*), based in part on the German critique of popular literature, which is generally identified with the pejorative term *Trivialliteratur*. The reading rests on a number of assumptions that are not yet explicit, and the ground from which it has been launched is not yet visible. The stance I have adopted thus far also omits a variety of other readings. Therefore, what follows is a discussion of previous work on popular literature, beginning with German scholarship and moving on to more recent American treatments of popular narratives, still using *Die hölzernen Teller* as an explanatory example. My purpose is both to shed some additional light on this particular text and to develop a position from which to analyze subsequent narratives from *Die Abendschule*.

The founding gesture in the German tradition of criticism directed toward popular narratives was a double move. On the one hand, beginning as early as the 1960s, scholars launched a concerted attempt to locate progressive texts that had previously been excluded from the canon. They turned to overtly political texts and to works produced and read outside the confines of the educated middle class (*Bildungsbürgertum*). Horst Denkler's *Berliner Strassenecken-Literatur, 1848/49* (Berlin Streetcorner Literature, 1848–49) and Jost Hermand's collection *Das Junge Deutschland* (Young Germany), significantly bearing the subtitle "Texte und Dokumente" in an effort to broaden the range of what might be considered "literature," are typical examples of the genre.[29] Coupled with these symptomatic rediscoveries was, on the other hand, a recognition that the traditional categories of literary evaluation, which had excluded such texts in the first place, were collapsing under the weight of sustained analysis. Once people took the trouble to look, they found that every supposedly "aesthetic" or "literary" use of language—every trope, metaphor, or other rhetorical figure—was just as prevalent in popular literature as in the accepted works of high culture. In fact, one could easily locate them in advertising and newspaper accounts of political events.[30] All this meant that the ground beneath the canon

---

[29]Horst Denkler, ed., *Berliner Strassenecken-Literatur, 1848–49* (Stuttgart: Reclam, 1977); and Jost Hermand, ed., *Das Junge Deutschland: Texte und Dokumente* (Stuttgart: Reclam, 1966). There are numerous other examples, particularly in connection with the revolution of 1848; Reclam and Leske are the two publishers most closely affiliated with these attempts.

[30]For a survey of the attempts to ground notions like the "literary" use of language as an evaluative category, see Jochen Schulte-Sasse, *Literarische Wertung*. Roland Barthes's *Mythologies*, trans. Annette Lavers (New York: Hill and Wang, 1972), is one of many places to look for "literary" language in everyday contexts. Recent

was shaky, to the extent that it had not disappeared entirely or indeed had ever existed in the first place.

One solution—that is, one way of rescuing some notion of high art while at the same time developing a means of evaluating more popular forms—is not to ignore traditional aesthetic categories but to argue that it is also necessary to include a work's political stance. The question of value then becomes not what aesthetic features a text contains, but whether the *use* of certain artistic innovations degenerated in the course of their appropriation by subsequent authors. To take a concrete example, one might ask if the novels of the 1850s, whether *Die hölzernen Teller* or Gustav Freytag's more "aesthetic" account of Anton Wohlfart's success in *Soll und Haben* (*Debit and Credit*), were artistically equivalent to the novels that had been the literary vehicle of bourgeois emancipation ever since the late eighteenth century. The question is actually quite difficult, and the answers are complex, but such ideologically based criticism might provide a reason why *Wilhelm Meister* was a better book in the context of Goethe's time than *Soll und Haben* was in Freytag's time. One can argue, that Goethe employed his "artistry" critically in the cause of advancing human freedom, whereas Freytag used roughly the same techniques and the same genre to glorify an emerging capitalist economy. Where *Die hölzernen Teller* fits, at least vis-à-vis Freytag, is still unclear from this perspective, but even if "better" becomes a political category that subsumes aesthetics, the question of evaluation has simply been displaced, not answered. Who ultimately decides, and on what basis, whether Goethe's stance was correct or how and why Freytag's was flawed?

In fact, proposing an ideological ground rather than seeking refuge in supposedly timeless aesthetic categories actually raises more questions than it answers. Deciding what is "good" now depends on already knowing what is politically correct, just as rejecting what is "trivial" depends on locating that same firm progressive ground. As for *Die hölzernen Teller*, despite its attack on absolutism, the novel's thrust is fundamentally conservative, and any critique of its ideologi-

---

usages that make it impossible to differentiate "high" and "low" culture range from McDonald's use of Brecht's "Mack the Knife" to sell hamburgers, after it had already been a popular song, totally divorced from its "literary" context, on numerous other occasions. Mike Deaver's staging of Ronald Reagan's "sound bytes" are among the "best" examples of the aesthetization of politics; those snippets of sound, framed by "memorable" background images, were overtly intended to eliminate the need for real content.

cal position has to ask why its happy ending is located so firmly in the past—and in the imaginary, intact world of preindustrial village life at that—rather than in the present or the future, where Freytag seems to be. Yet framing the question in that fashion implicitly rejects a set of political values that, at least in the United States, have recently enjoyed renewed popularity, even legitimacy. Their rejection by literary critics and others has even been held responsible for a decline in public morality, most notably in academia, as the norms and values that Americans supposedly once shared are called into question—or replaced by "literary theory," feminism, non-Western ideologies, or, if anyone in the 1990s still believes, Marxism.[31] On the other hand, let me suggest what was at stake in the founding gesture of ideological criticism in Germany: when Max Horkheimer and Theodor Adorno were confronted with works like *Die hölzernen Teller* they asked, "Why [is] mankind, instead of entering into a truly human condition, . . . sinking into a new kind of barbarism?"[32]

Horkheimer and Adorno posed the question in *Dialectic of Enlightenment*, a study written in the depths of World War II, when the barbarism of the "common" man very nearly succeeded in eliminating "high" art (and human civilization!) from Europe. *Dialectic of Enlightenment* became a key text in Germany in the 1960s and 1970s as the Frankfurt school of political philosophy and sociology reemerged during a period of conscious, hopeful, leftist radicalism, an age that seems incredibly remote now that communism has been so thoroughly discredited in Eastern Europe. Well before that change, when Marxism was still the most prevalent stance among European intellectuals, Horkheimer and Adorno could speak—without further reflection or proof—of an era's "objective social tendency," which in turn allowed them to characterize the function of mass entertainment: "Pleasure (i.e., the mere enjoyment of popular culture) always means not to think about anything, to forget suffering even where it is shown."[33] By way of contrast, "high" art pro-

[31]I allude to the controversy ignited by Allen Bloom, *The Closing of the American Mind: How Higher Education Has Failed Democracy and Impoverished the Souls of Today's Students* (New York: Simon and Schuster, 1987); and E. D. Hirsch, *Cultural Literacy: What Every American Needs to Know* (Boston: Houghton Mifflin, 1987).

[32]Max Horkheimer and Theodor W. Adorno, *Dialectic of Enlightenment*, trans. John Cumming (New York: Continuum, 1972), xi. Of course, the real founding document of ideological criticism was Marx and Engel's *The German Ideology*.

[33]Horkheimer and Adorno, *Dialectic of Enlightenment*, 122, 144.

vides a space where the lucky few, whom instrumental reason has not made incapable of understanding, can encounter the idea "that resistance is possible."[34] In other words, "high" art is valuable essentially because it promotes what Horkheimer and Adorno viewed as human freedom, while "low" art inhibited the transformation of society in that direction by placating the very people who were supposed to be the agents of change, the proletariat. Their analysis was, in short, based implicitly on a version of Marxism that is, like almost all versions of Marxism today, no longer very convincing, at least not without some discussion of its increasingly problematical grounding and the admission that ideological criticism might well be launched from a very different direction. This is not to suggest that Horkheimer and Adorno's insights into the functioning of the culture industry are completely wrong, but that one can make use of their position only with a number of reservations.

First, as Fredric Jameson has argued, there is no reason to believe that all "high" art actually has escaped the pressures of the marketplace and can therefore provide a refuge from the dictates of capitalism.[35] Whatever "high" art is, some of it is either less than hostile to the capitalist order or, at the very least, can be employed by critics and educators for purposes that may well be at odds with whatever the original readers in their very different context might have taken away from such works or with what critics of a different ideological bent might be able to discover there. Second, *Dialectic of Enlightenment* deals with only half of what might be considered popular literature; not only does the book exclude the large body of revolutionary and working-class popular literature that has recently been brought to light, but by means of the exclusionary gesture of its own peculiarly dated ideological certainty, it also refuses to judge various other works positively. For example, one obvious and significant alternative to Horkheimer and Adorno can be found in a number of recent feminist readings of popular narratives, discussed below in greater detail. At this point, however, it is already worth noting that some feminist critics have discovered their own version of the idea "that resistance is possible," which looks very different

---

[34]Ibid., 141.

[35]Fredric Jameson, "Reification and Utopia in Mass Culture," *Social Text* 1 (1979): 130–48. For an account that is in the mode of Horkheimer and Adorno but considerably more sensitive to the nuances of popular culture, see Michael Kienzle, *Der Erfolgsroman: Zur Kritik seiner poetischen Ökonomie bei Gustav Freytag und Eugenie Marlitt* (Stuttgart: Metzler, 1975).

indeed from Horkheimer and Adorno's fundamentally male vision. Moreover, they have identified that vision in works that Horkheimer and Adorno would never have considered for their own, contemplative canon.[36] Third, recent research has also demonstrated that "mass culture" has never been as undifferentiated as Horkheimer and Adorno suggested. For example, the opposition "Christian/unchristian," which underlay *Die Abendschule*'s view of the world, indicates not only that there have always been distinctions within popular culture, but also that for certain historically specific groups of readers these distinctions were very real indeed. Even if one ultimately rejects *Die Abendschule*'s world-view, one compelling reason for undertaking the present study is the opportunity it provides both to document the diversity of popular literature and to see whether and how the norms and values represented in a journal like *Die Abendschule* changed over time.

To address the latter concern first, one need only look briefly at other narratives published in the German-American press at roughly the same time as *Die hölzernen Teller*. Heinrich Börnstein's *Die Geheimnisse von St. Louis* (*The Mysteries of St. Louis*), for example, which was published serially in the *Anzeiger des Westens* feuilleton in 1850–51, is a sharp attack on the Jesuits that revolves around the widely held belief that they were engaged in a far-reaching conspiracy "to reconquer this infidel country for the holy Roman and apostolic church."[37] The Jesuits seem to have been the most popular target for nineteenth-century conspiracy theorists, before the rise of Zionism provided them with a new set of villains, but in spite of the anti-Catholicism they no doubt shared with him, Börnstein's canvas was painted with strokes broad enough to offend the pious readers of *Die Abendschule*, along with the Catholics. At one point, for example, while explaining why his own family does not attend church, one of the novel's heroes exclaims: "*German* Sunday, be greeted! . . . If thou wert wholly and totally at home in America, bigotry, false

[36]To cite but one example (as a taste of what is to come), see Elayne Rapping's review of Meredith Tax's *Union Square*, "PBS Meets Knots Landing," *The Nation*, April 10, 1989, pp. 492–94. Rapping tells what happened when she gave her fourteen-year-old daughter a copy of Tax's previous novel, *Rivington Street*: "[I] watched her pass it to her friends—Silhouette Young Love addicts all—and heard them discussing feminism, politics and what it means to be a Jew, with a seriousness that all my lecturing never aroused."

[37]Henry Boernstein, *The Mysteries of St. Louis; or, The Jesuits on the Praire de Noyers* (St. Louis: Anzeiger des Westens, 1852), 203.

devoutness and sacred hypocrisy would soon quit, and much in this country would be better."[38] Not only did certain popular narratives speak to one audience while offending others—all composed of people who took these differences very seriously—but at least some of the writers, editors, and publishers associated with such texts were also serious about the ideological, or in a sense pedagogic, intention behind them. In fact, the bifurcation of the literary market that began in the Enlightenment for both economic and aesthetic reasons[39] was probably followed by another split between those popular narratives that were conceived of as entertainment and those that were still attempting, however dubiously, to carry on in the reasoned tradition of the Enlightenment. *Die Abendschule* is one of the places to look for the latter type of text, and it is important to engage the texts published there on their own terms—that is, not to dismiss their sense of mission out of hand as a delusion. On the other hand, having decided to take these texts seriously certainly does not imply an acceptance of their implicit ideological stance. Admitting the possibility of an opposing view, which will become particularly important when discussing feminist critiques of popular culture, simply supplies a corrective to the standard form of ideological criticism because it exposes the problematic nature of its grounding in the critic's own, often unreflected, ideological certainty.

Again, this critique is not intended to dismiss Horkheimer and Adorno's contribution to our understanding of the culture industry. My initial analysis of *Die hölzernen Teller* should make it clear how important it is to try to explain how "all the trends of the culture

[38]Ibid., 163. The German version, Heinrich Börnstein, *Die Geheimnisse von St. Louis* (1851; St. Louis: C. Witters Buchhandlung, 1874), 2:89, is not nearly as stilted. It is interesting to note that the translator felt constrained to add a long explanation of this passage; it reads in part as follows: "The translator joins in with the author in his praise of the German Sunday. The American reader must not infer, from the description given above, that intemperance and debauchery are prevailing in our native country" (pp. 163–64).
[39]On the role of the marketplace, see Jochen Schulte-Sasse, "Literarischer Markt und ästhetische Denkform: Analysen und Thesen zur Geschichte ihres Zusammenhangs," *Li.Li. Zeitschrift für Literaturwissenschaft und Linguistik* 2.6 (1972): 11–31; and for the dimension of aesthetic theory, see Christa Bürger, "Das menschliche Elend oder der Himmel auf Erden? Der Roman zwischen Aufklärung und Kunstautonomie," in Christa Bürger, Peter Bürger, and Jochen Schulte-Sasse, eds., *Zur Dichotomisierung von hoher und niederer Literatur* (Frankfurt am Main: Suhrkamp, 1982), 172–207.

industry are profoundly (*in Fleisch und Blut*) embedded in the public by the whole social process."[40] And given the political and economic situation that the characters in the narrative shared with their audience of readers from *Die Abendschule*, it is also important to understand the ramifications of the reading that the text preprograms—in Horkheimer and Adorno's terms: "Immovably, they [consumers] insist on the very ideology that enslaves them."[41] As plausible as their conclusion sounds, in our present and far more conservative age, particularly after the collapse of communism in Eastern Europe, it would seem difficult if not impossible to make this kind of pronouncement from the olympian heights of ideological certainty that Horkheimer and Adorno seem to have occupied.

Recent American criticism, by way of contrast, has viewed popular narratives in a far more positive light. For example, while praising tales of adventure, mystery, and romance, particularly in their melodramatic incarnations, for their ability to embody "the thoughts and feelings unique to a particular period," John Cawelti proposes that such stories be judged according to different standards: "There is an artistry based on convention and standardization whose significance is not simply a reflection of the inferior training and lower imaginative capacity of a mass audience."[42] At first, Cawelti's attempt to justify popular fiction aesthetically seems to be nothing more than a sop thrown in the direction of conventional literary judgments, but his gesture is more complicated. In essence, Cawelti is caught on the horns of the dilemma that either tries to justify the study of noncanonical texts by opening the canon to works that have been excluded unjustly or, alternatively, that treats the same texts as cultural artifacts, which are interesting to the (literary) historian for what they reveal of a given society, quite apart from their artistic worth or lack of it. Because he wants to have it both ways, Cawelti's conclusion shows just how uncomfortable he is with the underlying tension: "The ability to express the spirit of the moment may not be as important an artistic characteristic as the appeal to universal human concerns in a lasting way; nonetheless, I

---

[40]Horkheimer and Adorno, *Dialectic of Enlightenment*, 136. The insertion is from the German edition, *Dialektik der Aufklärung* (1947; Frankfurt am Main: Fischer Taschenbuch, 1971) 122.

[41]Horkheimer and Adorno, *Dialectic of Enlightenment*, 134.

[42]John G. Cawelti, *Adventure, Mystery, and Romance: Formula Stories as Art and Popular Culture* (Chicago: University of Chicago Press, 1976), 299–300.

have come to believe in the course of my explorations that this is a distinctive kind of artistry worth studying in its own right."[43]

The underlying problem with this position is its unwillingness to question the ground on which it stands; American academics who wrote about popular literature in the 1970s seem to be perpetually embarrassed by the supposedly ephemeral object of their project.[44] And their response was often the attempt to stylize detective stories and westerns—both interestingly enough predominantly male forms—into high art. In the United States we have had to wait for feminist analyses of popular culture to undertake a radical critique of the notion of the canon and the supposedly neutral aesthetic criteria behind it. Because many if not most of the readers of popular fiction were and continue to be women, including the women who read *Die Abendschule* or had it read to them, popular narratives were an obvious choice for feminist critics.

One of the best examples of those recent reevaluations is Tania Modleski's treatment of mass-produced fantasies for women.[45] Modleski basically ignores "literary" criteria and focuses her attention on the oft-made claim that Harlequin romances, gothic novels for women, and soap operas fail to deal with the problems of real women. While admitting that these forms neither provide women with answers nor open a discursive space for them to look behind their anxieties—in fact, the "narcotic" effect of some women's continually increasing need for fantasies may increase their anxiety level[46] —Modleski still finds a moment of resistance there: "The so-called masochism pervading these texts is a 'cover' for anxieties, desires,

---

[43]Ibid., 300. The citation is from near the end of the book, but Cawelti begins his analysis with the same gesture (see ibid., 20ff.). It is worth noting that he faced precisely the same difficulty as the critics of German-American literature mentioned in the previous chapter, including their talk of "literary" versus "historical" interest.

[44]Will Wright, *Sixguns and Society: A Structural Study of the Western* (Berkeley: University of California Press, 1975), makes the same gesture in his preface: "And if your wife, husband, mother, or child asks you why you are wasting your time staring at Westerns on TV in the middle of the night, tell them firmly—as I often did— that you are doing research in social science." Wright's attempt to correlate shifts within the formula behind Westerns with social changes in the United States in the twentieth century is similar to the project I am undertaking here, except that he posits a fairly strict structural correspondence between Western (arche)types and social formations.

[45]Tania Modleski, *Loving with a Vengeance: Mass-Produced Fantasies for Women* (New York: Methuen, 1982).

[46]Ibid., 57.

and wishes which if openly expressed would challenge the psychological and social order of things."[47] Implicit in her project is a call to *un*cover the forces behind those needs, which can happen only if we accept the fact that, "while appearing to be merely escapist, such art simultaneously challenges and reaffirms traditional values, behavior and attitudes."[48]

To a certain degree both Cawelti's and Modleski's arguments can be applied to *Die hölzernen Teller*. As outlined above, that narrative not only speaks to political, social, and economic pressures that were very real to both Germans and German-Americans in 1854, but also captures the ideological framework with which they hoped to understand and resolve their difficulties. Is it, for that reason, as Cawelti asks, "worth studying in its own right"? Here the answer must be double. First, to the extent that a reading opens the canon and questions the basis of its existence, the answer would have to be yes—even though the kind of reading necessary to open up the category of what is worth reading in German, particularly in American German departments, is a critical reading. And it is also important to note that reading a text against the grain is not the same as discovering a lost classic, which raises the second and more problematical aspect of the reason for dealing with texts like *Die hölzernen Teller*. Is it enough to invoke "an artistry of the moment" as Cawelti does,[49] especially if the result is basically to treat the text as a historical artifact which can only bear witness to the lives of its German-American readers? Or could there also be a moment of resistance in *Die hölzernen Teller*?

Modleski waffles a bit at this point. For her the resistance in mass-produced narratives for women seems to be in her own critical reading and in her analysis of how "ordinary" women read these texts, or would read them if a critical moment could be inserted into their discourse, rather than worked out of the texts themselves. Harlequin romances, for example, seem to speak to real needs, but the reading they attempt to preprogram is, even in Modleski's own terms, scarcely liberating in and of itself. Most readers apparently find these romances to be an addictive drug whose ability to help them cope decreases with use and which therefore forces them to consume

[47]Ibid., 30.
[48]Ibid., 112.
[49]Cawelti, *Adventure, Mystery, and Romance*, 300.

ever larger doses of narrative.[50] At best, these texts point to a wide-spread dissatisfaction with the present state of male-female relation-ships, but those same texts never seem to question the cultural basis of such relationships or offer a space for reconsidering them. Short of offering a new mode of writing popular narratives, the point of projects like Modleski's can only be to impose a *critical* space on them from the outside. If readers cannot stop reading "mass-pro-duced fantasies," they can at least be taught to read them against the grain. Ultimately, they might start reading other kinds of texts as well. But before examining the question of whether any critique of *Die hölzernen Teller* or an analysis of that text's own implicit cri-tique of the productive relationships it represents necessarily stops this short, we first need to ask if popular narratives can ever model "positive" values.

Here again the ground from which the reading is launched be-comes absolutely critical, and it is this often insufficiently prob-lematized ground that separates the German tradition of ideological criticism from another strand of American feminism. Unlike their (male) forebears, quite a number of feminists are almost too eager to find redeeming instances of resistance in popular literature written by women. For example, writing recently of Harriet Beecher Stowe's major best-seller, *Uncle Tom's Cabin*, which appeared in 1852, just two years before *Die hölzernen Teller*, Jane Tompkins claims:

> that the popular domestic novel of the nineteenth century represents a
> monumental effort to reorganize culture from the woman's point of
> view; that this body of work is remarkable for its intellectual complex-
> ity, ambition, and resourcefulness; and that, in certain cases, it offers a
> critique of American society far more devastating than any delivered
> by better-known critics such as Hawthorne and Melville.[51]

The difficulties with Tompkins's assessment is whether its upward revaluation of sentimental narratives (largely melodramas written by and for women) is really sustainable. To begin Tompkins argues that the "religion of domesticity" elaborated by female writers in the nineteenth century was "a myth that gave women the central posi-

---

[50]See also, Janice A. Radway, *Reading the Romance: Women, Patriarchy, and Popular Literature* (Chapel Hill: University of North Carolina Press, 1984).

[51]Jane Tompkins, *Sensational Designs: The Cultural Work of American Fiction, 1790–1860* (New York: Oxford University Press, 1985), 124.

tion of power and authority in the culture."[52] Modern readers judge the submissive piety of their forebears too harshly because, as Tompkins puts it, they fail to realize that "piety and industry, both activities over which a woman has control, can set you free."[53]

Unlike Huck Finn, sentimental heroines did not have the option of running away; they stayed at home, coped as best they could, and transformed their oppression into a kind of moral authority. Particularly to the extent that the works in which they appeared were constructed in accordance with the Christian discourse that the vast majority of Americans used to frame their view of the world, Tompkins concludes: "I see their plots and characters [both admittedly stereotypical] as providing society with a means of thinking about itself, defining certain aspects of a social reality which the authors and their readers shared, dramatizing its conflicts, and recommending solutions."[54] For Harriet Beecher Stowe and her contemporaries real power in the world grew from individual faith; political and economic change, even the abolition of slavery, could be only superficial. Seen in these terms, *Uncle Tom's Cabin* was neither an insipid valorization of female sacrifice nor an appeal to submit to earthly power, however evil. Stowe's novel criticizes slavery from the only standpoint that its readers thought valid, and it presents an alternative, feminist utopia toward which they could strive in their daily lives. Therefore, according to Tompkins, the value of Stowe's work, and the value of the other sentimental novelists, lay in the "cultural work" they did. Such texts ought to be judged on the basis of how well they reached readers rather than on the extent to which they fulfilled various (male) standards of literariness—or, to include Horkheimer and Adorno, (male) standards of progressive ideology.

This summary of Tompkins's position leads directly to the question whether the same kind of argument could be made for *Die hölzernen Teller*. To be sure, *Die hölzernen Teller* is sentimental, but it is probably not a domestic novel; the anonymous author was probably a man, and the triumphant figure is also male. Although the idyll presented at the conclusion of the novel is located in the security of the home and family, it might be more accurate to use Cawelti's term and speak of it as a "social melodrama."[55] But is an

[52]Ibid., 125.
[53]Ibid., 168
[54]Ibid., 200.
[55]Cawelti, *Adventure, Mystery, and Romance*, 260–95. For Cawelti, social melo-

ideal construct based on the norms and values of the premodern village, where traditional modes of production still flourish, substantially different from the "effort to reorganize culture from the woman's point of view"? Granted, the nineteenth-century woman's world was largely indoors, but would Tompkins's hypothetical women readers have felt out of place in the world of *Die hölzernen Teller*? Or was the domestic sphere, and with it the artisan or agrarian idyll, actually an attempt to escape from the problems of the real world and a turn toward self-indulgence and narcissism?[56]

Certainly, neither *Die hölzernen Teller* nor *Uncle Tom's Cabin* can be accused of excessive quality according to the norms of formalist criticism, which is what Tompkins is really attacking. In both cases the books' characters are shallow stereotypes, their plots are contrived, and their language is anything but rich. Yet both texts addressed real problems within the terms of a widely shared ideological framework, and both offered solutions to those problems that would have empowered the weak at the expense of the dominant culture. Without claiming that female domesticity and the way of life associated with premodern modes of production were the same, the question then becomes whether we can valorize a feminist version of utopia without also accepting the world-view of *Die hölzernen Teller*, which was far more conservative and predominantly male. In addition, does it make a difference that the utopias they offered readers were indeed no-places, located either in a mythical past or in an idealized present, where the notions "that resistance is possible" could only be a rearguard action?

If we return to Tompkins's claim "that the popular domestic novel of the nineteenth century represents a monumental effort to reorganize culture from the woman's point of view,"[57] two fundamental ideological problems arise. And they are the same problems that would have to be dealt with in any attempt to view *Die hölzernen Teller* in a more positive light. First, female domesticity was more than likely a two-edged sword. Yes, the home was a realm

---

drama "synthesizes the archetype of melodrama with a carefully and elaborately developed social setting in such a way as to combine the emotional satisfactions of melodrama with the interest inherent in a detailed, intimate, and realistic analysis of major social or historical phenomena" (p. 261).

[56]For the feminist indictment of sentimental fiction, against which Tompkins specifically addresses herself here, see Ann Douglas, *The Feminization of American Culture* (New York: Alfred A. Knopf, 1977).

[57]Tompkins, *Sensational Designs*, 124.

in which women enjoyed a certain moral authority and personal autonomy, but as the masthead illustrations show, even in such apparently mundane activities as reading, the world of the family was not untouched by patriarchal authority. For all their power, female readers of *Die Abendschule* were generally reduced to the position of the read-to. To be sure, the evolution of that iconography points to the need to historicize any such judgments, but it should also underline the danger in assuming that the home or the preindustrial workplace was a realm of freedom, or that the resistance it represented was anything more than a hopeless gesture—no more than a literary refusal to deal with inevitable change. Second, as those masthead illustrations also demonstrate, the women for whom sentimental novels were supposedly carrying out their "cultural work" were primarily members of the middle class. While it is true that the bourgeoisie supplied many of the readers of popular fiction, care must be taken not to accept bourgeois authors' own attempts to reformulate literary discourse and stylize the representation of reality in literature into the *natural* order of things. Both the ideal of domesticity and the ideal of the household as a harmonious productive unit (*das ganze Haus*) were historical constructs that arose in the context of powerful social and economic developments, and although they may have provided some form of solace to their readers, the reason for reading them now need not be that the solutions they offered were somehow adequate to the situation in which they arose, or that they continue to bear witness to a tradition of liberating ideas.

A more cautious approach would be to argue, with Cawelti, that "the essential social-psychological dynamic of social melodrama is one of continually integrating new social circumstances and ideas to the developing middle-class sense of social value."[58] If popular narratives were one means by which readers, including middle-class readers, adapted to change, then a critical, diachronic reading of texts like *Die hölzernen Teller* can help chart those changes and provide an occasion for an assessment of the way popular literature helped the victims of change deal with the constantly evolving circumstances in which they found themselves, however inadequate, from our perspectives, the assistance they received might have been. Of course, history, including literary history, is also the story of how we arrived at the position we now occupy, and it offers some hope of an intervention based on that understanding. Any sensible read-

---

[58]Cawelti, *Adventure, Mystery, and Romance*, 284.

ing, therefore, has to proceed both with and against the text's grain, and such a reading can make sense only if it constantly historicizes not only the object of its inquiry but also the always problematical ground from which it is launched.

The reading I propose is therefore neither explicitly ideology-critical nor feminist, but to the extent possible both at the same time. As attractive as these two alternative positions might be—and I take them to represent the poles of a whole range of options—the only legitimate ground is to be found by constantly shifting from one to the other. I intend to examine the ideological stance of the texts published in *Die Abendschule*, knowing full well how insubstantial the foundation under that critique really is, knowing in other words that other critical—or even sympathetic—readings are certainly possible. Yet, while rejecting most of the "imaginary" solutions proffered in these narratives, I hope to treat them with as much seriousness as they were accorded by contemporary readers. For if those readers actually got something out of what they read, if the narratives published in *Die Abendschule* provided at least some of the material that German immigrants needed to construct new identities for themselves in the United States, then no matter how "wrong" or how fanciful those identities may have been, they were nevertheless adequate at some level to the challenge of the readers' historical circumstances. Moreover, they can help explain who those readers were and why, from the perspective of hindsight, they left us with the world we actually have rather than the one we might have preferred to inherit.

One could, of course, ask whether narratives transmit value or, if they do, whether it is their primary function. The question arises because the subject position any given text offers its readers probably has to coincide, in some not insignificant degree, with those readers' historically specific needs and experiences. Whether we then label the content of that overlapping an ideology, or whether we say that the text partakes of an era's hegemonic structures, is perhaps less important than the realization that narrations do not, for all practical purposes, have to manipulate their readers' beliefs. Readers expect to agree with a text's message, on the basis of genre conventions or the text's location in a trusted medium like *Die Abendschule*. Otherwise they would never have chosen to read it in the first place.

This is not to argue, however, that various specific contents are immaterial or interchangeable, but to note that the real satisfaction of reading may well have as much to do with pleasures in the realm of the psyche as with the satisfaction of seeing the right protagonist win. According to this hypothesis, identification (for example, the (male) readers' identification with the figure of Lukas in *Die hölzernen Teller*) not only allows readers to participate in the vicarious thrill of victory over the forces of capitalism *and* the remnants of a feudal aristocracy, but also permits them to escape, albeit briefly, from their own cares by entering into the life of another human being—in this case an imaginary one. In effect, the process of reading narratives, when one identity temporarily merges with another through an act of identification, might be likened to the child's feeling of symbiosis with the mother that Freud posits at the level of primary psychological processes, which remain as happy memories deep within the subconscious. By satisfying such primal desires, narratives are able to offer imaginary gratifications that are unconnected with any of the specific contents they might relate. The text's connection with reality is merely the first step in allowing for the satisfaction of universal human desires, which are satisfied only after an ideological "coincidence" permits that initial step into the text.

But even if this is the case—and there appears to be a good deal of evidence to suggest that it might be[59]—it still is not quite so easy to dismiss either the ideological or the thematic component of narratives. No matter what psychological model one employs, the subject positions texts offer readers often satisfy them only for a relatively short period of time, to say nothing of the limited appeal most texts have in terms of their readers' age, class, geographic location, and so on. And even if the need for narratives is universal, in projects like the present study it can simply and legitimately be bracketed in order to ask why some narratives seem to have worked for particular

[59]See, e.g., Gabriele Schwab, "Genesis of the Subject, Imaginary Functions, and Poetic Language," *New Literary History* 15 (Spring 1984): 453–74. See also Peter Brooks, *Reading for the Plot: Design and Intention in Narrative* (New York: Vintage, 1984); and Lennard J. Davis, *Resisting Novels: Ideology and Fiction* (New York: Methuen, 1987). Davis argues that novels have to be resisted precisely because of the psychological mechanisms they employ. But even if he is correct, as I argue below, it still seems necessary to go beyond his formal, instrumental approach in order to find specific instances of the traps that narratives set; otherwise Davis's approach is little more than the usual politically progressive criteria clothed in the fashionable garb of psychoanalysis.

readers in specific times and places. For example, that the happy ending accorded a craftsman like Lukas in *Die hölzernen Teller* probably appealed to *Die Abendschule*'s readers in 1854 because the narrative's successful closure provided them with some form of compensation for the harsh reality they experienced everyday in their new homeland. In other words, their gratification, even if it was confined to the imaginary realm and was perhaps a substitute for their taking action in their own lives, was nevertheless located in those readers' own mental presents; the displacement of the story to Saxony in an earlier age was, quite simply, a fiction.

The fact that such spatial and temporal dislocations are a common feature of popular narratives, which even nowadays are often located in the distant but still familiar European past or among the foreign but not impossibly remote English aristocracy, must mean that the shift occurs for a reason. Indeed, the relentless regularity of certain chronotopes must be more than a meaningless genre convention or pure coincidence. If the pleasure of narrative closure is the goal most readers seek, the text they read has to locate its happy ending in a time and space that renders such success plausible.[60] For Lukas to have returned home and settled into the comfortable life of a village schoolmaster in 1854, while the rest of the town's inhabitants happily continued to produce wooden plates in the manner of their forebears, would have flatly contradicted the experience of German immigrant readers who had recently left their homeland precisely because that image no longer corresponded to the reality they knew. The artisans, craftsmen, and their families who migrated to the United States certainly must have identified with Lukas's predicament, but they never would have left Germany if they could have imagined achieving his happy fate in their own real presents. Locating the plot a century earlier inserted the hero, who must succeed if the narrative is to work psychologically, into a time and place where his success becomes credible.

Of course, the setting has to not only permit Lukas's existence but also allow for the possibility of a meaningful conflict. Neither the cities of sixteenth-century Holland nor the United States in the nine-

---

[60]By the same token, this psychological function of narration—namely, the compensatory pleasure of identification followed by a happy ending—also explains why most "modern" or avant-garde texts can never be truly "popular" and can never have the disturbing effect they seek: The challenge of their open-endedness, and their principled refusal to allow sustained identification, mean that they necessarily fail to provide the satisfaction sought by "ordinary" readers.

teenth century, which were among the favored locales for later stories in *Die Abendschule*, could serve as plausible times or spaces for this particular narrative. It needs the Saxon court and the artisans of the surrounding countryside. In other words, the psychological moment of narration, far from eliminating the need for ideology, seems to demand something very similar to an assessment of the readers' sense of reality in order to explain why certain texts speak to the inhabitants of any one discursive universe while leaving other readers cold. Thus, not only must the act of offering a subject position still be understood ideologically, but the way narratives work for historically specific readers suggests, at the very least, a complex interplay between the world those readers occupied and the psychological mechanisms they shared with their fellow human beings, irrespective of the latter's location in time and space.

If narratives like *Die hölzernen Teller* supported a belief that happiness could be found only in a small community where the traditional values of the family and artisan production were still intact, many of the other texts published in the initial volume of *Die Abendschule* reinforced the specifically German aspect of its readers' ideology. I refer here to various histories of the Germans that were a recurrent feature of the magazine. These texts share a variety of formal features with other narratives published in *Die Abendschule*—for example, figures with whom readers can identify—and they are, in some cases, just as fictional. But from the standpoint of German immigrants, who were sure of the rightness of their faith but who were also confronted by numerous sects and by powerful nonbelievers, the following two quotations must have provided some comfort—especially if the Romans of European history are conflated with contemporary Roman Catholics. First, in an article entitled "Hermann, Germany's Liberator," they could read: "It was Germany and its tribes alone who resisted the terrible power of the Romans most forcefully, and they never submitted completely to the oppressive yoke of Roman rule" (I.3, 1).[61] Second, two weeks later, in an article about the enormous migrations that took place at the end of the Roman Empire, they were reminded: "It was decided by

---

[61]In an odd way, this text parallels the opening lines of the French comic-strip hero Asterix—except that *Die Abendschule*'s history was meant seriously: "The year is 50 B.C. Gaul is entirely occupied by the Romans. Well not entirely. . . . One small village of indomitable Gauls still holds out against the invaders."

God's providence that the same force that put an end to Roman rule in Germany would also crush it in Italy, indeed in all of Europe and in Northern Africa—the force of German weapons" (I.4, 3). As we shall see in greater detail in the next two chapters, such history not only helped to provide the German-American readers of *Die Abend-schule* with a specifically German component to their identities, but also gave them a sense of mission, however difficult things might become in their new homeland.

Of course, history is a mine that can yield any number of lessons, each appropriate to its own particular time. In the course of the next forty years *Die Abendschule* repeatedly explored the past, and the magazine's selection of topics is an important indication of how its editors read their audience. The historical narratives they chose ranged from nonfiction, admittedly written with varying degrees of poetic license, to the almost purely imaginary accounts of historical fiction, but the interesting question that such texts raise has less to do with their truth-content than with the values they contained. In other words, what role did history, understood as written accounts of the past, play in contemporary discourses? What did reading history mean to German-Americans?

The early years of *Die Abendschule* can offer only the beginnings of an answer, yet if the relatively small number of historical narratives published in the first few volumes do nothing else, they show how useful history could be in framing a discussion of values that were far from being merely historical. Because it is possible to use historical figures and events to refer obliquely (that is, in an age of censorship, safely) to the present, history was often the vehicle of choice in such discussions, and one could probably link the rise of historical fiction in Germany to the failure of 1848, and the subsequent muzzling of the press and publishing industry.[62] But, since *Die Abendschule* faced no such pressures, the reasons for its editors' frequent choice of historical fiction must have been grounded in the genre's popularity and, as will become clear below, especially in Chapter 5, in the uses to which historical fiction could be put.

Besides *Die hölzernen Teller*, the only other extended work of fiction published in the period before the Civil War was a historical novel, *Die Meergeusen* (The Water Beggars), which was written by

---

[62]Louise Mühlbach's turn to historical narratives is the example that comes to mind most readily.

the German pastor W. O. von Horn.[63] The title refers to the Dutch seamen who fought on the side of William of Orange against the Duke of Alba and the Spanish domination of the Netherlands during the sixteenth century. Like most historical fiction, Horn's novel ties real people and events to the fate of imaginary individuals in an attempt to bring history closer to its readers. Not surprisingly, the main interest revolves around a young woman, Elisabeth, daughter of the mayor of Antwerp, who is loved by her cousin, Wilm von Strahlen: "He loved Elisabeth faithfully, purely, and tenderly, and his belief in her purity was his heart's most precious possession" (V, 130–31). Completing the plot-propelling triangle is Jan van der Does, another cousin: "I hope for Elisabeth and—her money—oh, what a goal, what an opportunity! I have to reach this goal, even if my path leads over graves!" (V, 145). In contrast to Gertrud in *Die hölzernen Teller*, Elisabeth remains pure to the end, and she is eventually, after five years and an enormous number of adventures for all concerned, united with Wilm, who is able to defeat Jan—and much of the Spanish navy in the process.

That plot could occur in virtually any historical setting, but not every context would be of as much interest to the readers of *Die Abendschule*. The prize in the struggle between Jan and Wilm is not only Elisabeth and her money but also freedom for the Netherlands and the Protestants who support the house of Orange. In the final battle both Jan and his Catholic masters are vanquished, and the city of Briel becomes "a cradle of freedom" (VI, 51). Although the novel was written in Germany by a German author, for the readers of *Die Abendschule* the situation of German Protestants in Holland was certainly recognizable; the inhabitants of the American republic could look to the example of the Netherlands for legitimation in the two countries' parallel histories, and the German-American Protestant readers of *Die Abendschule* could also stylize themselves into the defenders of freedom against a foreign power, namely the Roman Catholic church.

This is not to say that history was the dominant feature of *Die Abendschule* in these early years. The magazine also contained short stories with contemporary settings, for example, "Victor Carabine" (VII, 133–35, mispaginated), which dealt with a soldier in the Crimean War, and there were numerous texts set in the timeless

---

[63]*Die Abendschule*, V, no. 17–VI, no. 7. For more on Horn, the pen name of Wilhelm Oertel (1748–1867), see Müller-Salget, *Erzählungen für das Volk*, 142–47.

world of preindustrial, rural life where "God is just" ("Der Meineid" [Perjury], II, 53) and Christian virtue is rewarded ("Die rettende Bibel" [The Saving Bible], VII, 144–47). Current events loomed large in the pages of *Die Abendschule*, both in news reports and in the form of short biographies: the new king of Italy, Victor Emmanuel II (VI, 4–6), and all three candidates in the presidential election of 1860, the Republican Abraham Lincoln (VI, 163) and the Democrats John Breckenridge and Stephan Douglas (VI, 190). One series that must have been particularly useful to German-Americans was composed of sixteen articles on the "The Fundamentals of Law in the United States" (II, 16—III, 9, 1855–56). There the new immigrant could learn how to become a citizen, buy property, and make a will. The law was, however, far from an ideologically neutral space; for example, it could not be used to justify an equitable redistribution of property:

If we inquire first into the reason behind the right of private property, we find what both reason and revelation teach, that God gave the earth and its bounty to humanity in general, to own and to use, but left the distribution of the same to mankind. (II.22, 163)

Of note here, too, is the fact that whatever the subject, *Die Abendschule* remained a Christian journal ("both reason and revelation teach"), but, lest the undertaking sound too easy and too coherent, it is important to remember the almost constant struggle for survival that plagued the magazine during the first decade of its existence. Some of the difficulties have already been hinted at in the survey of masthead illustrations in Chapter 1, but those images do not provide the complete story, particularly with regard to the financial risks involved as the new journal struggled to find and hold an audience. The editor's introduction to the initial issue already lists the chief problems: "Because of the illustrations, issuing this magazine involves considerable expense, and we therefore turn to all the friends of Christian education and training with the urgent request that they do everything possible to help disseminate it" (I.1, 3). By issue number twelve *Die Abendschule* claimed to have 1,600 subscribers, mainly scattered throughout the Midwest, and the paper declared its willingness to accept small advertisements. The final issue of volume one did contain an advertisement for Friedrich Rauchfuss's *Praktische Englische Grammatik* (Practical English Grammar), but unless a great deal of other advertising appeared in circulars that accompanied the magazine, the effort does not seem to have been very successful.[64] Irregularities in the dates of individual issues suggest that it was difficult to produce *Die Abendschule* according to schedule, and illustrations were an unending source of aggravation. In a poem written "Zum neuen Jahr 1856" (For the new year 1856), some of which was quoted at the beginning of Chapter 1, a writer (presumably the editor) promised his readers: "A lot about art, nature, and science / world commerce, riddles, songs / [And] God willing, also many a picture" (II, 186). God must have left the poor fellow in the lurch because by the end of 1856 the original publisher had bowed out of the enterprise. At that point the new editor, Pastor Diehlmann, moved to St. Louis, perhaps to serve a new parish there, and he took *Die Abendschule* with him (III, 144).

For several months Diehlmann also acted as publisher, but his printer, J. H. Buschman, assumed those duties just before the start of volume four (III, 185). By volume five (1858) both the editor and publisher had resigned, to be replaced by Otto Ernst, a local bookseller, who acted as publisher, and Alexander Saxer, the deputy rector of the Missouri Synod's Concordia Seminary, as editor. At this juncture *Die Abendschule*'s subtitle changed to "Eine Zeitschrift für Belehrung und Unterhaltung"; the limiting words "für die reifere Jugend" were dropped in what was apparently an effort to broaden the journal's appeal or at least bring the title into accord with its contents. The new publisher also promised "[that he] would spare no sacrifice and would employ the highest level of diligence to see that the readers of this magazine were completely satisfied by its pleasing external appearance, worthwhile pictures, regular publication, prompt delivery, etc." (V, 192). The specificity of his apology is a good indication of what readers must have had to endure in the previous five years, and one wonders how many of them were left.[65]

[64]The 15 February 1859 issue (V. 120) contains the following notice: "We respectfully draw your attention to the advertisements in the supplement to today's edition." Unfortunately, only one of these supplements from the early years of *Die Abendschule* has survived (V.3, November 1858), AL unnumbered. In addition to a large advertisement for the magazine itself, which is an indication that the space would otherwise have been empty, there are four notices for bookstores, three in St. Louis and one in Buffalo, New York. There is also an ad for a homeopathic apothecary. The largest of the bookstore ads is for the new publisher's own place of business, and the ad indicates that he is also an agent for the homeopathic medicines. In all, not much money could have changed hands here.

[65]The advertising circular mentioned in the previous footnote claims: "Since *Die Illustri[e]rte Abendschule*, which has a circulation of 2,500, is read in every state of

Ernst's brief tenure as publisher—May 1858 to November 1859—produced a new low-point in *Die Abendschule*'s existence, which was already quite precarious. Money—in this case, the lack of money—was the root of the problem; apparently there were simply not enough subscribers to make the undertaking pay. In the first number of volume six the editor reported: "Although a fair number of new subscribers have appeared in recent years, their number bears no relationship to the significant increase in expenses, which have arisen from the purchase of worthwhile illustrations and from the considerable improvement in the magazine's appearance" (VI, 1). Still, there must have been just enough money to make stealing it worthwhile. Issue number five was dated 15 September 1859, but number six did not appear until 1 November. Curious readers could have learned from the *Lutheraner* of 4 October that "Mr. Otto Ernst's secret departure has made the continued existence of the above-named journal [*Die Abendschule*] impossible."[66] Issue six appeared only because the magazine's printer, Moritz Niedner, bought the rights to the journal at a public auction for ten dollars, probably because he was hoping to make good on the debt Ernst had left him.[67] At that point *Der Lutheraner* seemed surprised, and genuinely gratified, that *Die Abendschule* would continue to appear.[68]

But the magazine's troubles were far from over. A few months later Saxer also resigned as editor, to be replaced by another pastor, C. J. H. Fick, who was also a close friend of Walther (VI, 129). He quickly reaffirmed *Die Abendschule*'s basic principles, most explicitly on the first page of the next volume:

It is well known that, since 1848, German newspapers have become increasingly anti-Christian. . . . [*Die Abendschule*], which stands firmly

---

the Union and in Canada, the success of the advertisements can be counted on with certainty." Given Ernst's subsequent behavior and the natural tendency to exaggerate in such circumstances, the number is to be treated with caution.

66"Illustri[e]rte Abendschule," a one-paragraph notice signed by Saxer. *Der Lutheraner* 16 (4 October 1859): 32.

67See Louis Lange, "Bericht an die Ehrwürdige Synode von Missouri, Ohio und a. St. über die Synodaldruckerei und die 'Abendschule,'" CHI, A & HL 1048. Upon reappearing, *Die Abendschule* reported: "Shortly before the date on which it was to appear, the publisher and sole owner [of *Die Abendschule*] disappeared without notice and without leaving any indication of what was to be done. He did leave behind a considerable debt for its printing" (VI,41).

68*Der Lutheraner* announced the reappearance of *Die Abendschule* on 29 November 1859, (16:64).

on the foundation of faith, intends to serve all the Germans in this country by attempting to promote Christian education generally. (VII, 1)

The last page of the same issue, however, also contained a fairly blunt appraisal of the journal's situation: "It remains to be seen whether the effort and expenditures we made in order to improve *Die Abendschule* will be acknowledged by our dear readers. So much is certain: if the circle of readers does not increase significantly we will not be able to pay the bills" (VII, 8).

Indeed, the physical appearance of the magazine had changed significantly; in 1860 it returned to quarto format under the third masthead, discussed earlier, which was far more inviting visually. The volume's opening number contained the first installment of K. H. Caspari's "Zu Strassburg auf der Schanz" [On the Parapets of Strasbourg][69] and the beginning of a series by Dr. Livingstone, "Früheste Bekanntschaft mit Afrika" (My Earliest Acquaintance with Africa). One must assume that the two authors were familiar enough to entice new readers and harmless enough to reassure the faithful few that the magazine was still worthy of their continued support. The first issue also contained a poem by the obviously pseudonymic G. Hilarius "An Göthe" (To Goethe), which regretted that the great poet was not a Christian, and that fortnight's picture was an engraving of the mounted statue of George Washington in Union Park in New York City. But apparently unable to count on significant newsstand sales, the publisher suggested that readers who wanted to see *Die Abendschule* continue each try to find one or two others who would subscribe. He and the editor decided, just like their predecessors who had begun the magazine six years earlier, to wait an extra two weeks with issue number two to see whether the requisite number of paying readers would be forthcoming: "[*Die Abendschule* will appear], but only in a month—not in 14 days—so that they can see if there is sufficient interest" (VII, 8).

It must have worked, because after 1860 *Die Abendschule* continued to appear, virtually without interruption or delay, until December 1940. For almost all of that period it was in the hands of the Lange family. Louis Lange's quiet purchase of the journal—an-

---

[69]Müller-Salget, *Erzählungen für das Volk*, 344, lists the following publication data: Karl Heinrich Caspari, *"Zu Strassburg auf der Schanz": Eine Erzählung für das deutsche Volk* (Stuttgart: Steinkopf, 1853).

nounced in a brief notice on the back page of volume seven, number fifteen, dated 1 April 1861—was the other significant change *Die Abendschule* underwent in its early years. According to information provided to advertisers in 1895, Lange, who had died two years earlier, was born in Zennern, Germany, in 1829.[70] He emigrated to the United States at the age of seventeen and worked as an apprentice at German-language papers in New York and Detroit before moving on to St. Louis. There he was employed as a bookkeeper by Moritz Niedner, printer and publisher of the *Missouri State Journal*, who had rescued *Die Abendschule* in 1859. The magazine Lange purchased in 1861—for $200!—supposedly had about one thousand subscribers, and the prospectus issued in 1895 described it as "a very poorly printed German story paper."

Lange's descendants may well have been trying to heroicize their forebear's undertaking, but in 1861 the enterprise certainly did look extremely shaky. The next chapter traces the development of *Die Abendschule* as it gradually acquired a firmer sense of itself and its audience, particularly once it reconstituted itself as *Ein Deutsches Familienblatt* in 1867. The changes that occurred were not just in the masthead or indeed in the magazine itself; 1865 marked the end of the Civil War, and in the decade after the cessation of hostilities mass immigration from Germany began again. In addition, with the creation of the second German Empire in 1871, Germans who came to the United States were coming from a redefined Germany, which would have a profound effect on the identity of Germans throughout the world. In short, once the founding gesture had finally been brought to fruition, *Die Abendschule* soon had to begin providing narratives to a new mix of people who were, or were becoming, German-Americans in a social, political, and economic context that was quite different from the world of the 1850s.

[70]"Abendschule," CHI, AL 648.

CHAPTER FOUR

Narrating an Identity Crisis:
German Unification in *Die Abendschule*

The Franco-Prussian War and the high point it reached with the proclamation of the Empire in January 1871 were political events of the first magnitude for Germany and indeed for the rest of Europe, but they were also significant symbolic events for German-speaking people throughout the world. For one thing, the foundation of a German state meant that German immigrants to the United States could finally answer questions about their origins in a manner that made sense to officials in the ports of New York, Baltimore, and New Orleans. They were no longer from Prussia or Saxony or some other place that scarcely anyone had heard of, but from Germany. Whether this automatically made them Germans or, because they had left their original homeland for the United States, German-Americans is the principal question this chapter will explore. I shall examine texts published during the half-dozen years leading up to 1871 and include the years that immediately followed the series of Prussian wars and the creation of the Empire under Wilhelm I and Bismarck because there was often a considerable lag before such tumultuous events began to echo through the pages of *Die Abendschule*. Yet it is not so much the events themselves that are of interest here; the real issue is how "1871" as a symbolic event helped focus attention on the question of German-American identity.[1] This

---

[1]In what follows I use the number 1871 in quotation marks as a referent not just for the year but also for the whole complex of events and symbols associated with "1871" and evoked by every mention of it. Similarly, "German," "American," "German-American," and "Lutheran" are supposed to denote a good deal more than some merely factual attribute based on national origin, place of residence, or

is not to suggest that something like a single subject position for German-Americans suddenly emerged in 1871, but rather that the fact of German unification added yet another variable to the multiplicity of forces already at work among German immigrants in the United States. The question of identity was reopened with a vengeance in 1871, but questions of identity—or perhaps identities, competing and unresolved—had already been thematized in earlier texts. And although identity was not always openly problematized, it was nevertheless inscribed in virtually everything published in *Die Abendschule* in this period. This chapter therefore maps some of those multiple inscriptions and also asks how *Die Abendschule*'s narratives might have helped readers develop their own answers to the question of who they were.

In general terms, to judge by the narratives published in *Die Abendschule*, the end of the Civil War seemed to signal a kind of identity crisis for the German population of the United States. The drastic decline in immigration during the conflict, and the relatively successful integration of German troops into the Union armies, made it appear as if the distinctively German ethnic group that had begun to develop in the 1850s would gradually melt into the larger American whole. And it is important to remember that before the onset of immigration from southern and eastern Europe in the 1880s, the white population of the United States was still remarkably homogeneous. In a very real sense, when measured in terms of sustained nativist prejudice, it was Roman Catholics from Ireland who constituted the white "other"; their religion often made them far more "foreign" than the predominantly Protestant Germans, who at least theoretically could have disappeared.

Readers of *Die Abendschule* were therefore confronted with what appeared to be a particularly serious dilemma—namely, the choice between three separate and for all practical purposes mutually exclusive identities. First, they could try to remain German, which involved the continued maintenance of Old World customs in an increasingly if often passively hostile environment, where there was little support for a way of life that was separated by thousands of miles—and a whole economic order. Second, they could attempt to become assimilated, but the voluntary abandonment of their German heritage in no way guaranteed successful Americanization. In-

religious affiliation. Those distinctions will become clearer in the course of the exposition.

deed, the risk of being caught between two worlds, symbolized by an imperfect grasp of English, was as great a danger as the loss of whatever it had meant to be German in a foreign land. Third, *Die Abendschule*'s readers had to deal with the particular demands placed on them by their Lutheran beliefs, which were, on the one hand, far more developed and far more exclusive than identities like "German" or "American" and, on the other hand, intimately connected with them both. For it was only in the United States that Walther and his followers could have created the eminently German but nevertheless thoroughly American Deutsche Evangelische-Lutherische Synode von Missouri, Ohio und anderen Staaten. Yet neither the Synod nor its members were fully German-American by 1865; that was an identity they would only approach—in part, with the help of various subject positions offered them by narratives like those published in *Die Abendschule*—in the course of the next half-dozen years, thereby paralleling the "pretext" provided their erstwhile compatriots in what became Germany in 1871. As Hawgood put it:

> The year 1871 saw two new unified Germanies in existence rather than one, very different from each other, but sharing a sense of self-satisfaction most annoying to the rest of the world and ultimately of great disadvantage to both. One was the German Empire under Prussian hegemony erected by Bismarck, and the other was German-America.[2]

Of course, it was not that simple in either country, and one of the interesting developments traced in this chapter is the continued tension between the all-inclusive "German-American" and the still militantly exclusive "Lutheran" as those identities were negotiated in the years leading up to the foundation of Bismarck's Reich. How those

[2]Hawgood, *Tragedy of German America*, 265. Although he claims that German immigrants had already become German-Americans by 1860 as a result of nativist agitation, Hawgood undercuts his argument when he admits, in a wonderfully mixed metaphor, that the German-Americans had again lost that sense of identity by the end of the Civil War and therefore had to recreate it anew: "His boats were burned but he still gazed longingly out to sea, grasping the oar that was the relic and the symbol of his old-worldliness in a new world; and of this oar he fashioned the hyphen that was to serve for so long at one and the same time as both a link and a bar between his Germanism and his Americanism, and as an obstacle to all his endeavours" (pp. 253–54). See also Hans L. Trefousse, "The German-American Immigrants and the Newly Founded Reich," in Trommler and McVeigh, *America and the Germans*, 1:160–75.

negotiations fared in the last two decades of the nineteenth century is the subject of the final chapter.

Popular narratives like those published in *Die Abendschule* often provide a space where identities can be proposed and tested and where conflicts between various identities can be mapped and articulated. As Tony Bennett and Janet Wollacott have argued, such texts function "not by simply putting the reader or viewer back into the ideological subject positions from which, implicitly, the narratives start, but by moving him/her on to a new set of ideological co-ordinates."[3] Moreover, when popular fictions "establish or shift subject identities," they do so "with the active consent of their readers."[4] As one might expect, the narratives published in such an unsettled or unresolved period are far from monologic, and the texts published in *Die Abendschule* in the half-dozen years between the end of the American Civil War and the foundation of the second German Empire are particularly rich and varied. The year 1871 really was a decisive one for those who would become German-Americans, and what they read in the preceding few years shows why they might have longed for some form of resolution. Not only are the short stories and serialized novels filled with a variety of answers to the questions of what it meant to be "German," "American," "German-American," and "Lutheran," but history—that is, the discourse of history, where notions like the "nation" and "national identity" were almost invariably grounded in the nineteenth century—played a particularly important role. And it was the history of the German people, from their almost mythical beginnings to the events that had just culminated in the new Empire, that was a specific focus of readers' attention in *Die Abendschule*. After Bismarck's success, all of German history was reinterpreted with the telos of "1871" in mind, and among German immigrants in the United States the "mission" of the Germans in Europe was believed to parallel the special destiny of Germans in the United States.

Yet even before the success of 1871, which came to be symbolized in the annual celebrations of Prussia's decisive victory over the French at Sedan, history was apparently a special source of comfort to American Germans who worried that they would disappear as an identifiable group, and so the history of Germans in the United

---

[3]Tony Bennett and Joan Wollacott, *Bond and Beyond: The Political Career of a Popular Hero* (New York: Methuen, 1987), 5.
[4]Ibid., 280.

States was another recurrent topic in *Die Abendschule*. In other words, both fiction and nonfiction shared the narratological task of socializing German immigrants, of proposing, negotiating, reproducing, and reinforcing German-American identities. If the result at this point—through 1871—was still a decided schizophrenia, if texts that proposed a subject position of pan-Germanic identification could coexist with texts that modeled Lutheran exclusiveness, we have an indication of how deep the fissures within any potential German-American whole were, and of how much work remained to be done in the ensuing decades of the nineteenth century, when at least some of the multiple variants of those German-American identities would be consolidated—but then only at considerable cost to the little content that remained. Still, "1871" continued to exist as a key symbolic "event"—complete with its own set of emotionally charged semantic markers, for example, Bismarck, Wilhelm I, Sedan—that could anchor whatever it meant to be German anywhere in the world.

Of particular interest here are the conflicting representations of the fundamentally different subject positions offered readers by several texts that appeared in the same volume of *Die Abendschule*—volume eighteen—from the years 1871–72. Reading these narratives with the question of identity in mind is often to read them against the grain and to search for levels of meaning below the surface of content, especially to the extent that contradictions within and between texts become apparent, although multiple variants would probably be a more accurate term.

Of course, not every text fits so neatly into the category of an identity crisis, at least not an identity crisis defined solely on the basis of national origin. The overtly religious component of nearly all these texts—in a sense, the connection between "Belehrung und Unterhaltung" in the magazine's early subtitle—raises the question of what other functions such narratives might have had. While religious values were also constituent elements in the identities proposed for readers of *Die Abendschule*, the apparent purpose of these narratives and their relationship to modes of narration initially defined in the early German Enlightenment also merit particular attention. For the writers and editors of *Die Abendschule*, moral instruction, albeit "entertaining" moral instruction, was serious business indeed. This second reading, which reexamines the same texts in order to analyze the norms and values they espoused, is clearly with the grain, but my thesis is that the two readings actually complement one another. The chapter therefore skips about between history and the everyday difficulties faced by fictional Germans in the United States and back again, in an effort to show how the discussion of identity was joined simultaneously with and from a variety of different subject positions.

One cautionary note is in order here, concerning the question of what these narratives represent. While the question may not seem so pressing or so difficult for texts labeled "history," when it comes to fictional accounts of the life of German immigrants in the United States, one might well wonder to what degree the stories were accurate. But that question seems misplaced in both instances. First, as already discussed in Chapter 2, any approach that reduces either literature or the supposedly "factual" accounts of history to the status of documents necessarily limits the number of texts worth reading, both by excluding the thematically noncontemporaneous and the "unrealistic" and at the same time by demoting the texts that remain to the second-class status of mere illustration for whatever can be verified elsewhere.[5] From the standpoint of modern academic historiography, the so-called historical texts in *Die Abendschule* would probably suffer most under these criteria, for they are often not very different from their fictional counterparts—either in form or content. To be sure, fictional texts represent something other than "just the facts," but this is not to say that either history or fiction is "false," just that the question of truth-value is poorly put. It not only privileges the history of the few people powerful enough to have left traces in official archives, but also overlooks the very different "truth" of fiction—for example, the insight that fiction might provide into the less public realms of experience.

Second, posing the question in terms of the relationship between "reality" and the text automatically posits the latter as a closed, ultimately unified entity, which can refer only to "events" that took place beyond the text and outside of it. Yet when history, or what we can know of the past, is also treated as a text, distinctions between "reality" and the text, or between the inside or outside of any particular text, including history, break down irreparably. I believe, with Mikhail Bakhtin, that what narratives really represent is not

---

[5] I direct the reader's attention back to the discussion of Dorothy Skårdal's *Divided Heart* in Chapter 2. See also Dominick LaCapra's treatment of the difficulties involved when historians read novels in his *History and Criticism* (Ithaca, N.Y.: Cornell University Press, 1985), 125–34.

"reality" per se but discourses in which various realities, or various versions of "reality," are constituted by the way individual speakers, mostly narrators and the characters they create, react to their fellow fictional human beings in a specific historical time and place. In this sense Bakhtin can provide a workable answer to the question at the beginning of this paragraph when he defines the novel, and by implication other texts as well, as the "dialogized representation of an ideologically freighted discourse."[6] In short, this chapter shows that the texts analyzed below represent the material and discursive reality faced by German immigrants in the United States without necessarily being a reflection of any particular verifiable set of facts or events.

As a mass phenomenon, German immigration to the United States began in earnest in the mid-1840s and continued almost until the end of the century, but observers writing in the mid-1860s could easily believe that it was already a passing phenomenon. The absolute annual peak of 215,000 German immigrants was achieved in 1854, only to decline to one-third of that number in the following year. By 1862 the annual number of German immigrants had fallen below 30,000, and the floodtide of 1854 did not return again until the early 1880s, long after the abrupt but temporary decline of the 1860s had passed. In these confusing times for Germans in the United States, in May and June 1868 to be exact, *Die Abendschule* published a three-part article titled "The Population of the United States and the German Element of the Same," written by a professor with the appropriately reassuring name of H. Baumstark ("strong as a tree"). After comforting readers with his claim that the situation of the Germans in the United States was still far from decided, and certainly not for the worst ("The process of assimilation [*Verschmelzung*] is not yet complete, and so long as immigration from our old homeland continues it will not be complete," XIV, 129),[7] Baumstark admits that there is nevertheless cause for worry:

Unfortunately, so many of our compatriots are so lacking in character that, in order to make rapid progress in the process of shedding their skins, they soon become neither Germans, nor Americans, but rather a race of pathetic hermaphrodites (*ein elendes Zwittergeschlecht*), semi-

[6]M. M. Bakhtin, "Discourse in the Novel," in *The Dialogic Imagination*, 333.
[7]Subsequent references to Baumstark's text will omit the volume number.

Americanized German-Americans by their nature, habits, and indeterminate language—disgusting and despicable to both Germans and Americans. (p. 137)

Although the sense of loss continues to reverberate in every ethnic group's reaction to the "promise" of assimilation into an American society that was and remains pluralist largely only in theory, nowadays we would worry more about the racist tone of Baumstark's metaphors than about any danger to "German" culture. It is, however, worth noting that there is often more than a quiet hint of racism in much of the discourse about the fate of Germandom in the United States. Here, for example, not only are Germans who forsake their heritage members of a "race of hermaphrodites," but in the same article the stream of German immigrants has also become "muddy and impure, . . . dirtied by [among other things] base passions and vices (*trüb und unrein . . . beschmutzt durch [u.a.] niedrige Leidenschaften und Laster]*" (XIV, 130). Unlike the Germans in Europe, who are apparently free from drinking, gambling, and whatever sexual temptations one might term "base passions and vices," Germans in the United States run the risk of producing "mixed races" (*Mischvölker*) like the French and Spanish, whose few positive qualities are the result, respectively, of their Frankish and Gothic—that is, Germanic—blood. Compared with the Germans in their midst, the Americans (and here Baumstark is referring only to the descendants of British settlers) can best be described as "depraved, enervated, and degenerate (*verkommen, entnervt, und entartet*). Luckily, however, "whoever views the history of the world in all its complexity as a work of divine providence has to recognize that the German people, as a result of its particular talents, have been selected by God to be the bearer and mediator of Christian culture among the peoples of Europe" (p. 138). The solution would therefore seem to be easy, and God has apparently been busy preparing the way for the German colonization of the United States. Not only has the decline in moral standards (*Sittenverfall*) among the Yankees resulted in a drastic reduction in their birth rates,[8] but, as Baumstark is quick to note, German immigration is also on the rise again. Then too, German culture is making particularly welcome

[8]The moral decline of the American people, in both the public and the private sphere, was a recurrent topic of concern in *Die Abendschule*; see, e.g., "Der moralische Zustand des Volkes der Vereinigten Staaten" (The Moral Condition of the People of the United States), a six-part series that ran in volume eighteen, pp. 121ff.

progress in the Midwest, where its only real competition comes from the Irish—and then just in terms of numbers because the Germans are far more advanced in terms of "intellectual strength and training" (p. 146). Yet, as convincing as his arguments might have been to proponents of German culture, who were never a reticent lot, Baumstark's conclusion is surprisingly sober: For all their supposed superiority, the Germans in the United States will only be able to delay (*hinausschieben*, p. 147) the process of assimilation, which means that there must be a huge faultline running through the middle of all Baumstark's racist claptrap.

During the nineteenth century, one of the unresolvable contradictions in any appeal to pan-Germanic values was religious in nature. The dilemma raised by a "people" divided along religious lines since the sixteenth century is to be found especially, but not exclusively, in arguments based on German racial or cultural superiority, and the difficulty of being or becoming "German" while at the same time remaining "Lutheran" echoed through all the narratives published in *Die Abendschule* in this early period of German-American identity formation. Baumstark's attempt to demarcate the border between Germans and Americans is a good example of how convoluted such arguments could become. He is, of course, forced to admit that there are "among the Americans honest, conscientious people and true Christians." In other words, some Americans are almost virtuous enough to be considered German, "while [at the same] time many Germans lead the life of scandalous, unholy knaves, . . . bringing shame to the German name in this country and becoming Americanized precisely by quickly adopting American vices" (p. 138).[9] At this point the opposition "German" / "American," which translates into virtuous-Christian / degenerate-heathen, has been almost completely divorced from semantic markers based on national origin. This tension between a (pseudo-)biologically grounded category of national origin and a religiously defined category of national culture ultimately makes it impossible for Baumstark to advocate anything like a unitary German-American identity. Consider the following injunction:

[9] In view of *Die Abendschule*'s act of negative self-definition discussed in Chapter 3, it is worth noting whom Baumstark includes among the "non-Germans" and how he justifies their exclusion from the real Germans, namely, with the aid of pseudo-biology: "In particular, it is the German revolutionary heroes of the year 1848, who are not the 'flowering of human intellectual development,' as Dr. Schenkel in Heidelberg would say, but rather a real plague upon the country" (XIV, 138).

> Particularly we German Protestants have to be seriously concerned
> about the preservation of the German language (and therefore with the
> German character, because the two are inseparable). For it is in our
> robust, gritty, emotional German mother tongue that the rich treasure
> of our sacred literature and spiritual poetry have been deposited. The
> richness, fullness, force, and purity of divine truth that are expressed
> there have not been matched by the corresponding literature of any
> other people, nor can their majesty and power be recreated in any
> other language, not even in English. (p. 138)

Baumstark is not just addressing *Die Abendschule*'s readers directly
("we German Protestants"); he is also making the implicit claim that
German Protestants alone are the true heirs of everything that is
"essentially" German—that is, both that they are connected with
the essence or transcendent center of German culture and that they
represent everything that is really "German," rather than just factu-
ally so—on the basis of some accident of birth or residence. Holding
the German center therefore becomes as much a religious imperative
as a national or cultural imperative, because it is only with the anchor of the German language—"and therefore with the German
character, because the two are inseparable"—that this particular
brand of Protestantism can continue to flourish. In a sense, whenever Baumstark says "German" he means "Protestant," just as his
use of "Protestant" always implies "German," but with the unfortunate difficulty that each term always undercuts the other. Not all
"Germans" are "Protestants," nor are all "Protestants" "Germans."
Try as he might, Baumstark is ultimately not very reassuring, not
only because he sees delay as the sole answer to the danger of assimilation, but also because he is unable to offer his readers a coherent
subject position. In effect, he leaves them suspended between the
contradictory alternatives of two separate identities, without the
means or even the reflective space for a resolution and
certainly without a sense of what it might mean to become German-
American.

There were other variables in this unsolved equation, not the least
of which was *Die Abendschule*'s own continued struggle for an identity and, as both a precondition and a result, commercial viability.
Volume eighteen, which began in September 1871 (after the successful conclusion of the Franco-Prussian War and German unification)
opens as usual with a long foreword, which once again attempts to
explain the magazine's own peculiar sense of mission, namely, "to

preserve the Christian, German character (*Art*) in America." (1) Aside from the continued tension between "Christian," "German," and "in America," the immediate difficulty is twofold; both within the United States and from Europe, other journals are impinging on *Die Abendschule*'s market. First, in the United States, where by 1871 there are already dozens of German-language competitors offering their own mix of "*Belehrung und Unterhaltung*," utility is apparently a problem: "If we were to provide regular market reports, we would make a lot of anti-Christian weekly newspapers unnecessary" (XVIII, 1). The editor is aware that *Die Abendschule* would have to become a weekly to displace them, and he promises to spare no effort toward that end.[10] Second, German family journals, principally *Die Gartenlaube* and *Daheim*, seem to have been making inroads into *Die Abendschule*'s readership. Barth reports, for example, that *Die Gartenlaube* sold some 10,000 copies in North America in 1873.[11] Interestingly enough, the response from St. Louis mixes piety with an overt appeal to the readers' identity as German-Americans:

> While the one (*Gartenlaube*) has quite openly taken up arms against the Christian faith, *Daheim* is also not completely free of objectionable articles. Such warnings, however, will be successful only when you help to allow your own German-American and in every aspect unobjectionable *Daheim* to develop here in North America. Don't we have our own government on this side of the ocean? Our own churches and schools? Our own schoolbooks, yes, even our own religious and business publications? Why then should we continue to suffer under the guardianship of Berlin or Leipzig or some other European locality with regard to entertainment and instruction? (XVIII, 2)

Apparently the problem was so acute that the attack on *Daheim* extended even into the pages of the major narrative published in this particular volume, a twenty-two-part novel entitled *Die Wittwe und ihre Kinder: Erzählung aus dem deutsch-amerikanischen Volksleben* (The Widow and Her Children : A Story of German-American Popular Culture).[12] Without giving away too much of the plot before the

---

[10]Reports from the major commodity markets began to appear in volume nineteen in 1872, but *Die Abendschule* did not become a weekly until 1874, with the start of volume twenty.

[11]Barth, *Zeitschrift für alle*, 285.

[12]When it was published, the text was as good as anonymous because the author is

detailed analysis presented below, it can be revealed that one of the widow's children, her son Gottlieb, has been sent to the neighboring town's *Gymnasium* so he can prepare to enter a seminary. When one of the other boys there suggests that the pupils pool their money and subscribe to *Daheim*, everyone but Gottlieb agrees. Even the principal approves, but Gottlieb, the character with whom male readers can identify, nevertheless writes his hometown pastor for advice and receives the following reply:

> To be sure, there is nothing in *Daheim* that grossly offends against morality or that is written with the intention of heaping scorn upon our Savior or his Gospels, but the magazine is by no means therefore to be recommended, least of all for young pupils. (XVIII, 154)[13]

The pastor continues by remarking that if Gottlieb is really serious about his studies he will not have time to fill his head with useless information and that *Daheim* "contains absolutely nothing that he would need to know at some point in his life." Yet the difficulty with *Daheim* is not just its purported uselessness; in fact, this Christian alternative to *Die Gartenlaube* was positively dangerous, at least if it found its way into the wrong hands:

> *Daheim* (and like it, all similar journals) contains nothing at all that must be planted in one's memory; rather, its contents serve primarily to deform the imagination or fantasy of the soul, to corrupt it forever. If the stories in *Daheim* are not openly immoral, they are nevertheless not permeated by a Christian spirit, and that is an enormous failing. Reading these stories and novels allows numerous absurd ideas and concepts to flow into youthful souls, carnal desires are awakened, improper desires called forth . . . .

To be sure Gottlieb's pastor does not go so far in his letter as to condemn fiction altogether, but he does want to limit its readership: "Older, more experienced people can read stories of this sort with-

---

identified only as J.C.W. Not until an extended obituary appeared in XXV, 376–78, following the final episode of another of his novels, did readers of *Die Abendschule* learn that J.C.W. was none other than "Direktor" Lindemann (1827–79), editor of the Synod's *Evangelisch-Lutherisches Schulblatt* and director of its teachers' college in Addison, Illinois. See A. C. Stellhorn, "J. C. W. Lindemann: First Director of the Evangelical Lutheran Teachers' Seminary in Addison, Illinois," *Concordia Historical Institute Quarterly* 14 (October 1941): 65–92.

[13]Subsequent references to *Die Wittwe und ihre Kinder* will omit the volume number.

out harming themselves in the process, but for young souls they are nothing short of poison" (pp. 154–55).

The happy conclusion is that the other boys decide not to subscribe to *Daheim* after all, and they come to respect Gottlieb for the role he played in their decision. However, especially given the novel's location in *Die Abendschule*, the question of what German schoolboys in the United States should have read remains painfully unanswered. Can they be entrusted with magazines like *Die Abendschule*, if the texts they find there include novels? Granted, on the strength of the previously quoted passages *Die Wittwe und ihre Kinder* does reflect, however inadvertently, on its own reason for being, as well as on the dangers associated with fiction in general, but the text's very existence as a novel seems to undercut whatever legitimacy its contents might otherwise possess. And if novels per se are unsuitable reading material for young people, what can possibly be left of *Die Abendschule*'s claim to be *ein deutsches Familienblatt*, as the magazine's subtitle still proudly proclaimed? Could the father really read *Die Wittwe und ihre Kinder* to his wife and children, or was it, too, better left to "older, more experienced people"? And what of the editor's intention of producing his "own German-American and in every aspect unobjectionable *Daheim*," right down to the stolen masthead illustration that graced each issue containing this particular novel? Given the fictional pastor's condemnation of "*Daheim* (and like it, all similar journals)," one is left wondering whether or even how he could still have found some tortured rationale for recommending *Die Abendschule* to his younger charges.

On the other hand, if *Daheim*'s real sin was the fact that it represented the principal German competition for the self-assuredly German-American periodical *Die Abendschule*, why is the latter nevertheless filled with texts that are imported from Germany? Of course, one reason was the need for suitable texts; there were apparently just too few German-American authors to fill the journal. Moreover, part of *Die Abendschule*'s mission had always been both to transmit and to mediate the culture of their homeland to the German-speaking immigrants in the United States. In his foreword to the 1867–68 volume, for example, the editor wrote: "Finally, we would like to note that the publisher has returned from his trip to Germany with some very worthwhile writings, from which we will communicate the most interesting elements" (XIV, 2). As noted before, *Die Abendschule* often contained texts that were presumably pirated from German publications, and they must have resonated loudly enough among the readers to keep the whole undertaking afloat. The point is not that the editors were hypocritical or incompetent but that they were trapped by the difficulty, if not impossibility, of providing a single coherent identity for either the magazine or its readers. All of them—readers and editors alike—had to keep a number of mutually exclusive identities in the air simultaneously, and they were constantly trying to juggle the whole lot without either dropping or catching—fixing—any single definition. Just how intractable the magazine's plight was can be seen by examining two texts that ran concurrently through much of volume eighteen: first, *Die Wittwe und ihre Kinder*, and second, "Die Geschichte des deutschen Volks, nach den Quellen für die 'Abendschule' erzählt" (The History of the German People, Narrated for *Die Abendschule* according to the [Original] Sources).

Besides Gottlieb Brand, the boy of fourteen introduced above, the novel concerns the widow's brother-in-law, Franz Heller, her daughter Elizabeth, age nineteen, and Heller's son Heinrich, who seems to be roughly Elizabeth's age. The two families live across the yard from one another but in substantially different circumstances. Franz Heller, his wife, and his son enjoy the comforts of a large farmhouse, while the widow and her children occupy an old log hut, where the Heller family had started out. The yard also separates two vastly different world-views and in a sense two versions of what might become of German immigrants in the United States. Franz Heller's wealth is the product not so much of his successful farming as of his practice of moneylending—with "Interessen," as the author's mixture of German and English would have it (XVIII, 34)[14] The first loan we read of is one that Heller makes to a poor shoemaker whose wife is ill and who expects an act of Christian charity from his fellow member of the local church. What the man actually

---

[14]As an earlier quotation from Baumstark indicates, "language maintenance" (Sprachpflege) was not just a cultural task; for German Lutherans it was also a moral duty, which is why the numerous Americanisms in these early texts are somewhat surprising. Although it is not the purpose of this study to document such "mistakes," the publisher's position, recorded in his foreword to volume nineteen (1873–74), is nevertheless worth quoting: "We will accord very special care to the German language, our dear mother tongue. We regard this as one of the most important tasks of German-American writing, for reasons that are not obvious to everyone but that are of enormous meaning and consequence for our most holy (evangelical-Lutheran) Christianity, as well as for the secular and historical mission (*Beruf*) of German adopted citizens. Our task is made all the more urgent because German-American newspaper prose is not only morally and religiously corrupt but also, in particular, often linguistically corrupt" (Louis Lange, "Vorwort," XIX, 1).

gets is a promissory note, which he has to sign before receiving Heller's "help." Later Heller goes as far as to sue another parishioner
for nonpayment, even though he has promised to donate a similar
amount of money to the church. At this point the narrator apparently felt compelled to intervene lest his readers miss the point, and
he therefore characterizes Heller and the bailiff who is supposed to
collect the money—ironically and disapprovingly—as follows:
"Their calling is 'business,' and they can perform such tasks devoid
of heart and conscience and nevertheless be good Christians!" (p.
99). The theological difficulty is that Heller's stance would seem to
be anchored in Luther's claim that every profession, and not just
that of the priest, can be justified in the eyes of the Lord, but the
local pastor takes up the narrator's position and warns, "Heller, the
miserly devil has got you completely and utterly in his power!" (p.
131). In fact, the pastor calls Heller a heathen and threatens to ban-
ish him from the congregation if he does not mend his ways. To mix
a few metaphors, by paying so much attention to the literal meaning
of his name, which implies the phrase *Heller und Pfennig* (nickels
and dimes), Gottlieb's evil uncle proves himself penny-wise and
pound-foolish.

By way of contrast, while the widow is not exactly unmindful of
her poverty, she firmly believes that her needs and, more important,
her children's needs will somehow be met. The question becomes
acute when the pastor and the teacher decide Gottlieb has what it
takes to study theology. Heller, who believes the boy has an obliga-
tion to repay his uncle's "kindness" by aspiring to nothing more
than the life of an unpaid farm laborer, is unwilling to help, as are a
number of the wealthier members of the congregation. For example,
a woman who brought a large dowry into her marriage with a much
weaker man comments: "Twenty dollars more or less is really not
the issue! But I cannot abide this arrogance, that some beggar's son
wants to become a minister, who will ultimately appear in our pulpit
and say, 'It is easier for a camel . . .'" (p. 53). In the end, however,
the other, poorer members of the congregation manage to scrape
together enough money to finance Gottlieb's education. They con-
tribute a pig or whatever else they can afford to the greater glory of
the Christian community, which is always in need of more pastors.
Gottlieb is therefore free to attend the *Gymnasium* in a neighboring
city, and he acquits himself well, in spite of a few intervening episodes whose major purpose is to retard the happy ending we all
expect.

Of course, these complications also provide the author with an opportunity to discuss a number of questions that must have troubled Lindemann and his readers, and because Gottlieb's problems are integrated into the narrative, their solutions carry the additional weight of the character's presence. Instead of the author lecturing his or her readers, one of the figures in whom those readers have invested a certain amount of emotional energy is allowed to succeed or fail and thereby make the author's point. For example, in addition to the question of a subscription to *Daheim*, which made him something of a moral authority, Gottlieb persuades his fellow students not to present a "classical drama" as part of their graduation exercises, because he considers the plays in question—Körner's *Night Watchman* and Immermann's *The Foolish Countess*—to be immoral: "We have a rich selection of quality texts, so why should we debase ourselves by memorizing and presenting the works of carnally oriented people, in whose works vice [here, adultery] is glorified and real virtues are made to appear ridiculous!" (p. 163). In short, *Die Wittwe und ihre Kinder* shows a fairly narrowly circumscribed version of virtue triumphing over a wide variety of sins.

There is more to this particular novel than the eternal struggle of good and evil. One additional layer of meaning concerns the personal identities of individual characters and, by way of implication, the novel's readers. Franz Heller is not only guilty of the sin of avarice, but he has also succumbed to the temptations of the developing capitalist economy, which this novel consistently associates with "America." Heller is, after all, successful in terms that are well understood in his new homeland, and his success comes at the expense of what *Die Abendschule* elsewhere represents as fundamentally German traits. For example, "Die Geschichte des deutschen Volks," which ran concurrently with *Die Wittwe und ihre Kinder*, maintains rather straightforwardly: "Making money into a business or lending it with interest is unknown among the Germans" (XVIII, 6). In a European setting this might have been the place for an anti-Semitic comparison between Germans and Jews, but here it is the "ex"-German Heller who has moved from a log cabin to his comfortable farmhouse as the result of usury. The lesson is underscored in Gottlieb's portion of the plot, when the boy lends money to some of his schoolmates although, unbeknownst to him, the practice is forbidden. Rather than risking expulsion should their own actions in soliciting the loans become known, the illicit borrowers manage to convince the headmaster that Gottlieb has stolen another pupil's watchchain. The upshot is that Gottlieb is forced to leave the *Gym-*

nasium in disgrace, only to return in triumph in the next episode once the real thieves have been exposed. In the process Gottlieb learns of the dangers of moneylending and thereby affirms his essentially "German" nature.

Yet, while he does embody the other half of the opposition defined by Heller's acceptance of money/capitalism/America, the version of Germanness Gottlieb represents certainly does not include the whole population of German immigrants in the United States. In fact, the religious diversity of the German immigrant population of the United States actually seems to have intensified one of the chief difficulties faced by German Protestants in their new homeland. It was the old question of who they were, this time clothed in the details of who was to be excluded from their number. When the author of *Die Wittwe und ihre Kinder* describes a ball in a short story titled "The Fourth of July: A Story of German-American Popular Culture," which also appeared in *Die Abendschule* during 1871, he writes: "The people in the dance hall were standing around, crowded closely together, watching the wild movements. There one could see Catholics and Jews, [Prussian] Unionists and Lutherans, churchgoers and mockers; they all *seemed* to be brothers!" (XVIII, 5; emphasis added).[15] The ramifications of these subgroups' fundamental differences, which existed just barely beneath the surface of their supposed ethnic unity, are worked out more fully in Lindemann's longer narrative by Gottlieb's sister Elizabeth, who is basically the female half of the "German-Lutheran" subject position that this text offers to its readers.

Elizabeth's role in the plot is propelled by Franz Heller's fear that she harbors secret designs on his son Heinrich—that is, that she hopes to marry into the wealthy side of the family. To avert the catastrophe he foresees for his property, the elder Heller attempts to arrange marriages for them both. Admittedly, the plan is somewhat

---

[15]"Der vierte Juli" also contains another indication that Heller's reprehensible behavior was not just the result of his own sinful nature but of his unfortunate Americanization, in this case his refusal to obey the pastor's injunction not to sue a fellow parishioner for nonpayment of her debts. When someone in "Der vierte Juli" tries to convince a young man not to attend the dance, the older of the two is unjustly admonished: "Be reasonable [already the wrong ploy], then you would quickly see that young people need a bit of freedom. We live in America now, and no official and no pastor has anything to say here" (p. 6). Disobedience vis-à-vis one's pastor is therefore marked as an "American" trait. Of course, the fact that the dance and the drinking associated with it takes place on a quintessentially American holiday also links this behavior to "American" values.

premodern and could therefore be considered contrary to Heller's Americanism, but his potential aberration is nevertheless in the service of a thoroughly modern and "American" end. The match would not increase the size of the family farm, a traditional value, but the balance in its bank account. But Heinrich refuses what his father considers a good match—"A cow, a bed, a wardrobe, a table, chairs, and four thousand!" (p. 83)—for the legitimately bourgeois reason that he does not love the woman in question. Elizabeth's case is more interesting. She is willing to accept her uncle's choice if it also reflects God's will, which she ascertains by asking of her prospective husband, "Is he a Lutheran Christian?" After a bit of initial confusion about his pastor's name and about the precise nature of the church in his home village, the man, whose name, Michael Streit (quarrel), certainly is no accident, replies: "A [church] like you have here? No! Luckily, it is not like that! We let everyone believe what he wants to! Now I remember. Our congregation is called Evangelical-Reformed-Lutheran!" (p. 92). This answer—namely, that the man does not belong to a Missouri Synod church, but rather to the slightly more liberal competition, is proof enough for Elizabeth. She realizes that there is scarcely anything worse than the wrong kind of Lutheran and adamantly refuses to have anything to do with the fellow, undoubtedly because she is convinced that it could not be God's will for her to marry a member of a different branch of Lutheranism in the United States.[16]

At this point the question of identity is apparently resolved in favor of an exceedingly narrow band in the already limited spectrum

[16]Franz Heller's measure of the man is worth noting here: "You don't know him? You don't know him? Haven't I said that his name is Michael Streit and that he has acres of land? Isn't it enough when you know that he has money?" (p. 92). Twenty-five years later the novel resurfaced in an interesting manner in volume 3 of *Blätter und Blüten, Die Abendschule*'s annual premium for readers who renewed their subscriptions on time and were willing to pay a small additional price. (In 1898: "Price in Bookstores, $1.50. For prepaid readers of *Die Abendschule* 50 Cents including postage." The title of the supplement, incidentally, was stolen from a similar undertaking launched by *Die Gartenlaube*.) The revised version of the text seems to refer to some change in the history of Lutheranism in the United States, for in 1897 Streit is rejected not for his membership in the "Evangelical-Reformed-Lutheran" church but apparently to avoid offending some of the magazine's subsequent readers in a congregation that is "Free-Protestant" (p. 134). Despite the subsequent softening, as E. Clifford Nelson, ed., *The Lutherans in North America* (Philadelphia: Fortress Press, 1980), notes in its description of such conflicts: "Even more than others, the Missouri Synod had boundless confidence that it represented the only real Lutheranism in America" (p. 377).

of German Protestantism in the United States. In essence we have the Missouri Synod personified, with its own peculiar mixture of absolute self-confidence, even self-righteousness, coupled with a curiously defensive rejection of anyone else's attempt to claim some of the same moral and theological ground. At this point the plot can finally proceed to what readers must have expected would be a happy ending. In the penultimate episode the elder Heller dies unrepentant, still clutching his ledger and the keys to his strongbox, and his long-suffering wife invites the widow Brand to move into the farmhouse and to bring her daughter along. Elizabeth refuses, because she thinks it would look like she really is trying to ensnare Heinrich, but the two of them nevertheless really do seem destined for one another. Still, instead of moving in with her aunt, cousin, and mother, Elizabeth takes a job as a maid and moves to the town where Gottlieb is once again successfully attending school.

Now, after slogging through all of the previous twenty-three installments, readers must have been waiting expectantly for the twenty-fourth, confident that in the ensuing two weeks until its publication everything would finally work out for the widow's two children. They already know that Gottlieb is about to graduate from the *Gymnasium* and will finally be able to begin studying theology in earnest at what must have been the right kind of "German" Protestant seminary, and Heinrich is also free to act according to the dictates of his heart and propose to his cousin. In fact, he is under way from the family farm to the—perhaps evil—city to do just that when we learn that Gottlieb has contracted smallpox. Fortunately, Elizabeth is nearby, and she can comfort her brother as death approaches. Gottlieb's end is therefore happy, although principally not because of Elizabeth's presence but because God, for some unfathomable reason, seems to have willed his passing from the scene. For her part, Elizabeth finds solace in the hymns she sings at Gottlieb's deathbed, but the Lord, inscrutable as "He" is, has decided to end her life also, for she too has contracted smallpox. As the narrative closes, literally and in narratological terms as well, Heinrich arrives—just in time to learn of Elizabeth's funeral—and the puzzled reader can only conclude that the ways of the Lord are indeed mysterious.

Of course, habitual readers of *Die Abendschule* may not have found *Die Wittwe und ihre Kinder* as puzzling as the modern reader might. Indeed, if we turn briefly to a narrative entitled *Bonifacius: Sittengemälde aus einer deutschen Ansiedlung in Nord-Amerika*

(Bonifacius: A Portrayal of the Customs of a German Settlement in North America), which ran for twelve issues in volume sixteen, during 1869–70, it becomes clear that unhappy endings were certainly not unknown in *Die Abendschule*. In addition, the Bonifacius story reinforces—or perhaps prepared the way for—a number of the themes later raised in *Die Wittwe und ihre Kinder*. It too concerns a group of Germans faced with the choice between the norms and values of their homeland and those of their adopted country. Set in 1844 in a village on the prairie of Illinois, the plot revolves around a band of settlers who seem to have completely given up their old "German" ways. They drink, dance, curse, and play cards—in short, carry on "like the heathens." But they nevertheless prosper as farmers. Interestingly enough the text represents their actions as a tangible result of the villagers' acceptance of "American" values. When one of the farmers eventually raises the question of forming a proper, "Lutheran" congregation so they can call a pastor, his chief opponent uses the opposition "Germany"/"America" to argue against the idea, at first, with considerable effect:

> Do you want—he said to the first—to be robbed of your freedom, so that you can no longer eat, drink, sleep, and dance without first asking your spiritual leader for permission? Up until now you were free. Do you want to become a slave and not drink any more liquor as a favor to the pastor, not dance anymore or play [cards]? . . . Well, pretty soon you'll be able to tip your hat to the pastor and piously wish him "Good morning," just like you enjoyed doing in Germany! (XVI, 99)[17]

Note that the semantic marker most clearly associated with the United States is freedom—here freedom from what the text had previously characterized as the "yoke of German princes and priests" (p. 43), which is also seen to include economic freedom and the rewards it brings: "People in America are not so stupid that they believe in God! Work, work—that's how you get happiness and money!" (p. 51). For one set of characters, therefore, the terms "American" and "America" stand for social and economic freedom, while "German" and "Germany" represent visions of religious intolerance and a paucity of economic opportunity.

Another group seems to yearn for something they had left behind, but until the accidental arrival of a forlorn unemployed schoolmas-

---

[17]Subsequent references to *Bonifacius* will omit the volume number.

ter named Gottlieb Kreuzer their desires remain indistinct and unarticulated. The settlers are only dimly aware that something is missing, but especially for the males in the group the pressures of starting a new life have relegated religion to the background. In fact, it is Kreuzer's presence and the pious example he sets for the villagers who found him exhausted and hungry alongside a trail in the wilderness, that allows the opposing group to develop and then contest Kreuzer's vision of life for the community. Like his metaphorical referent Bonifacius from the narrative's title, Kreuzer is destined to become an "apostle to the Germans," converting the newly heathen descendants of the original Germanic tribes.

The crisis comes when "German" Lutheranism confronts its American counterpart. Having already received copies of Walther's new periodical Der Lutheraner, which arrived free of charge when they ordered some schoolbooks,[18] the villagers decide to write to St. Louis for help in securing "an upright Lutheran pastor" (p. 90). Until then they have been served by a traveling minister, who appears periodically to marry people, baptize their children, and provide his congregation with "the most varied bits of news—good and evil, comic and serious, moral and frivolous, all in large number" (p. 84). In other words, the man is portrayed as being scarcely religious and everything other than a good example for his parishioners; he can certainly outdrink most of them. When he learns of Kreuzer's presence, the Reverend Möbler accuses the new schoolteacher of undermining his pastoral authority: "He tempts my flock, turns them into fanatical pietists and dejected hypocrites. Is that not shameful, particularly in this country?" (p. 85). Again the opposition is couched in terms of freedom, whereby the choice between "freedom" and "slavery" is also a choice between a life that is "American" and one that is "German." Thus the "American" pastor's sermon is directed against false prophets who would deny the "bright sunshine of the Enlightenment" and the "light of reason," which he links to the founding principles of the American republic. Indeed, his version of Christianity is almost a caricature of the Enlightenment rationalism that the Lutheran Church–Missouri Synod fought so hard to destroy: "Mankind carries the true sparks of divinity in its own breast! We need do nothing else for our salvation than follow our innate feelings, which will inspire us to action!" (p.

---

[18]Because the story was set in 1844, it was ten years too early for them to have received Die Abendschule, but Der Lutheraner had just begun publication.

85). Unfortunately, all his talk of freedom ends in a drunken revel, described in a paragraph that uses the words "reason" and "freedom" in heavily ironic quotation marks no fewer than six times.[19]

The lesson, as well as the correct choice, is obvious, and in the end the majority of the villagers form an alternative Lutheran congregation so they can call a pastor. After waiting for well over a year because of the Synod's "shortage of preachers," a young candidate from Germany—by way of St. Louis—is scheduled to arrive. Since a village's pastor is invariably also its schoolmaster, Kreuzer realizes that his work is done, but initially no mention is made of what his subsequent fate might be. Apparently he is destined to move on to another school, but in the final episode, while preparing his young charges to welcome the new pastor, the son of his worst enemy falls into a river, and Kreuzer drowns trying to save him. Again the reader is left to contemplate the mysterious ways of the Lord.

No matter what these authors may have had in mind in so severely disappointing their readers' expectations of a happy ending— if indeed contemporary readers expected one as much as I did—two positive lessons still remain. First, from the point of view of both stories, but especially of *Die Wittwe und ihre Kinder*, there are indeed certain invariable moral verities. And it is interesting to note that whether German Protestants could attend dances or the theater, whether they could charge interest on the money they lent, or whether they could play the stock market, buy fire and life insurance, and install lightning rods were hotly debated issues in the 1860s and 1870s, and indeed into the twentieth century.[20] The leaders of the Lutheran Church–Missouri Synod were clear and adamant in their rejection of what they regarded as sinful behavior, and their position in this discourse is clearly represented in narratives like *Die Wittwe und ihre Kinder*. Moreover, the fact that the novel in large part simply seems to illustrate such positions suggests that journals like *Die Abendschule* were committed to a mode of writing

---

[19]Another example might help underscore the nature of the opposition: After a particularly disastrous encounter with the "Americans," during which Kreuzer's protector is severely wounded, the schoolteacher shouts (the original is in italics): *"These are the fruits of culture and enlightenment without the fear of God"* (p. 52).

[20]See Meyer, *Moving Frontier*, 344–52. To cite but one example: In 1864, after a series of seven congregational meetings, Walther's home congregation in St. Louis endorsed a statement that included the following conclusion: "God Himself here [i.e., in Scripture] denies eternal salvation to him who practices usury" (p. 345). Franz Heller's fate is therefore obvious.

based in the early Enlightenment. However, since developing that line of argument, which will include a rereading of both *Die Wittwe und ihre Kinder* and *Bonifacius* from a slightly different perspective, but still without claiming to have explained everything in them, it will have to wait until the end of the chapter, when a larger variety of narratives can be considered.

Second, the two narratives both resolve the question of identity quite narrowly by rejecting all the major temptations that confronted German Protestants in the United States in the latter third of the nineteenth century. Readers who either already identified with the single subject position represented by the widow's two children and by Gottlieb Kreuzer, or who were searching for an identity while already occupying a starting position similar to the villagers in *Bonifacius*, were given the opportunity to see precisely what dangers lurked behind the alternatives of Americanization and undifferentiated German-Americanization. And because they were assured eternal salvation as long as they remained on that straight and narrow path, their success or failure in this world was more or less immaterial. What God then chose to do with the souls entrusted to him was perhaps unfathomable, but it was also of little concern to those whose identity alone guaranteed "His" eventual favor. As we shall soon see, however, this version of the answer is too easy because it is still incomplete.

While the ways of the Lord might have seemed mysterious to readers of *Die Abendschule* if judged by the fate of isolated individuals, when it came to nations, especially in view of the remarkable events of 1870–71, God's handiwork was apparently clear for all to see. Summing up those momentous years, the journal's editor wondered rhetorically who or what was responsible:

> To which circumstances do we have to attribute this miraculous change in [Germany's] fate? Perhaps to the perfection of its firearms? To the superiority of its armies? To the intelligence and the bravery of its soldiers? To the skilled battlefield tactics of its generals? To the wisdom of its statesmen? To the unity of its princes? To the weakness and delusion of its enemies? No, certainly not. On the contrary, the honor of this great work belongs to Him, who alone with his heavenly legions could perform such deeds, who gave the fire-spitting mouths [of the weapons their] power, the young warriors their gallantry and enthusiasm, the princes their vision, and who blinded the impudent, treacherous, godforsaken enemy. (XVIII, 57)

In fact, as a result of God's direct intervention, the new emperor, a "second Barbarossa," will be able to preside over the "rebuilding of the ancient and honorable German empire" (XVIII, 57). Moreover, reconstituting the Empire is not, in the editor's view, simply a political act. The tradition to which he alludes is the Holy Roman Empire, which had, as this version of history emphasized, united all the Germanic peoples of Europe under a single creed for a period of some seven hundred years, roughly from the year 800 to 1500. At that point the Reformation had returned Christianity to its original (in Die Abendschule's view) pure form, but only at the expense of dividing Germany along religious lines. In other words, the political unity of 1871 is only a first step:

> May these brilliant successes also contribute to invigorating the religious belief that lies dormant in our German brothers, so that not only the German people's earthly power and honor becomes a shining example for all other peoples, but also its belief in our God and Savior! (XVIII, 57)

Aside from the text's pointed and unmistakable arrogance, which is probably more offensive to modern readers than it was to its contemporaries, there is another enormous difficulty with this line of argument, one that is encapsulated quite succinctly in the phrase "our German brothers." For readers of Die Abendschule the "brotherhood" of Germans necessarily included not only all the residents of the new empire but also the entire "German" population of the United States. Any individual reader would therefore be likely to find "Catholics and Jews, [Prussian] Unionists and Lutherans, churchgoers and mockers" among his or her "brothers"—the very people about whom J.C.W. could write in the very same volume: "they all *seemed* to be brothers!" (XVIII, 5; emphasis added). Again, the point here is not to accuse the magazine's editors, authors, or readers of being inconsistent, but to note the problems they all must have faced either in simultaneously proffering a number of competing and even mutually exclusive identities in the texts they wrote or edited, or in encountering a series of virtually incompatible subject positions in the texts they read.

Again it is in volume eighteen, which covers the period from 15 September 1871 to 1 September 1872, the year in which "1871" reverberated most loudly, where the confrontation of conflicting subject positions is most readily visible. Besides Die Wittwe und ihre

Kinder, the volume's other major text was a seventeen-part series titled "The History of the German People." A more detailed analysis of this particular text follows below, but at this point it is already worth noting that what is being presented here is neither the history of the German nation as a political entity nor the history of the various Germanic tribes. At least to judge by the title, the emphasis in this particular history will be on a kind of Pan-Germanic unity rather than on diversity, whether religious or not.

Of course, given the fact of "1871," the choice of texts in this volume is hardly surprising, but it is worth noting that history had long occupied a central position in *Die Abendschule*. There was often as much history as fiction in the magazine; in fact, sometimes there was even more history. For example, the 1869–70 volume contained a twenty-four-part history of "Der bömische Krieg" (The Bohemian War), which emphasized, in a curiously prescient display of Prussian patriotism, the 300-year-long conflict between Prussia and Austria for hegemony in Germany.[21] Then toward the end of the volume, when the Franco-Prussian War broke out in July 1870, a brief announcement of the news displaced everything else—including the suddenly more distant, historical account of the war with Austria—from the lead position on the magazine's front page, and the editor promised his readers that extensive reports from the battlefield would henceforth be featured just as prominently.[22] By volume eighteen, which began appearing in September 1871, readers were apparently clamoring for an exhaustive account of the recent conflict, but in vain. The necessary source material, most notably the accounts traditionally issued by the German general staff, had not yet been issued.

However, readers would not have to feel too disappointed, because the magazine had procured "the diary, written exclusively for us, of a knight of the Iron Cross . . . whose sword had glittered [at the battles of] Weissenburg, Wörth, and Sedan and within view of the French capital" (XVIII, 1).[23] In fact, the entire difficulty was ap-

[21] "Der bömische Krieg," XVI, 2ff.

[22] "An die Leser," XVI, 161. In lieu of reports from the battlefield, which were presumably not yet available, this issue contained a text entitled "France and Germany" that began with this sentence: "There is a hereditary animosity between France and Germany" (XVI, 161). Of course, St. Louis was a long way from the war in Europe, and because *Die Abendschule* was still published only every other week, the amount of actual "reporting" it could provide was severely limited.

[23] The anonymous account was entitled "My Experiences in France," XVIII, 2ff.

parently soon overcome. A full account of the "Deutsch-Französischer Krieg" (The Franco-Prussian War) ("Prepared using German, French, and English Documents") began to appear in the final two issues of volume eighteen and was continued in twenty-three more installments in volume nineteen.[24] It is not unlikely that the decision to begin this particular history at the end of volume eighteen was not only intended to satisfy the presumed demand for an authoritative account of the war but also to induce readers to renew their subscriptions. And for new subscribers—those who had just begun to receive the journal with volume nineteen, the publisher promised to include the last two numbers of the previous volume free of charge, "as long as supplies last."[25] "1871" apparently sold magazines, and this series was clearly not the end of reader interest in the Franco-Prussian War. Reports of the conflict continued to be a staple of the German-American press—and for that matter the German press—for years to come.[26] A decade later, for example, *Die Abendschule* published a five-part series of personal memoirs, "Vor zehn Jahren: Erinnerungen aus dem Kriegsjahr 1870" (Ten Years Ago: Reminiscences of the War Year 1870), written by a German pastor who before emigrating to the United States had served an exile congregation in Paris.[27] And to cite one German example, Anne-Sussane Rischke reports that during the years 1870–71 *Die Gartenlaube* contained "more than 300 prose texts, numerous illustrations, and more than twenty relevant poems." The sheer mass of war stories, she concludes, "turned the family journal into a collection of war reports [*eine Art Kriegsfeuilleton*]."[28]

One could extend this list almost at will, but I shall argue that

---

[24]"Der deutsch-französische Krieg von 1870 und 1871," XVIII, 180–82, 185–86.

[25]"Sprechsaal" (Consulting Room, but really Letters to the Editor with replies), XIX, 8.

[26]In 1905, thirty-five years after "1871," *Die Abendschule* was still offering its readers "a richly illustrated, deluxe volume" entitled *Bismarck und seine Zeit* (Bismarck and His Times), written by H. Dümling, the man who had edited the magazine from 1881 to 1893. See *Blätter und Blüten* (St. Louis: Louis Lange Publishing Co., 1905), 11:391. In 1891, Georg Köppen, editor-in-chief of the Milwaukee paper *Germania*, published a thick volume (564 pages plus a foldout map!) under the title *Der Deutsch-französische Krieg, 1870 und 1871: Den Deutschamerikanern erzählt* (The Franco-Prussian War of 1870 and 1871, Narrated for German-Americans) (Milwaukee: Verlag von Geo. Brumder, 1890).

[27]G. Stöckhardt, "Vor zehn Jahren: Erinnerungen aus dem Kriegsjahr 1870," *Die Abendschule*, XXVII, 104ff.

[28]Rischke, *Lyrik in der "Gartenlaube,"* 78.

there was more to the discourse of history in *Die Abendschule* than its merely quantitative status. At the level of identity formation, as I shall demonstrate, historical narratives served essentially the same purpose as their fictional counterparts. Not only did the conventions of nineteenth-century historiography tend to produce narrative histories, which were basically structured like novels—complete with "identifiable" heroes and all the other narrative devices of realist fiction—but German history was an obvious source of information, or a readily available discourse, about what it meant to be "German." In addition, for readers of *Die Abendschule* the actual physical distance from events in Germany made contemporary history all the more relevant to any developing sense of "Germanness." It was, after all, in history as well as in "Culture" (both understood as discursive formations—that is, as readily available institutional locations for any number of cultural-political activities) where the issue of German unification had been kept alive in the years before its political realization. In this connection one should also note that during the nineteenth century history had achieved a central position in the German educational system. Along with religion, German, and the ancient languages, history was accorded a major role in fostering love of God and country.[29] In fact, both the rise of history as an academic discipline during the latter half of the nineteenth century, and the large number of popular histories and historical novels published in the same period, suggest that history occupied a central position in the institutionalized reproduction of "German" culture as it was reshaped in the image of an increasingly feudalized bourgeoisie. At the very least, history provided an excellent means for raising the issue of a "German" identity, or in the present context a "German-American" identity.

In this context the decision to publish the series "Die Geschichte des deutschen Volks" in the fall of 1871 is indeed scarcely surprising. In fact, the editor seems to have envisioned a clear, developmental line running through the German past to his own present—to "1871." In essence, history's teleological movement had reached its provisional high point in Wilhelm I and Bismarck (and in the Lutheran Church–Missouri Synod). Thus, after apologizing for not yet being able to offer an authoritative account of the Franco-Prussian War, the editorial foreword continues:

[29]See Margret Kraul, *Das deutsche Gymnasium, 1780–1980* (Frankfurt am Main: Suhrkamp, 1984), esp. 74–126.

> Since in the meantime the history of the German people has undeni-
> ably arrived at an important turning point, we hope we are not pro-
> ceeding against the wishes of our readers when we present them with
> the history of this our people from Ariovistus [a Germanic chieftain
> defeated by Caesar in 58 B.C.] to the [ascent of] the first emperor from
> the Hohenzollern dynasty. (XVIII, 1)[30]

The plan was to sketch the course of German history in twenty-four
installments, including such high points as "Barbarossa," "Saint Jan
—that is, Jan Hus," and "Old Fritz [Frederich II]," but the whole
undertaking soon went off course. It took an extra episode to get as
far as Hus, "the precursor of Martin Luther" (p. 86), and Luther
himself occupied three chapters, instead of the single chapter that
had been planned. The author's difficulty in charting Luther's life
briefly is understandable. As the text's narrative voice put it: "He
[Luther] is not only the most important man in German history, but
rather in all of history!" (p. 118), and Luther's importance for the
Lutheran Church—Missouri Synod is also undeniable. What is more
curious is that the series then ended with the next installment, which
was only the seventeenth and was dedicated to Charles V. One explanation might be that Luther's principal opponent was to be understood as a failed precursor to Wilhelm I. The text attempts to
show "how Emperor Charles used his immense secular power in
vain in order to obstruct the blessed work of the Reformation and to
reestablish the sinister rule of Roman anti-Christianity" (p. 132).
Especially in light of Bismarck's struggle with the Catholic church
(*Kulturkampf*), which had already begun in the summer of 1871,
Wilhelm's united Germany could be viewed as the successful Protestant counterpart to the earlier failure of Charles V.

Whatever changes crept into the text in the course of its being
written, it is clear from the outset that the question of German or
German-American identity was a principal focus of the narration.
Not only did the editorial introduction speak of "this *our* people,"
but the first installment, "*Our* heathen Ancestors," begins with a
question that asks the reader directly who he or she is: "From whom
are *you* descended, reader?" (p. 6; emphasis added). Even on the
surface the answer, "from the Germans," suggests that Germans
have a great deal in common—namely, a set of ancestors going back

---

[30]Subsequent references to "Die Geschichte des deutschen Volks" will omit the
volume number.

to Adam and Eve and, in the course of the Germanic peoples' subsequent development, the characteristics that all Germans have supposedly inherited. In fact, although "from the Germans" is only a very short answer, it implies orientation of the entire lengthy treatment of German history that is to follow.

There are at least two other levels at which this rhetorical interchange functions. First, the use of the familiar form of address, "du," rather than "Sie," is a concrete example—and for *Die Abendschule* a relatively rare one—of what Dieter Barth calls the "intimate form [*vertrauliche*] of address," which he claims was typical of the family journal as a genre.[31] The strategy, which included letters to the editors, the so-called *Briefkastenwesen*, as well as the policy of expressly encouraging readers to participate in the magazine's activities by submitting their own texts, was no doubt meant to bind readers to the journals they read.[32] Just as the magazine was to become a part of their families, so too were readers to become members of the larger family of editors, writers, and subscribers.

Second, the direct, familiar form of address is also an example of what Louis Althusser has termed "hailing" or "interpellation."[33] For Althusser the question "From whom are *you* descended, reader?" involves an implicit recognition on the part of the reader that he or she is being addressed. The answer "from the Germans" is therefore doubly voiced. It is both an authorial reply to the writer's own rhetorical question and it is a report in the form of indirect discourse or reported speech, of the reader's presumed response.[34] Moreover, according to Althusser, this brief exchange actually produces the reader as a subject. Of course, any reader is always already a subject, whose subjectivity is constantly being reproduced and reinforced. Indeed, as should be clear from the foregoing discussion, *Die Abendschule*'s readers generally seem to have occupied a number of

[31]See Barth, *Blätter für's Volk*, 193–202. Baumstark's history had also been addressed to "us German Protestants" (XIV, 138).

[32]The first issue of volume nineteen contained a small box labeled "Sprechsaal" on the final page, but it was the sole occurrence that year. Three of the ten responses dealt with texts produced by readers. "H.N. in A.," for example, was advised: "Send the continuation of the 'adventure' that has already been delivered. Personal experiences are always preferable" (XIX, 8).

[33]Louis Althusser, "Ideology and Ideological State Apparatuses (Notes Towards an Investigation)," in *Lenin and Philosophy*, trans. Ben Brewster (New York: Monthly Review Press, 1971), 127–86.

[34]"Double-voicing" is another idea associated with M. M. Bakhtin. See his "Discourse in the Novel," *The Dialogic Imagination*, 259–422, esp. 324ff.

overlapping and at times contradictory subject positions simultaneously, but it is nevertheless true that the opening lines of "Die
Geschichte des deutschen Volks" really do interpellate the magazine's readers into the "story" of German history. By hailing those
readers as "Germans," the text offers them an ideological anchor; it
"identifies" them as individuals who are no longer isolated but
rather part of a larger whole.

It is also important to point out that syntactically this act of identification is to be understood not just transitively—that is, not just
as the process of recognition or pointing, but also reflexively, in the
sense of identifying with. In fact, interpellation is a kind of dialec-
tically doubling process of identification. In Althussarian terms, the
newly designated individual subject is both centered around the
"Absolute Subject" and at the same time decentered as his or her
boundaries dissolve in the midst of that collective. In the present
case, the Absolute Subject is Germany or the German people, both
of which are imaginary collectives and which can therefore, according to Althusser, provide "the absolute guarantee that everything
really is so, and that on condition that the subjects recognize what
they are and behave accordingly, everything will be all right."[35] In
other words, *being* "German" is, in and of itself, an answer to the
author's rhetorical question, and that answer also contains an implicit set of norms and behaviors appropriate to the label.

Whether this analysis somehow suggests that the interpellated
subject is necessarily unitary and self-conscious, as some of Althusser's critics have suggested, seems to me immaterial.[36] Readers of
Die Abendschule certainly must have accepted the implications of
something like the interpellative form of address, and therefore their
own part in the larger story of German history, in order to have
continued reading. Yet not only were they simultaneously situated
differently by other texts, even by other texts within the same issue
of the magazine, but it was also immediately clear that even this
narrative history of the German people was itself everything but unitary. German history is filled with problems for "Germans" who are
both Protestants and residents of the United States. Thus the author
of "Die Geschichte des deutschen Volks" had to begin by explaining
away the readers' heathen forebears and their pre-Christian and

[35]Althusser, "Ideology and Ideological State Apparatuses," 181.
[36]See, e.g., Smith, *Discerning the Subject*, esp. 3–23; and Silverman, *The Subject of Semiotics*, 215–20.

therefore objectionable practices. At the same time, however, the narrator also attempts to establish a sense of continuity with the present: "The attentive reader will have drawn the conclusion that they [their heathen ancestors] possessed large and noble, natural talents. The same talents that explain their descendants' ability to have waged the wars of 1813 and 1871—namely, physical strength, bravery, and loyalty." And at this point, interestingly enough, the text also attributes to them a trait well suited to the demands of the German immigrants' new homeland: "an instinct for civil rights [*bürgerliche Freiheit*]" (p. 7).

The rest of this historical account, which moves from the medieval empire to the Reformation, need not concern us here. Its content is so predictable that there is nothing to be gained in summarizing it. The important point is that the discourse of history in *Die Abendschule* spoke to the same question of identity that was raised in texts like *Die Wittwe und ihre Kinder*. That is not to argue that it provided the same answers—far from it. In fact, volume eighteen is rent by the conflict between the "Lutheran" exclusivity of the fictional texts and the Pan-Germanic inclusivity of the history it contains. If there was a unifying aspect to the narratives, it was to be found in the norms and values that all these texts espoused. Not only was there a good deal of overlap in terms of specific recommendations, but, more important, the gesture of recommending specific behaviors for their readers is identical in both sets of texts. What that gesture implies about the larger undertaking and how it relates to the question of identity is the subject of the remainder of this chapter.

Although the problem of German-American identity is clearly inscribed in both the fictional and nonfictional narratives published in *Die Abendschule* in the years surrounding "1871," it should be clear from the discussion of the other themes mentioned above that an examination of the quest for a "national" or "religious" identity by no means exhausts the range of meaning that those texts contain. On the other hand, the moral lessons to be examined below should not be understood as somehow distinct from the question of identity, for no matter how the dilemma of "German" or "American" or "Lutheran" was (provisionally) resolved, that balancing act involved no more than a relatively small portion of the complex subject positions offered to the readers of these narratives. We turn our attention now to what would otherwise be the normative gaps left in all these potential identities once the question of "national" identity had been answered, however contradictorily and however tentatively. Indeed, if the competing versions of German-American identity outlined above suggest a kind of schizophrenia on the part of *Die Abendschule* and its readers, it is important to remember that there was nevertheless a good deal of consistency at the level of norms and values that served to unite these texts. Still, to the extent that the texts of this period were also engaged in representing a "Christian" worldview, they were staking out positions in a discourse that was everything but settled. In addition, the fact that such texts were still a principal site for moral instruction in the late nineteenth century would suggest that a number of theoretical issues that had apparently lain dormant since the early German Enlightenment were also far from decided.

As institutional religion lost its hold on society's conscience in the course of the eighteenth century, the inculcation of norms and values was gradually secularized and fictionalized.[37] Literature was the principal arena of combat, and the discourse of literature, which included both literary texts and the theories that grew up around them, provided a location where the bourgeois proponents of "reason" could develop and display their own alternative version of the social order. The result was a near classic ideological confrontation that pitted an outmoded hegemonic system against its temporarily counterhegemonic successor. Without delving into the question of how or why absolutism had come to the end of its days, it is important to note that the position of literature as a legitimizing discourse made it the obvious vehicle—in fact, the only conceivable vehicle—for any attempt at wresting control of the public sphere from the court and its supporters in the church. In practice, this meant that literature's "representational" function, which at the beginning of the eighteenth century still referred to the courtly function involved in the positive portrayal of established social and political hierarchies, had to be reappropriated. Representation henceforth came to refer to the "realistic" or even "natural" staging of norms and values that would foster a bourgeois order.

For the texts produced during the early German Enlightenment, the result of this struggle was twofold. First, the religious tradition

[37]For a more detailed account of these developments, see, e.g., Rolf Grimminger, ed., *Hansers Sozialgeschichte der deutschen Literatur, 3: Deutsche Aufklärung bis zur Französischen Revolution 1680–1789* (Munich: Hanser, 1980), esp. 251–326.

of edifying texts (*Erbauungsliteratur*) lived on generically, if in secular garb, in the *moralische Wochenschriften* (moral weeklies), whose high point was reached in the years 1720–60. Second, so-called high literature also increasingly concerned itself with the portrayal of bourgeois values—for example, love and the nuclear family as opposed to the arranged, political marriages typical of the absolutist order. Such writings were originally intended to educate princes, but authors soon shifted their attention away from the court in an effort to promote a genuinely bourgeois public sphere that could then function as a countervailing moral instance. Enlightenment optimism about the efficacy of literature as a means of initiating social change soon diminished, and with the advent of romanticism "high" literature's explicit and active social role soon atrophied to the point of virtual disappearance. This is not to say that the Romantics, especially the early German Romantics, viewed their poetic enterprise as apolitical, but that the political failure of the German Enlightenment made it impossible for them to believe the moral regeneration of society could be effected simply by means of rational discussion of and through literature. Yet, although by the beginning of the nineteenth century the tradition of social engagement had been discredited intellectually, it would be a mistake to assume that every writer abandoned the notion that literature could effect social or political change. "Young Germany" (*Junges Deutschland*), the "social" novelists of years before the Revolution of 1848, and their heirs in the revolutionary tradition of proletarian and then socialist realism certainly tried to keep that belief alive, and I would argue that the specifically pedagogic function of literature was also taken up by some forms of popular narrative.

There is a certain irony involved in the fact that, of all people, it was *Die Abendschule*'s writers and their conservative counterparts throughout the world who eventually shouldered the burden left behind by their arch-foes, the rationalists, and it is particularly ironic in view of the fact that the initial Enlightenment gesture involved an attempt to substitute literature and the bourgeois public sphere for the moral authority of the church. Enlightenment authors would also have been appalled to learn that one of their principal "weapons" had been abandoned and then recaptured by the enemy. Of course, in reality the lines of transmission were neither so clear nor so direct, but tracing the historical trajectory of that heritage would be a far larger task than can be attempted here. At a minimum one would have to consider both the politically progressive elements mentioned above, as well as what Friedrich Sengle has termed "spiritual Biedermeier."[38] The next step would probably be to writers like O. Glaubrecht, W. O. von Horn, and the other pastor-authors discussed by Müller-Salget, some of whom periodically appeared in both *Die Abendschule* and its close German relative, *Daheim*.[39] Meanwhile, popular literature itself had split into literature that was apparently mere, even base, entertainment, as opposed to the more refined and intellectual stimulation supposedly offered by "high" art, and literature that still maintained the Enlightenment's pedagogic optimism, albeit with vastly different objectives. *Die Abendschule* is obviously connected to the latter tradition, although in a manner too complex and as yet too little explored to detail here. Whatever the path of its transmission, this particular mode of writing persisted beyond the early German Enlightenment, and it is almost uncanny to read texts from *Die Abendschule* while remembering Johann Christoph Gottsched's (in)famous recipe for constructing a narrative:

> First of all, one selects a moral (*einen lehrreichen Satz*) that is appropriate to the objectives one intends to achieve; this moral should serve as a foundation for the entire poetic work. One then recollects an utterly commonplace story, in which some event takes place that obviously reminds one of this previously selected moral.[40]

If the comparison between the early phases of the German Enlightenment and a nineteenth-century German-American magazine sounds farfetched, an examination of several of the narratives published in *Die Abendschule* in this period should prove that the distance was not really so very great. I begin with a fairly detailed summary of a five-part story entitled "Die Lebensversicherung" (Life Insurance), which appeared in *Die Abendschule* in volume sixteen (1869–70), in an attempt to show how everything in the text was subordinated to an explicit moral lesson. Not coincidentally, the

[38]Friedrich Sengle, *Biedermeierzeit: Deutsche Literatur im Spannungsfeld zwischen Restauration und Revolution, 1815–1848* (Stuttgart: Metzler, 1971), 1:137–51. See also Hartmut Draeger, "Vom Kulturasketismus zum geistlichen Biedermeier: Protestantisch-konservative Literaturkritik im preussischen Vormärz," diss., Freie Universität, Berlin, 1981.
[39]For example, *Die Abendschule* published Glaubrecht's *Der Kalendermann von Veitsberg* in twenty episodes during 1865–66 (XII, 35ff).
[40]Johann Christoph Gottsched, "Versuch einer Critischen Dichtkunst," in his *Schriften zur Literatur* (1730), ed. Horst Steinmetz (Stuttgart: Reclam, 1972), 96.

narrative's point concerned a hotly contested issue within the Lutheran Church–Missouri Synod—the question of whether its members should purchase life insurance. The story's plot involves a German-American family of five whose life is so settled, so loving, and so perfect that the reader cannot help but expect disaster. Tension arises first because of the husband's ambition; Erwin Stein hopes that his single-minded devotion to the farm implement factory he and a partner have founded will provide his family with an increasingly comfortable life. His wife, Agnes, regards any success as a gift from God, and she is more concerned about her husband's soul than about the family's material well-being or lack of it. Thus when Erwin claims "Only someone who exerts himself will be made rich by God!" Agnes replies, with a slightly mixed metaphor: "Oh, my dear husband, pride makes you blind so that you do not see how Satan is forging chains in order to plunge you into greed" (XVI, 124).[41] The initial family idyll has clearly been threatened, and temptation soon rears its ugly head in the form of an insurance salesman who appears one morning at the beginning of the second episode.

The salesman begins by trying to explain the idea behind life insurance to Agnes, but she is unable to comprehend why she or her family would be any better off if she had an insurance policy. Her husband and children prefer her alive, and Agnes herself would have no use for the money in the event of her death. When the agent finally leaves in a state of utter frustration, Agnes is still puzzled. She calls the very notion of life insurance "a lottery with death," a phrase she repeats when the agent returns that evening to speak to the *rational man* of the family (pp. 132–33). It is interesting that the agent's appeal is couched in terms that are both recognizably "American" and tied to the Enlightenment's belief in progress: "It is one of the advances of the nineteenth century that one can, for so little money, protect and sweeten the lives of one's loved ones" (p. 133). Insurance is therefore linked to progress, to money, and to the belief that *man* can control *his* own fate without, or even in spite of, God's designs. Agnes, however, is still afraid that an insurance policy could sometime tempt her to want her husband dead. As a result of her fears, Erwin does not take out a policy on his own life, but he insures Agnes's life for $5,000—to protect the family's long-term security.

---

[41] Subsequent references to "Die Lebensversicherung" will omit the volume number.

Episode three portrays the family two years later and in far different circumstances. Apparently Erwin's business has turned sour, and Agnes's attempts at consoling him backfire badly: "Drop it. Your stupid chatter annoys me! It's easy for you to trust in God when I provide for you" (p. 139). Then, when Erwin's partner absconds with their firm's few remaining assets, the conflict between the husband's and the wife's world-views becomes a matter of life and death. Agnes is so shocked by her husband's attitude that she actually, but only momentarily, wants to die, and it soon occurs to Erwin that the money from her life insurance policy would solve all his problems. At first, he is able to resist the temptation ("Satan get thee hence!" p. 140), but because Erwin is ultimately unwilling to put his life in God's hands, he soon begins to rationalize and to imagine that Agnes would indeed be better off dead, rather than being forced to live in straitened circumstances. In short, the insurance really had been purchased at the cost of their relationship and of the family's true happiness; moreover, the policy is on the verge of imperiling their immortal souls as well.

When episode four opens, Agnes has just died. A doctor from the insurance company examines her body, finds nothing wrong, and by the end of the day Erwin has his $5,000. As suspicious as Agnes's death appears to the neighbors, who suspect that Erwin poisoned her, a subsequent autopsy again reveals nothing. At this point the townspeople finally decide that Erwin's remorse is actually a sign of undying love for his departed wife. In fact, Erwin is plagued constantly by her image, and in spite of his renewed business success he is unable to find peace because he cannot confess some sin, presumably her murder. Not surprisingly, then, in episode five the reader learns just how cleverly the murder had been carried out, but there is one unexpected development. Again it is the mysterious ways of the Lord, who has for some reason chosen not to punish Erwin directly with business failure or ill health—or with anything other than remorse. As a result, the pastor to whom Erwin finally confesses concludes, "He [God] has allowed your terrible crime to remain hidden from other people. Your children don't suspect it either, so keep and preserve them, otherwise they will be completely orphaned" (p. 156). As the narrative closes, Erwin has given up his implement business to become a farmer, and once he is safely established in the countryside he tries to be both a father and a mother to his children. The fact that he also became enormously pious almost goes without saying.

In the end the moral of the story has to be something like "Trust in God and don't buy life insurance!"—sentiments that the authorities in the Lutheran Church–Missouri Synod could have endorsed wholeheartedly.[42] And if the author, whether consciously or not, had really begun with such a "lesson," he or she could scarcely have invented a better tale to illustrate it, at least within the limits of talent and world-view. How the process of writing actually proceeded is of course unknowable and largely immaterial, but the end product does look very much like what Gottsched had prescribed more than a century earlier.

Nor was "Die Lebensversicherung" an isolated example. Volume fourteen of *Die Abendschule* contains a novel that revolves around the sin of pride: *Das Pfarrhaus im Harz* (The Parsonage in the Harz Mountains); it was written by Henry Liebhart, a Cleveland pastor who was apparently not affiliated with the Missouri Synod.[43] Liebhart's narrative contains enough plot to fill sixteen episodes, but the novel ultimately concerns a young girl's unhealthy ambition; she wants to follow in her parents' footsteps and to become a missionary in India. In spite of her exemplary piety she is finally disappointed, because it was actually for her own sake, and not for the benighted natives of India, that she wanted to go in the first place. In spite of her disappointment, there is a kind of happy ending: "Her life lay behind her. Everything she had thought, learned, and wished for had been destroyed; her dearest desires and plans had failed— but God had nevertheless richly blessed her: He had humbled her" (XIV, 125).

With all the twists and turns of an entire novel it is sometimes difficult to reduce the plot to a single lesson. Shorter narratives were generally better suited to Gottsched's ideal because they could more easily be limited to one "moral." However, even the more complex novels published in *Die Abendschule* in this period often contain

---

[42]See Meyer, *Moving Frontiers*, 347, for an excerpt from a 1908 report on the Synod's attitude toward life insurance.

[43]The narrative appeared anonymously, but it was also published in book form, *Das Pfarrhaus im Harz* (Milwaukee: Verlag von Georg Brumder, n.d. [1869?]). The National Union Catalogue attributes it to Liebhart (1832–95), probably on the basis of a foreword he added to the volume. There he speculates that the book was written by a woman (p. 5), but he seems to be following the well-established narrative convention of supposedly finding or editing someone else's manuscript. Except that he also published his own family journal, *Haus und Herd*, from 1873 to 1877, Liebhart was too obscure to have left a record of his life in any of the usual sources of information on German-Americans or on notable Americans of any sort.

individual scenes that appear to have been constructed to illustrate a particular point. Although discussed above in a slightly different context, Gottlieb's rejection of *Daheim* and of classical drama in *Die Wittwe und ihre Kinder* is a good example of that tendency.[44] Dancing was another frequent target of this kind of moralizing, and Lindemann's other narrative, "Der vierte Juli," concerns the dangers of a ball that one character claims is only "innocent entertainment" but that others see as a potential first step on the road to eternal damnation. However, although disaster strikes one of the participants (he drinks up all of his earnings and then dances—that is, sins and starts sliding down the slippery slope into hell), another is awakened to dancing's potential for lasting harm (XVIII, 5–6). Similarly, in an interesting scene in *Bonifacius* Kreuzer's principal protector decides to dance just once with his wife before returning home from a barn-raising, but the man's enemies use the occasion to start a brawl in which he is stabbed and nearly killed (XVIII, 51–52). In other words, up through the early 1870s it seems as if there is a moral for every story, and a number of stories for every moral. The frequency of the pointed moral lessons in these texts is such that one has to believe they were written not merely as entertainment but to illustrate the dangers of dancing, of the theater, and of more serious sins like pride and avarice.

In this connection the dangers associated with drinking presented a difficult problem for the writers of *Die Abendschule*. On the one hand, drunkenness is frequently presented in the narratives of this period as a frightful problem. In "Der Freie und seine Sclavin" (The Freeman and His Female Slave), for example, "a respected businessman in St. Louis" abandons his wife and children for the pleasures of his lodge, where he drinks to excess and as a result is ruined financially.[45] Kreuzer's initial difficulties with the villagers in *Boni-*

---

[44]Somewhat earlier, in 1860, *Die Abendschule* (VII, 58ff.) published a three-part story entitled "Die Bettlerin" (The Beggarwoman), which concerns the ruin brought about by the theater: A woman is seduced by a young nobleman while she is a member of his amateur theater company, and when he then marries a woman of his own class the actress is reduced to begging with her young daughter. Numerous complications ensue, but the interesting point is that the story was published just when Heinrich Börnstein's St. Louis theater company was reaching its high point, only to disappear for other, more compelling reasons during the Civil War. See Börnstein's *Fünfundsiebzig Jahre*, 229–46.

[45]"Der Freie und seine Sclavin: Eine Begebenheit aus der neusten Zeit" (The Freeman and His Female Slave: A Very Contemporary Story), *Die Abendschule*, XVIII, 5ff. As the title perhaps suggests, this particular narrative also contains a good deal

facius are also explained to a large degree by his refusal to drink
with them, which they take as a rejection of their hospitality and an
insult. On the other hand, drinking—especially families drinking
beer together on Sunday afternoons in the local beer garden—was
an important part of nineteenth-century "German" culture, in the
United States as well as in Germany, and attempts to limit this particular custom in the name of temperance or Sabbatarianism were
(however well or ill disguised by the language of moral outrage)
often little more than thinly disguised nativist or know-nothing attacks on the "foreign" lifestyle of German immigrants, who were
after all the largest group of non-English-speakers in the country.
Alcohol was, simply put, one sign of the Other, and it therefore
represented both a challenge and a threat to some people's "American" values. In addition, the debate over alcohol consumption was
also about political and economic power. Numerous election cam-
paigns from the 1850s on were fought over the authority to restrict
the sale of alcoholic beverages or to allow their sale under certain
circumstances—indoors and not on Sunday, for example. Indeed,
the electoral issue of drink raised the specter of immigrant political
majorities, and it often led to politicians either pandering to the so-
called "German vote" or attempting to limit the franchise drastically—excluding new and therefore insufficiently Americanized immigrants. Indeed, while machine "corruption" in various American
cities was sometimes nothing more than a means of providing much-
needed jobs to loyal newcomers, the Progressive movement has been
analyzed as little more than an attempt to maintain the old order's
political power through the ruse of "good" government. Brewing
was also an important industry, and it was soon dominated by
German immigrants. So it is not surprising that the alcohol question reverberated through many of the narratives published in *Die
Abendschule*, and the magazine jumped into the quagmire editorially
as well.[46]

In the six-part series entitled "Der moralische Zustand des Volkes

---

of heavy-handed irony about what freedom really is. Basically it asks whether the
Enlightenment's definition of freedom was adequate for a moral life. Thus at one
point, in answer to her son's question, the "Freeman's" long-suffering wife answers:
"What your father understands freedom to be I can't say; but I can tell you what I
understand. It is, my dear son, the freedom to follow God's will gladly" (p. 6).
[46]On the alchohol problem in Germany, see James S. Roberts, *Drink, Temperance,
and the Working Class in Nineteenth-Century Germany* (Boston: Allen and Unwin,
1984).

der Vereinigten Staaten" (The Moral Condition of the People of the
United States), which has been referred to more than once above, the
editor cautioned against overzealous attempts to regulate human behavior. Far from being effective weapons against drunkenness, temperance laws "simply force alcohol addiction into concealed hiding
places. . . . When human rulers draw the boundaries around what is
permitted more narrowly than God has drawn them, immorality is
not thereby hindered, but rather, in a different manner than before,
encouraged" (XVIII, 121). Gottlieb Kreuzer, the hero of *Bonifacius*,
is a good example of a character who attempts to occupy this middle
ground. Unlike the villagers who seem to need a schnapps to start
the day, and a few more while they are working, Kreuzer refuses
hard liquor altogether. As a result, in spite of his relatively small
stature, Kreuzer is actually a much more efficient worker than the
rest of the company, and he avoids their more serious sins (e.g.,
blasphemy) as well:

> Father and son drank out of a single glass, while carrying on blas-
> phemous discussions. It was not yet 10 o'clock [A.M.!], when a few
> men were lying about behind the barn in a condition such that the
> resident pigs could have recognized them as one of their own. The
> further the work progressed, the smaller became the number of
> workers. (XVI, 51)

True to his German heritage, however, to say nothing of the realities
of life among the German-Americans, Kreuzer is willing to drink a
glass of beer. In so doing, he is able to disprove accusations that had
been made about his character and about his feelings of solidarity
with the other villagers: "The fool is a teetotaler! . . . He's a dumb
greenhorn! . . . In America you drink liquor like water! . . . Anyone
who doesn't want to drink here despises us!" On the other hand, by
drinking only beer ("I never drink distilled spirits!"), and beer only
in extreme moderation ("I'll empty this [one] glass [of beer]. . . . I
never drink more than that!"), Kreuzer is able to demonstrate that
drinking is neither inherently evil nor essentially "American" (51).
Significantly, however, Kreuzer does make abstinence on the job a
condition for the otherwise willing workers who want to help him
build a new schoolhouse, and at the school's dedication, which
marks the beginning of the village's return to the fold of proper,
Lutheran Christianity, Kreuzer's protector declares: "Distilled spirits
will never again pass my lips" (76). Of course, the man is neither so

pious nor so hypocritical that he forswears beer too. Moderation in the defense of liberty, whether it be religious tolerance or the freedom to drink as much or little as one will, can be a virtue. In short, both the characters themselves and their actions—the protagonists' as well as their opponents'—serve to illustrate *Die Abendschule*'s editorial position, and they also show that German immigrants could live a morally acceptable life in their new homeland without embracing as "un-German" an idea as temperance.

At this point one can well imagine how attractive such narratives, particularly those for which the adjective "popular" denoted their potential appeal to a large readership, must have appeared to writers who shared *Die Abendschule*'s moral and moralizing agenda. As the analysis of *Die hölzernen Teller* demonstrated, nineteenth-century literary texts often functioned by deploying constellations of characters who were able to represent various norms and values indirectly. The reason is simply that people, even fictional people, are far more believable and far more effective bearers of ideas—that is, of ideology—than any editorial could ever be. Unlike the editorial's reasoned appeal to the intellect, and to the intellect alone, individual figures can operate on several different levels at the same time. Whenever opinions are voiced by the "well-rounded" characters of realist fiction, for example, the figures also automatically project those ideas with the credibility of their whole existence. Moreover, along with the characters' implicit or explicit "messages," the text provides readers with the opportunity to see these ideas in action. In fact, the whole point of most of the narratives published in *Die Abendschule* up through 1872 seems to have been to stage the confrontation between opposing sets of norms and values. Thus in *Die hölzernen Teller* the characters' positions, by which I mean what individual figures are made to say and do in the narrative, define a comprehensive, well-articulated opposition to the modernizing tendencies found in the German economy of their day—and in the readers' own experiences too. Together, Lukas and his cohorts "represent" the broad ideology of antimodernism. They both embody and give voice to the values of the preindustrial family, the intact village community, and the artisan's mode of production. Yet as effective as this particular strategy of ideological "representation" was, or, perhaps, given the disjointed nature of the text in question, could have been, the authors favored by *Die Abendschule* in the 1860s and 1870s seem to have adopted a different mode of narration, which resulted in texts with a far more limited purpose.

As the next chapter shows in far greater detail, opposition to economic progress and the social change it brought about was a recurrent theme in many of the texts published in *Die Abendschule*, including those dealt with here. In "Die Lebensversicherung," for example, the father's decision to sell his implement business and take up life on a farm, where he can devote more time to his children, clearly echoes an opposition to factory production that is coupled with an idyllic view of rural life. However, the texts that appeared in the 1860s and 1870s tend to thematize a far narrower set of concerns. At their center one can almost invariably locate a single, easily recognized moral lesson, and it is the presence of this solitary "moral" that connects these texts so strongly to the mode of writing originally practiced in the early German Enlightenment. Without belaboring the point by digressing into an extensive comparison of two historically very distinct actualizations of this particular mode of writing, it is still too early to drop the subject altogether. The thematic treatment developed above has so far necessarily overlooked a number of the important generic features common to all these texts.

First, the convention of employing narratives to illustrate the advantages of a particular virtue or the dangers of some vice means that there is often little room in these texts for the development of character. As even their names suggest, figures like Gottlieb [dear to God] Brand in *Die Wittwe und ihre Kinder* and Gottlieb Kreuzer in *Bonifacius* already appear on the first page as fully formed embodiments of virtuous German Lutheranism. Although they are both tried, neither is ever really tempted, nor do they either backslide or grow more virtuous. Even though he progresses from childhood almost to maturity in the course of the novel, as a young man Gottlieb Brand is precisely the same person as the boy readers encountered in the first chapter of the novel. The story of his education is by no stretch of the imagination, or of the genre, a novel of education (*Bildungsroman*); Gottlieb Brand has already been educated or formed (*gebildet*) by his beliefs. Similarly, Gottlieb Kreuzer arrives in the United States penniless and forlorn but everything other than a "dumb greenhorn." The simple religious faith that constitutes the center of his being is already fully developed, and it remains unshaken throughout the text. Moreover, even the minor characters who are persuaded to alter their behavior by the force of either of the two Gottliebs' examples do so essentially by rediscovering in themselves traits that had lain dormant rather than by undergoing some form of conversion. The boys at Gottlieb Brand's school, for example, are willing to forgo their subscriptions to *Daheim* on the basis of the pastor's appeal to their already well-developed moral sensibilities, and the settlers on the Illinois prairie seem to have been waiting for years for someone like Kreuzer to come along and lead them back to their old ways. To give but one example of their feelings, the first time Gottlieb Kreuzer sings a hymn for his host family, the narrator remarks: "Long-forgotten memories were awakened in them. They had to think about their homeland. It seemed to them that until now they had done without a great deal" (XVI, 36).

Since such characters are not intrinsically very interesting, one reason for killing off the protagonists at the end of the two major narratives discussed here might have been that, having illustrated the points they were intended to make, there was nothing left for them to do. Neither Gottlieb Brand nor Gottlieb Kreuzer was ever progressing toward a specific goal, so neither of the narratives could be resolved by having their protagonists achieve some concrete result. Once their antagonists, who also arrive full-blown, are defeated, the narratives simply end. For whatever reason, these authors seem not to have been aware of any narrative devices that might have helped them produce more subtle conclusions, but to no small degree the authors were also simply done in by the genre. All the fictional texts discussed in this chapter are structured by plots that pit virtue against vice, rather than "realistic" characters against one another. Not surprisingly, given the nature of *Die Abendschule*, virtue always wins—though victory is certainly Pyrrhic for the protagonists. Since every line is always clearly drawn from the outset, since there is never any ambiguity about who the heroes and villains are, and since there are no triangular constellations of characters but only the simple opposition of good versus evil, the result is almost invariably figures who are even more wooden than is usually the case in popular narratives. Part of the difficulty may indeed have stemmed from the individual authors' lack of skill and from the relatively small number of German-American practitioners and the resultant paucity of appropriate texts, which apparently necessitated the publication of pirated German texts like Horn's *Kalendermann*. Yet, as Horn's example demonstrates, the problem of character was no mere "artistic" pitfall but a problem inherent to the genre. Even though the novel contains a lost heir and some accompanying intrigue, Horn's protagonist is as upright and as humble on the first page as he is in the final paragraph. And although the danger should have been obvious since Gottsched's time, the promise presented by the narrative as an instrument of moral instruction must have outweighed any aesthetic reservations. As flat as these characters are, readers were apparently still drawn in by the plots the two Gottliebs and their assorted counterparts stumble through.

A second interesting feature of this mode of writing is its implicit model of human subjectivity. Narratives employed as a means of internalizing values and behavior patterns presuppose readers who have, or are in the process of acquiring, strong superegos. Essentially, such texts are either supposed to reinforce behavioral codes that their readers have already accepted, or are intended to help readers acquire new sets of values. The model necessarily implies the existence of powerful, external authorities, in this case certainly including the church and probably also the "father" in *Die Abendschule*'s typical family of readers, and the superego itself also functions as an authority internally whenever individuals make decisions rationally according to the norms and values inscribed in their psyches. Coincidentally, this model, like the mode of narration in which it is embedded, is completely compatible with the Enlightenment's view of humanity, which Missouri Synod Lutherans shared at some level. Grace might be a condition for eternal salvation, but until their deaths or the Last Judgment people are responsible for their actions. This is not, however, to suggest that the texts function only at this purely rationalistic level or that reading them simply involves the "identification" of their moral lesson. Although identification, like interpellation, clearly can include the conscious apprehension of what a text is seemingly intended to transmit, the way texts work is by no means that limited. When viewed in psychoanalytic terms, these narratives also employ another sort of identification, which can be defined as the "psychological process whereby the subject assimilates an aspect, property or attribute of the other and is transformed, wholly or partially, after the model the other provides."[47] Curiously, although the end result is the same, the latter form of identification actually seems to undercut the prospect of human agency involved in the deliberate representation of virtue. Yet far from being flawed or a mass of contradictions at this level, one could also term the result a particularly successful marriage of "Belehrung und Unterhaltung," at least to the unknowable degree that readers actually followed the advice they received.

[47]J. Laplanche and J.-B. Pontalis, *The Language of Psychoanalysis*, trans. Donald Nicholson-Smith (New York: Norton, 1973), 205.

A third aspect of the genre is also connected with these texts' implicit reliance on established authorities, but in a totally unrelated manner. Unlike the texts of the early Enlightenment, from which they drew their inspiration, however indirectly, the emancipatory moment is almost totally missing from the narratives published in *Die Abendschule*. One reason is that in the United States in the latter half of the nineteenth century the essentially bourgeois norms shared by both sets of texts no longer represented an attack on the values of an absolutist state. Whereas Enlightenment texts pointed forward, toward a utopia that could be established only in the future, *Die Abendschule*'s utopia, to the extent that it was worldly at all, was located firmly in the idealized past of intact, organic, and essentially rural communities populated by artisans and their nuclear families. As we have seen, this orientation is clearly present in *Die hölzernen Teller*, and it exists, albeit more discreetly, in virtually all of the texts under consideration here. The happy ending on a farm in "Die Lebensversicherung" is the best example, but the village renewal Gottlieb Kreuzer brings to the Illinois prairie and the lifestyles of the survivors in the other narratives fit this pattern too. It is therefore understandable that one of the questions apparently troubling readers, a question that will be a central concern in the next chapter as well, was whether "America" would continue to symbolize the wrong sort of values—for example, rationalism and industrialization—or whether it could become the location for the rebirth of some form of preindustrial society, just as it had served as the location for the rebirth of the authentic version of "German" Lutheranism.

Finally, both the rational, normative dimension and the psychological aspect of these narratives meant that their "morals" functioned essentially as another means of providing an identity for the readers of *Die Abendschule*. In a sense, the double act of identification that they foster is simply one more way of describing how texts offer their readers subject positions. Thus, Laplanche and Pontalis continue, "It is by means of a series of identifications that the personality is constituted and specified."[48] In the texts discussed above, readers were given a preview of the kinds of values and patterns of behavior that were expected of "German" "Lutherans" in the United States. Seen in this light, the analysis of what was essentially an early Enlightenment mode of writing in the second half of the

[48]Ibid.

chapter in no way contradicts the search for traces of "German-American" identities that preceded it. Reading the texts published in and around the symbolically crucial year of 1871, whether with or against the grain, produces more or less the same results. The norms and values that these texts proclaimed on their surface were part and parcel of the same unresolved and unresolvable triangle of oppositions that pitted "German," "American," and "Lutheran" against one another in the still unsuccessful struggle to define an inclusive ethnic identity for German immigrants in the United States. And while the contents of the readers' superegos were not nearly as problematic as their cultural-political identities, the fact that undesirable activities could never be conclusively labeled "German" or "American"—that it was indeed possible, at least within the confines of various fictional and nonfictional narratives, for virtue to succeed on both sides of the ocean—meant that the juggling act of simultaneously keeping at least three competing identities in the air was far from over.

In this chapter I have explored the textual basis of German-Americans' psychological acrobatics without attempting to impose either an order or a hierarchy on the resultant subject positions. No matter how unitary the subject position that any *single* text offered its readers, and no matter how satisfying that particular resolution of those readers' apparent identity crisis might have been, the narratives published in *Die Abendschule* in this period, taken as a whole, certainly did nothing to arrest the movement from one subject position to another. In other words, despite the success of "1871," and despite its undeniable significance to the German-speaking population of the United States, nothing like *the* German-American as a single anchor for their identity had yet emerged. Even within the relatively small and fairly homogeneous readership of *Die Abendschule* the question of identity was still unanswered, as it had been for some time. For all its significance, "1871" may have only refocused a question that had already been reopened—if it had ever been closed—by the cultural-political precipitates of the Civil War and the temporary decline in German immigration in the 1860s and 1870s. Certainly "1871" could never provide answers for the larger group of German immigrants who were still so deeply split along religious, political, class, and other lines and who therefore were worried about the prospect of assimilation, even if it only meant melting into the larger group of German-speakers in the United States rather than into the intensely more diverse caldron of "America." The people who read these narratives might have been united behind various norms and values and firmly convinced of their essential validity, but the same readers must also have been acutely aware that in their new and "foreign" environment virtue's hold on their lives was extremely tenuous. Every step in any particular direction, whether toward the subject position "German" or "American" or "Lutheran," was potentially the beginning of an irreversible slide down the slippery slope of loss, whose end result was the forfeiture of cherished aspects of the other two positions.

In fact, without the tension between their surface of moral certainty and their underlying defensive posture, which is generated by the prospect of impending loss, these narratives would not make for such fascinating reading today. And it is specifically in this fear—whether manifested in anger at evil incarnate, in the rejection of a specific form of national identity that was momentarily linked to some form of dangerous behavior, or in righteous wrath directed against Jews, Catholics, Mormons, and, most vehemently, against the wrong kind of Lutherans, who apparently represented the most acute threat—that one can uncover the most detailed inscriptions of the readers' search for an identity. Obviously, this was a process that continued beyond "1871." Everyone is always involved in shaping or reshaping his or her own identity in response to the pressures exerted on him or her by altered circumstances. On a larger scale, changes both in the economy and in the culture and society of the United States during the final two decades of the nineteenth century, as corporate capitalism began to work its way into the lives of hitherto virtually independent producers, meant the position of German immigrants also changed significantly. So did the arrival of the so-called new immigrants, the peoples of southern and eastern Europe, who began to arrive in significant numbers in the 1880s. It should therefore not be surprising that the narratives published in *Die Abendschule* toward the end of the century differed markedly from those published in the years around "1871," but to explore the traces of those changing circumstances requires another chapter.

CHAPTER FIVE

Myths of German-American Identity: From "German" Antimodernism to Our Anglo-Saxon Cousins

Periodization is always a dangerous undertaking. Only the heuristic necessity of interrupting the flow of history—in this case, the almost continuous publication of *Die Abendschule* from 1854 to the end of the nineteenth century and beyond—in an effort to understand what was happening at various points along the way can ever justify interventions like chapters, especially chapters that claim to be "from" something "to" something else. Even if the last quarter of the nineteenth century did represent a new era in *Die Abendschule*'s existence, the change was neither rapid nor abrupt. In fact, when the magazine finally became a weekly with volume twenty-one in 1874, after years of weighing the advantages and risks, the inaugural editorial promised: "it is still the old, proven friend, who will now visit his patrons twice as often as before. . . . What the reader found in previous years of subscribing—stimulation, entertainment, instruction—he will also find in the future" (p. 1). On the other hand, the new weekly publication schedule can be read as an indication not only that the magazine itself was more secure financially but also that its readers had established themselves in the United States well enough to be able to afford both the minimal added cost (an increase of fifty cents a year, from $1.50 to $2.00) and the far larger demands that twice as much reading material would make on their leisure time. Thus it is probably not accidental that none of the implied readers in *Die Abendschule*'s final three mastheads (Figures 7–9) is personally engaged in the production process. In the 1874 image the "man" of the family is still a farmer—and not a reader like the women represented there. Particularly in the penultimate masthead, which appeared between 1878 and 1881, the readers' role in the production process has changed considerably. These people, who are reading on the front porch of their farmhouse, seem content to watch as others work for them. By the final masthead, 1881– 1907, the world of work has disappeared entirely.

In a sense, this shift in the position of the magazine's readers represents the shift from the so-called old middle class of craftsmen and farmers (*Bauer*), who often lived and worked with their apprentices and farmhands (*Knechte*), to the white-collar employees of large, impersonal corporations, who constituted a "new middle class."[1] The transition from one type of middle class to another, as corporate capitalism gradually became the dominant form of economic organization in the United States after 1880, was anything but smooth, particularly not for the artisans and small producers who had originally fled Germany for the New World in an effort to avoid precisely that threat to their traditional lifestyles. For the old middle class, industrial production and the ensuing expansion of the world marketplace, which quickly brought virtually everything produced anywhere under its sway, raised the specter of personal decline into the proletariat. Middle-class members of the German immigrant community therefore often viewed the process of industrialization and modernization with particular alarm. Change posed an acute danger—to the immigrants' status as well as to their pocketbooks— rather than an opportunity for advancement. The ideological precipitate of these developments was a vague and largely unarticulated sense of anxious opposition that Jackson Lears and others have labeled "antimodernism."[2] What that concept implies and how it permeated the texts published in *Die Abendschule* during the 1880s and and 1890s will be discussed more fully below. For now, suffice it to say that the magazine responded to the altered circumstances of its readers as the promise of "1871" was gradually replaced by other, more pressing concerns. To help its readers cope with the changes,

[1]The national-liberal politician Hugo Böttger apparently invented the distinction around the turn of the century. See Werner Conze, "Mittelstand," in Otto Brunner, Werner Conze, and Reinhart Koselleck, eds., *Geschichtliche Grundbegriffe: Historisches Lexikon zur politisch-sozialen Sprache in Deutschland* (Stuttgart: Klett-Cotta, 1978), 4:49–92, esp. 88ff; Jürgen Kocka, ed., *Bürger und Bürgerlichkeit im 19. Jahrhundert* (Göttingen: Vandenhoeck and Ruprecht, 1987); and Jürgen Kocka, ed., *Bürgertum im 19. Jahrhundert: Deutschland im europäischen Vergleich*, 3 vols. (Munich: DTV, 1988).

[2]Jackson Lears, *No Place of Grace: Antimodernism and the Transformation of American Culture, 1880–1920* (New York: Pantheon, 1981).

Die Abendschule had to provide them with a different kind of narrative.

In the specific historical situation of the United States at the end of the nineteenth century, the anxiety produced by the decline of the old middle class was focused by a number of related problems, which reverberated with special resonance for middle-class German-Americans, no matter how they otherwise constituted their identity. To begin, for most of them, emigration was a relatively recent memory, and no matter what dislocations they had experienced there, the society the emigrants left had been their home. Now they found themselves in a new and very different culture. To cite but one particularly significant example, the privileged status of the artisan was much more firmly rooted in European traditions than in the United States. For centuries these occupations had provided German cities and towns with their social, economic, and political elites. For the fortunate few, advancement into the new middle class, even though it meant successfully avoiding the dangers of proletarianization, certainly did not guarantee anything like the position of the *Bürger* in preindustrial Germany. Corporate capitalism brought with it an entirely different elite, which was clearly not equivalent to the middle class that had existed in the old world. And just as the members of the old middle class were once again distinctly separate from those located ever further above them, so too was the gulf between the old middle class and the expanding working class wider and deeper than ever before. Parrying threats to the ideological hegemony of the middle class therefore involved maintaining boundaries in several directions simultaneously.

In the 1880s and 1890s, *Die Abendschule* was filled not only with texts that stress the values of the old middle class vis-à-vis corporate capitalist encroachments, but also with texts that attempt to differentiate its readers from an increasingly militant working class. The latter presented middle-class German-Americans with a particular difficulty, because working-class German immigrants were heavily implicated in socialist and anarchist movements in the United States. In the summer of 1877, for example, St. Louis, where *Die Abendschule* was published, was the scene of a full-fledged general strike, which had erupted there in the course of nationwide labor unrest. Of the 1,000 members of the Workingman's party who formed the core of the strike in St. Louis some 600 were of German descent.[3] Similarly, a few years later, six of the eight men tried in connection with the infamous Haymarket Affair were of German origin. As a result, to judge by the texts published in *Die Abendschule* in this era, it became important for middle-class German-Americans to prove—both to themselves and to the powerful, English-speaking majority—that "German" did not necessarily imply radical or dangerous. In fact, in *Die Abendschule* "German" would eventually signify the only real source and embodiment of the label "American." In other words, in the 1880s and 1890s, the discourse of German-American identity was structured by a wholly different set of oppositions than it had been in the years around "1871."

In addition, during the late nineteenth century the situation of German immigrants in the United States was further complicated by the arrival of very different and far less easily assimilable groups of immigrants from southern and eastern Europe, who looked much less like the favored Anglo-Saxons, who frequently came from underdeveloped and largely precapitalist societies and who were often Catholic or Jewish. While these new ethnic minorities made excellent strike-breakers—that is, while they initially entered American society near the very bottom of the social and economic scale—they nevertheless represented a visible challenge to "Anglo-Saxon" hegemony. The new immigrants provided the traditional Eastern elite, which was itself endangered by the process of modernization, with the perfect excuse to raise bulwarks against change in every form. German immigrants, who had previously defined themselves defensively in opposition to an "American" norm, were suddenly caught in the middle. Quite unexpectedly there was another "them," another "other," and the question was whether German-Americans would be able to become part of the hegemonic "us" or whether they would be relegated to a newer and far less desirable version of "them." Thus, particularly toward the end of the nineteenth century,

[3]Philip S. Foner, *The Great Labor Uprising of 1877* (New York: Monad Press, 1977), 159; see also David T. Burbank, *Reign of the Rabble: The St. Louis General Strike of 1877* (New York: Augustus M. Kelly, 1966). It is significant that the workers' proclamations were generally issued in English and German but not in other languages. For *Die Abendschule*'s account of the strike, see XXIII, 382–83. The magazine also used the occasion to argue that railroad workers were actually better off than they had been in 1860 (pp. 388–89) and to propose Christianity as the only answer to "Deutscher Sozialismus" (German Socialism) (pp. 369–70) and "Arbeiternoth" (Workers' Destitution) (pp. 393–94).

texts published in *Die Abendschule* attempted to appropriate the notion of "Anglo-Saxon exceptionalism" that was part of the English-speaking mainstream's response to the new immigration. After all, German-Americans could argue, the Anglo-Saxons were nothing if not Germans. Yet, as will become clear below, this was a dangerous strategy. By accepting an "American" definition of what was acceptable, middle-class German-Americans ran the risk of undercutting the rationale for their own continued existence as a separate group. In other words, for German-Americans the stakes in all of these social, economic, and ideological conflicts were extraordinarily high, and while the popular narratives published in *Die Abendschule* in the final quarter of the nineteenth century were still connected with the idea of an ethnic community, the discourse of German-American identity continued to change along with and in response to the world in which it was manufactured.

The question of German-American identity had certainly not been resolved by "1871." In its overt form, however, the dilemma posed by the multiple choices between "German," "American," and "Lutheran" simply disappeared from the pages of *Die Abendschule*. On a purely factual level the reason for the change is easy to see. Because all three of the identities were set in a world that was already beginning to disappear during the Civil War, when the North mobilized its considerable industrial resources to preserve a more modern version of the American state, they rapidly became irrelevant in the postwar era as economic development continued apace. By the 1870s, middle-class German-Americans were confronted by the same threat as their English-speaking counterparts, and their discourse was therefore increasingly structured by a new set of oppositions. Inasmuch as it threatened their very existence, economic and social change seems to have forced more strictly ethnic considerations into the background, at least temporarily. In 1880, for example, readers of *Die Abendschule* could read a story whose beleaguered hero is an "American," and there is not the barest hint that his difficulties are connected with the negative values that term had conjured up a decade earlier.

The man's name is Amos Sparks, and he is "Der Schlosser von Philadelphia" (The Locksmith from Philadelphia). Subtitled "Nach einer wahren Begebenheit" (In Accordance With a True Story), the narrative, written by Wilhelm Ziethe, appeared in *Die Abendschule*

in three successive issues in August 1880[4] (XXVI, 769ff.). One after-
noon Sparks, the city's most skillful locksmith, is called on to open a
rich merchant's safe. It seems that the merchant, a man by the name
of Drummond, has lost the key. Drummond's problem is compounded by the fact that he needs some of the money in the safe
immediately in order to pay off a bill of exchange; otherwise he will
lose his reputation for creditworthiness, which is the key to his success as a businessman. Sparks quickly picks the lock and demands
five dollars for his services. When Drummond complains about the
fee ("What? Five dollars? You're not really very sensible. The whole
job hardly lasted five minutes" [p. 770]), Sparks responds by explaining how much skill and training are involved in his trade and
concludes: "You should, therefore, . . . not evaluate my work by the
amount of time that I spent on it, but rather according to the value
that it has, indeed, has to have, from your perspective" (p. 770).
Drummond nevertheless offers him a much smaller sum and says
Sparks can sue him if he is dissatisfied. Not to be outsmarted, Sparks
shuts the safe, tells Drummond to hire someone else, and prepares to
leave. At this point the merchant has little choice; the bank is about
to close, and no one but Sparks can open the safe. Sparks, however,
decides to teach the merchant a lesson, and he demands ten dollars
to open the safe again. Drummond is caught: "I would rather spend
a thousand dollars than have the bank close before I can redeem my
note there" (p. 771).

In the next episode Sparks is seen late at night near the Pennsylvania Bank. When a robbery is discovered there the next day, Drummond sets the police after Sparks, who is after all the only Philadelphia resident capable of having broken into the bank's vault.
Sparks was actually following a wayward journeyman, the orphaned
son of his own former master, but, once arrested, Sparks decides to
rely on his own reputation for honesty, so he refuses to answer any
questions lest he compromise the young man who had been placed
in his charge; the poor fellow is already endangered by "all the
temptations of the big city" (p. 771). Although Sparks is found innocent, enough suspicion remains to ruin his reputation, and he gradu-

[4]Ziethe (1824–1901) seems to have been a pastor whose sermons were published
in Berlin. The rest of his life is so totally obscure that he did not even merit mention in the *Deutsche Bibliographisches Archiv*. *Die Abendschule*'s reliance on German authors in 1880s and 1890s was particularly heavy, one supposes, because of
J. C. W. Lindemann's unexpected death in 1879.

ally sinks deeper and deeper into poverty. Eventually, after he wandered from place to place with his long-suffering family, the real culprit, a New York safecracker, is discovered. Drummond apologizes, and Sparks returns to Philadelphia in triumph. At first he refuses to sue the bank for damages because "his good name and his honor had, after all, been saved, his business was flourishing again, and his family was quite comfortable and satisfied" (p. 803). When he finally does accept ten thousand dollars from the bank, he uses the bulk of the money to set up a fund "from which needy master craftsmen and apprentices are to be supported" (p. 803).

The question is how and why this narrative about an "American" locksmith could speak to the readers of *Die Abendschule*. The answer is obviously connected with the expansion and consolidation of the U.S. economy in the decades after the Civil War. By and large, industrialization meant that steam replaced human muscle, steel replaced iron, and large-scale enterprises, with their rational, hierarchical organizations, replaced small-scale production—with disastrous consequences for craftsmen like Amos Sparks, although initially his particular trade was probably somewhat less threatened than many other occupations. For my purposes, however, the important variables are not the *facts* of economic development in general or of Sparks's trade in particular, but the discursive precipitates of the social and economic changes that can be found in texts like Ziethe's.

The text is structured by the differences between Sparks and the merchant Drummond. The semantic markers that define the principal characters propel the narrative forward because they also create an unavoidable conflict between the two antagonistic world-views they represent. As an artisan, Sparks is part of an essentially precapitalist economic order whose values are at odds with everything Drummond stands for. Sparks is an autonomous, independent producer, whereas Drummond, for all his wealth, lives from others' labor and is nevertheless at the mercy of his creditors. Moreover, as Sparks admonishes Drummond, the artisan's unalienated labor is to be rewarded not according to the abstract, quantifying measure of time but "according to the value that it has, indeed, has to have, from your perspective." Sparks is also characterized by the trait of loyalty to his family and the community of satisfied customers and fellow craftsmen. Not only are Sparks's wife and three children named in the course of the exposition, but his father, who is repeatedly characterized as "venerable," also plays a significant role in the narrative. Moreover, Sparks's difficulties with the law arise when he is unwilling to sacrifice his adopted journeyman's reputation for the sake of his own security. In contrast to the locksmith's *ganzes Haus*, where work and family life are still united, Drummond's residence is important only as the location of his money. Besides the altercation that occurs when Sparks opens the merchant's safe, the only other action that takes place there is Drummond's successful attempt at persuading a master cabinetmaker to testify against the locksmith. The exchange is interesting for what it reveals about the two men's beliefs. The first speaker is the cabinetmaker, who explains his reluctance as follows:

> "Sparks and I have always always been good neighbors, and I have no real desire to accuse him on the basis of a mere suspicion and, perhaps, destroy his good reputation forever."
>
> "Neither here nor there!" replied the businessman angrily. "This doesn't concern your neighborliness in the least, but rather the peace and quiet of our city and its inhabitants." (p. 786)

For Drummond, incidentally, the phrase "peace and quiet" refers almost exclusively to the security of the Pennsylvania Bank's vault. Note too the importance the cabinetmaker ascribes to his friend's reputation. The topos, which is repeated nearly two dozen times in the course of the narrative, underscores the contention that people's *true* worth is determined neither by the commodities they are able to produce nor by the money they have accumulated, as Drummond falsely believes ("Mr. Drummond looked joyously at the full rolls of coins and the bundles of bank notes that the iron safe hid and preserved in its interior"), but by the position an individual like Sparks can earn through his or her "honest behavior [*rechtschaffenen Wandel*]" (p. 770).

Taken together, the set of values represented by the autonomous individual, by unalienated production, by unquantifiable worth, and by the family and the community—which define Sparks and, by way of contrast, his adversary Drummond—are virtually synonymous with what Jackson Lears calls antimodernism. For him the term couples the longing for an intact, organic community with the rejection of urban market society, because in the course of historical development the market had "undermined individual autonomy and promoted social interdependence. Ordinary people's livelihood depended increasingly on decisions made in distant cities, on circumstances largely beyond the individual's control."[5] Men like Drummond—that is, capitalists, particularly merchants and bankers—were viewed as the chief villains in a system whose continual expansion threatened the existence of the independent producers who would have been reckoned to the old middle class in Germany. For these German artisans and their counterparts in the United States, the danger of a gradual or even sudden fall into the ranks of the proletariat was very real. When Jay Cooke's Philadelphia bank closed its doors in 1873, for example, the ensuing panic threw the whole American economy into a tailspin.[6] In the fictional world of *Die Abendschule*, however, traditional modes of production and, more important, traditional values triumph. As we have seen, for example, the bank is even forced to finance a fund for "needy master craftsmen and apprentices." Seen against this background, "Der Schlosser von Philadelphia" is anything but apolitical entertainment. The story clearly spoke to the real concerns of its readers.

In translation Ziethe's text could just as well have addressed the problems of English-speaking craftsmen,[7] but in the 1880s and 1890s *Die Abendschule* was filled with texts that located these same values in a specifically "German" environment, generally in the past. As will become clear shortly, the time and space represented in these narratives was often anything but unmotivated. To begin, one can scarcely imagine a more convenient setting for the success of traditional values than in the period before the incursion of capitalism. For German-Americans the fact that the historical narratives they read took place in the heroic past of the German peoples was no doubt an important means of fostering and cementing a specifically German component to their identity. The historical accounts discussed in the previous chapter were certainly part of this process, but as the texts to be explored below indicate, neither general histories of Germany nor accounts of the victory of "1871" were sufficient for the readers of *Die Abendschule*. At least toward the end of the nineteenth century they seemed to have required a much more rigorously delimited myth, whose contours and function will become

[5]Lears, *No Place of Grace*, 34.
[6]See Howard Zinn, *A People's History of the United States* (New York: Harper and Row, 1980), 237–38. The involvement of prominent members of the Grant administration and of the Congress in the Crédit Mobilier scandal earlier in that same year added to public sentiment against banks. The worldwide depression, into which the United States was also dragged, was triggered by a bank panic in Vienna.
[7]See Denning, *Mechanic Accents*.

apparent only after we examine several other narratives from roughly the same era. Not coincidentally, however, these texts propagate and reinforce many of the same values as those espoused in "Der Schlosser von Philadelphia."

Take, for example, Luise Pichler's "Der Sohn der Witwe" (The Widow's Son), which was published in four parts during May and June 1880—that is, in the same volume as Ziethe's text.[8] Set at the end of the twelfth century during the reign of Kaiser Friedrich Barbarossa, the narrative is structured by the opposition between two mothers and their sons. Competing interests pit an apprentice swordsmith and his widowed mother against the area's ruling countess, another widow, and her ne'er-do-well son. A month before the widow's son Guntram is to submit his masterwork, which would enable him to rebuild his late father's decrepit workshop, the young man is drafted into the imperial army. Since he is the sole support of his mother, the order is apparently illegal, but the power-hungry countess is unwilling to overturn it because she was bribed by an official who wanted to protect his own son. Meanwhile, the young count, who has reached the age of majority, prefers "to spend his time at the imperial court or traveling to tournaments rather than occupy himself with the administration of his properties" (XXVI, 564). On the imperial front, Kaiser Barbarossa, although hard-pressed to defend his Italian territories, is unwilling to sell off any of his German possessions to raise money for mercenaries: "I am not a businessman who barters [verschachert] souls for money!" (p. 581). Guntram is now a soldier because, as he puts it, "when the emperor is in need, then shame on anyone who can bear arms but remains behind" (p. 582). When the imperial army is defeated, Guntram saves the obviously grateful emperor's life and is promised a reward. In order to raise more troops, however, Barbarossa first needs the financial support of the Pavian nobility, who believe him to be dead. Guntram therefore helps him return to Pavia to make an appeal for funds, but once there, instead of behaving imperially in front of the

---

[8]Pichler was the pen name of Luise Zeller (1823–89), a pastor's daughter who apparently resided exclusively in Germany; she was the author of numerous historical narratives. See Franz Brümmer, *Deutsches Dichterlexikon*, vol. 2, 1877, *Deutsche Bibliographisches Archiv*, p. 1408. I mention her father's profession only because it is remarkable how many of *Die Abendschule*'s authors had some sort of direct connection with a parsonage. "Der Sohn der Wittwe" bears the subtitle "bearbeitet für [adapted for] *Die Abendschule*"; just what this meant should become clear below in the discussion of the Raabe text.

assembled notables, Barbarossa embraces his wife in their presence "while his young sons jubilantly hugged at his knees" (p. 612). Ultimately Barbarossa conquers his enemies; the countess apologizes to Guntram, who brings news that her son is alive and ready to assume his position in the county; and Guntram turns down a knighthood in favor of the house and workshop Barbarossa had initially promised him. He later explains to his mother, "I have my own house, with a wife and children who love me inside—what do I want with empty honors? I enjoy my work and it feeds me, I therefore thank God, who has done so much for me and who has guided me so well" (p. 616).

In spite of the seven hundred years that separate their settings, in ideological terms the two narratives discussed so far are virtually identical. In "Der Sohn der Witwe" the regressive utopia inhabited by the artisans in "Der Schlosser von Philadelphia" has simply been projected into the more distant and, as I will argue below, therefore far more plausible time and space of German history. Like Amos Sparks, Guntram is an artisan, and the semantic bundle that defines him in the narrative includes the same characteristics of autonomous individuality and support for the family, which is again portrayed as an example of *das ganze Haus*. Kaiser Barbarossa, with whom Guntram shares these traits, adds the anticapitalist dimension. Loyalty to his German subjects cannot be reduced to the money he desperately needs for his Italian campaign. The young count, by way of contrast, is initially dependent on the court for his entertainment, and he neglects both his family and his profession. Unlike the emperor, the countess values a bribe more than the demands of justice and traditional law. The fact that Guntram's success occurs in the hoary German past adds another dimension to the text's antimodernism, and it is interesting to note that in the figure of Kaiser Barbarossa some of the German ruling class has taken on a positive role quite different from the one ascribed to the King of Saxony twenty-five years earlier in *Die Abendschule*'s initial narrative, *Die hölzernen Teller*. Even though the young count in "Der Sohn der Witwe" still represents the negative side of courtly life, by 1880 the monarchy can represent a bulwark against the encroachment of modernizing capitalism and its system of quantifiable values.

Before turning to the much more complicated questions raised by the historical dimension of Pichler's text, the religious component of Guntram's final statement ("I therefore thank God, who has done so much for me and who has guided me so well") is worth considering.

Lears makes much of the decline in evangelical fervor and of the secularization of American life in the late nineteenth century, but his focus is largely on "high" culture.[9] I am convinced that throughout the late nineteenth and early twentieth century traditional religion continued to play an important role in the ideological framework of the middle class—and of much of the working class in the United States, if not in Germany, where Social Democracy was much more effective in displacing some of the institutional functions of the church. In any case, no matter how powerful religion was in either society taken as a whole, it was invariably important to the positive characters in the narratives published in *Die Abendschule*. After he is arrested, Amos Sparks consoles his wife by telling her, "The ancient God of Israel still lives, and he will rescue the innocent and bring the guilty party to light" (p. 786). The locksmith's father is also present in this scene, and his reaction is worth noting. Although the "venerable, old" man speaks only four times in the course of the narrative, Grandfather Sparks nevertheless establishes his own unmistakable voice. While none of the sources behind the old man's utterances is specified, they are nevertheless all recognizable quotations from Luther's translation of the Bible. In this particular instance he comforts his son, saying, "Your innocence will and must soon see the light of day, for it is written: 'The Lord will bring to light the hidden things of darkness and will make manifest the counsels of the hearts'" (p. 786). One must assume that a fair number of *Die Abendschule*'s readers were familiar enough with the scriptures to have known that the elder Sparks is quoting 1 Corinthians 4:5. If nothing else, those readers certainly recognized the biblical flavor of Grandfather Sparks's language, which I have rendered with the help of the King James Version of the Bible, and as a result they were undoubtedly supposed to accord the character a special measure of respect. Note too that the verse quoted here underscores the old man's emotional reassurance linguistically. He echoes the locksmith's key phrase, "to bring to light," and thereby lends his son's prediction the moral authority of the Bible. The Pichler text is much less elaborately marked in this regard, but it is probably not accidental that the countess is undone not only by her greed but also by her

[9] E.g., Lears, *No Place of Grace*, 32–47. For a very different view of developments on the religious front, see George M. Marsden, *Fundamentalism and American Culture: The Shaping of Twentieth-Century Evangelicalism, 1870–1925* (New York: Oxford University Press, 1980).

reliance on secular power relationships. The empress provides an interesting contrast. She reads "the Gospels in the original Greek text, for Beatrice was a woman who was as highly educated as she was pious" (p. 611). Of course, Guntram and his mother both trust God implicitly, and the widow's son's eventual triumph is really God's, "who has done so much for me and who had guided me so well." In short, religion is an additional semantic marker that helps structure the oppositions at the heart of these two texts, and the religious message is an important part of the ideology they share.

Saying that the two texts are virtually identical in ideological terms does not mean that the "historical" location of "Der Sohn der Witwe" is somehow insignificant. In fact, in the period under consideration in this chapter "Der Schlosser von Philadelphia" is one of the relatively rare examples of a "contemporary" text. Most of the narratives Die Abendschule published in the last quarter of the nineteenth century were set squarely in the past. Inasmuch as historical fiction was enormously popular with readers both in Germany and in the United States, its frequency in Die Abendschule should come as no surprise; in order to survive, the magazine's editors simply had to develop a sense of what sold. Still, there was ultimately far more than commercial success or fashion at stake in Die Abendschule's historical narratives. Indeed, the topos of history played such a significant role in the discourse of German-American identity that much of the remainder of this chapter will be devoted to the analysis of various historical narratives, but before turning to the ethnic component of specific texts, it is first necessary to discuss the institutional position of historical fiction in somewhat more general terms, using Pichler's narrative as an initial example.

The genre of historical fiction basically sprang into existence full-blown with the publication of Walter Scott's Waverley in 1814, for as Lukács says of the texts that might be considered its predecessors, they were "historical only as regards their purely external choice of theme and costume."[10] In other words, before Scott history was more of a prop than a theme; the history in such texts was itself meaningless. Lukács argues persuasively that it was far from accidental that the birth of the historical novel coincided with the decline of the Napoleonic Empire and the rise in nationalist fervor fostered by opponents of the French emperor—based, curiously

---

[10]Georg Lukács, The Historical Novel, trans. Hannah and Stanley Mitchell (1937; Lincoln: University of Nebraska Press, 1983), 19.

enough, on the model of revolutionary France. Yet, although the historical novel was certainly connected with this new form of collective consciousness that came into prominence throughout Europe after 1789, to assess the genre's continued popularity in the face of other social dislocations—for example, industrialization and emigration—something has to be said about the particular manner in which Scott and his disciples were able to appropriate history. At the same time, it is important to remember that historical fiction soon began to compete with the new discipline of history, whose origin was a related and more or less contemporaneous phenomenon. Academic history and historical fiction also shared most of the narrative conventions—for example, an omniscient narrator who affects a pose of objectivity that we would now label "realistic."[11] In short, history—whether fiction, "fact-tion," or "scientific"— had become an important discursive realm whose function remains to be delineated. However, to avoid raising such far-reaching and perhaps intractable theoretical issues in the limited space of this book, the question posed by historical fiction is better restated as follows: What advantages were there in locating a text like "Der Sohn der Witwe" in the past rather than in the present? I shall offer four distinct answers, all of which help explain the role of historical fiction in *Die Abendschule*.

The first, partial answer is simply that distance from contemporaneous events permitted much more plausible happy endings. The psychological mechanisms common to most of the texts published in *Die Abendschule* (see Chapter 3), could function only when authors were able to locate their narratives in a hospitable time and space, and in the 1880s and 1890s neither Europe nor the United States provided much of an opportunity for a journeyman swordsmith like Guntram. And although locksmiths were probably able to survive the pressures of industrial competition far longer than their fellow craftsmen, who happened to have been weavers or lathe operators, even Amos Sparks's experiences often stretch the bounds of credulity—for example, when his workshop is portrayed: "Cheerful

[11]See Philip James Brewster, "Wilhelm Raabes historische Fiktion im Kontext: Beitrag zur Rekonstruktion der Gattungsproblematik zwischen Geschichtsschreibung und Poesie im 19. Jahrhundert" (Diss., Cornell University, 1983), esp. 18–35, 53–133; and Karlheinz Stierle, "Erfahrung und narrative Form: Bemerkungen zu ihrem Zusammenhang in Fiktion und Historiographie," in Jürgen Kocka and Thomas Nipperdey, eds., *Theorie und Erzählung in der Geschichte*, Theorie der Geschichte 3 (Munich: DTV, 1979), 85–118.

conversation or lively, happy songs almost always accompany the work" (p. 769).[12] Of course, weavers and lathe operators do not appear here by accident. Those were both trades whose decline and miserable end were represented in contemporary narratives that the editors of *Die Abendschule* no doubt deemed absolutely inappropriate for their readership. The fate of the Silesian weavers had been thematized repeatedly, long before Hauptmann's 1892 play *Die Weber* (*The Weavers*), and the master lathe-turner Timpe, who was done in by his factory-owning neighbor in Max Kretzer's 1888 novel *Meister Timpe*, was a far more believable representation of reality than Amos Sparks. Unfortunately Timpe and the weavers failed to establish the idyllic community of artisans that apparently appealed to the readers of *Die Abendschule*. Because these readers and the authors who wrote for them knew full well that they were living in an era of profound labor unrest, it was certainly far easier and far more plausible for the harried craftsmen who populated so many of the magazine's narratives in this period to be located in the past. Thus Guntram is a contemporary of Kaiser Barbarossa, and Siegfried Brunstorp, an apprentice painter who is the hero of Otto Rüdiger's *Handwerksmann und Handelsmann: Kulturgeschichtliche Erzählung aus der Zeit der Zunftunruhen* (Craftsman and Businessman: A Cultural-Historical Tale from the Era of Guild Unrest), resides in fourteenth-century Hamburg.[13]

The list could go on and on, which is not to suggest that "history" was an irrelevant space. Quite the contrary. An advertisement that accompanied the initial episode of Rüdiger's text proclaimed: "This particular tale, even though it takes place in the fourteenth century, is as contemporary as any [story] could be!" (XXXII, 320). Among its many morals, readers could find both an attack on merchants, who often profit unjustly from the work of others ("Work is, above all, the production of new objects" [p. 610], and a series of statements directed against the supposedly dangerous restraints on trade fostered by the outmoded traditions of the guilds. What is most important here, however, is not the specific content but the fact that contemporary difficulties—for example, strikes and other labor un-

---

[12]The passage so faithfully echoes lines 11–12 of Schiller's "Lied von der Glocke" (Song of the Bell), which many nineteenth-century German readers knew almost by heart, that Ziethe's phrase must be regarded as a kind of embedded quotation: "When cheerful conversation accompanies it, / Then work flows happily along."

[13]XXXII, 308ff. Rüdiger is too obscure to have left behind any traces whatsoever; he is not among those identified in the *Deutsches Biographisches Archiv*.

rest—have been relegated to the past, where they can be resolved with far less trouble. Because these narratives basically existed to offer readers imaginary solutions to problems that were all too real and, given the conservative political orientation of *Die Abendschule*, virtually unsolvable in those readers' "presents," their distant historical location is in effect an enabling condition for that compensatory function.[14]

A second answer to the question "Why historical narratives?" is connected with the narratability and readability of history. Even though the academic history produced by such masters as Theodor Mommsen, who was, after all, the first German to win the Nobel prize for literature, was regarded as eminently readable, the conventions of historical fiction allowed authors far more freedom to recast even the driest events in more human terms. In a sense, the novelistic concentration on character in historical fiction is a reflection of the division of labor that resulted from the implicit bargain the writers of historical fiction had struck with historians. Because academic history was thought to be the record of essentially political events— that is, because historians basically chronicled the movement of great *men* through the intricacies of war and diplomacy, on the basis of what they could document from very narrowly defined archival sources—there was a great deal of material left over for the storyteller, even if he or she narrated the same "events" from roughly the same fundamentally omniscient perspective.

One of the principal advantages that historical fiction enjoyed vis-à-vis academic history was the former's ability to establish a fictive presence for the reader, generally in the form of ordinary people who either witnessed significant events or who actually experienced the triumphs and disasters first-hand. For example, the character Guntram, should he have existed, was far too insignificant to have left behind any traces in the official documents of Barbarossa's cam-

---

[14]Harmut Keil argues that radicalism among working-class German-Americans was, at least in part, the result of the same fears and frustrations. Unable to rise into the ranks of independent businessmen and small entrepreneurs—and, I would add, unsatisfied or unplacated by whatever narratives they shared with them—workers turned to unionism, socialism, and anarchism. See Keil and Heinz Ickstadt, "Elemente einer deutschen Arbeiterkultur in Chicago zwischen 1880 und 1890," *Geschichte und Gesellschaft* 5 (1979), 103–24. For a sample of "authentic" narratives in which the hard life of the journeyman is thematized, see *The Autobiographies of the Haymarket Martyrs*, ed. Philip S. Foner (New York: Humanities Press, 1969), esp. the accounts of Georg Engel and Michael Schwab, both of whom were German immigrants, pp. 93–130.

paigns in Italy, but the young swordsmith could nevertheless be used to show what the emperor's battles were "really" like.[15] In this particular instance Guntram, with whom the reader is led to identify, also demonstrates just how important the common soldier—in effect, the ordinary reader—could be, for it is Guntram and not some well-known general who saves the wounded and unconscious Barbarossa when the imperial army is defeated. In addition to the generically determined absence of such figures as Guntram, the other element missing from nineteenth-century histories, due in large part to the kind of evidence favored by historians, was the human side of its heroes. In Pichler's narrative, for example, readers could find out something about Barbarossa's wife and his children; moreover, they saw that the truly great were not only warriors and diplomats but also pious family men.

This particular side of the historical narrative was not confined to the longer works of fiction, nor was it limited to figures from the remote past. *Die Abendschule* apparently had an abundant supply of short articles to fill the white space that might otherwise have been left at the bottom of its columns by narratives that were just a bit too short. Along with scraps of advice and extremely tame jokes, scarcely an issue goes by in which readers are not offered a tidbit from the life of Friedrich the Great, King Gustav Adolf, who was the seventeenth-century Swedish champion of Protestantism, or Bismarck, to name but a few of the favorites. Here is an example of the genre published in 1881:

> *A Remedy for Duelling*: Gustav Adolf, the great king of Sweden, was an enemy of the duels that were so common in his day. He repeatedly declared in the presence of his officers that duelling was a crime, that it was unnatural, and that it robbed the fatherland of its bravest men. He wanted soldiers and not fencers in his army. Once two of his generals got involved in a dispute and asked him for permission to resolve their difficulty with a duel. After trying in vain to convince the two that their notions of honor were false, he gave his permission, with the condition that he be present at the duel. The king appeared at the time agreed upon with an executioner and a contingent of soldiers, whom he ordered to form a circle around the duelists. "The moment that one

---

[15]In no small measure historical fiction answers Brecht's question "Who built the seven-gated city of Thebes?" The readers of fictional accounts can often find out who actually won the wars and built the monuments afterward—even if their names go unrecorded in *real* history.

of them falls," he said to the executioner, "you chop the head off the other one." Dismayed, the officers fell at the king's feet and begged for his forgiveness. Since then, no one else ever asked him to approve a duel. (XXVII, 352)

According to this account, Gustav Adolf was not only a leading combatant in the great cause of religious freedom but also a king with the judgment of Solomon, an attribute that only a fictionalized account, which may well have made use of biblical models, could grant him.

The presence of men like Barbarossa or Gustav Adolf in historical fiction provides a third answer to the question of the genre's popularity and acceptability. Historical narratives were generally believed to be a more palatable and therefore more effective means of imparting the historical knowledge that members of the middle class had to have at their command in order to be able to demonstrate rhetorically their status as educated citizens (*Bildungsbürger*). Heinrich Börnstein's defense of the historical novels he reprinted in the *Anzeiger des Westens*, which has already been quoted in part in Chapter 2, is worth citing at greater length in this connection:

I paid particular attention to the cultural [*feuilletonistischen*] sections of my paper and attempted, by reprinting the better works of modern German literature, primarily by publishing historical novels like *Emperor Joseph and His Court*, *Frederick the Great*, and *Napoleon I*, to disseminate historical knowledge among the great mass of the population.[16]

To be sure, even Börnstein could not justify every work of historical fiction as a disguised opportunity to augment the largely undigested set of facts that passed for historical knowledge in the nineteenth century, and beyond. Rüdiger's account of the guilds in fourteenth-century Hamburg, for example, is bereft of recognizably important figures, and the events it relates are of no particular consequence in the larger scheme of things. Here, it seems to me that Lukács simply overstated the case he was making against Scott's predecessors. For reasons that should be obvious from the discussion of the plau-

---

[16]Börnstein, *Fünfundsiebzig Jahre*, 2:221. The novels he mentions were all written by the phenomenally popular Luise Mühlbach; see Lieselotte E. Kurth-Voigt and William H. McClain, "Louise Mühlbach's Historical Novels: The American Reception," *Internationales Archiv für Sozialgeschichte der deutschen Literatur* 6 (1981): 52–77.

sibility available in the past, some nineteenth-century historical fictions were indeed set in the past "only as regards their external choice of theme and costume." On the other hand, it is certainly true that much of the value ascribed to historical fiction by contemporary writers, editors, and readers was its ability to convey "facts."

The fourth and final answer to the question posed by the presence of so much historical fiction in *Die Abendschule* is connected with the specific content of the history that was related in these narratives. I hope to demonstrate that many of the works of historical fiction published in *Die Abendschule* contributed to the creation and articulation of a specifically German-American "myth of ethnic descent," to use a phrase coined by the British anthropologist Anthony D. Smith.[17] Although he never deals with the actual constitution of such myths or with how they might have changed over time, Smith nevertheless recognizes that the elaboration of any myth often involves a detailed but generally implicit and even unconscious cultural-political program. However, if ethnic myths only "reflected" some underlying political or social-psychological agenda, if their purpose were purely instrumental, one could never answer the question "Why the turn to the past?" Smith's answer, which echoes Lukács's treatment of the historical novel and is drawn in large part from Max Weber's sketchy treatment of ethnicity, has to do with the rise of nationalism, a phenomenon that he interprets as little more than the demand for a form of collective identity:

> By placing the present in the context of the past and of the community, the myth of descent interprets present social changes and collective endeavors in a manner that satisfies the drive for meaning by providing new identities that seem to be also very old, and restoring locations, social and territorial, that allegedly were the crucibles of those identities.[18]

While it is certainly true in general terms that the history of Germany discussed in the previous chapter was also part of a German-American myth of ethnic descent, my reading of Smith's model sug-

[17]Anthony D. Smith, "National Identity and Myths of Ethnic Descent," *Research in Social Movements, Conflict and Change* 7 (1984): 95–130. See also Smith's "Ethnic Myths and Ethnic Revivals," *Archives Européennes de Sociologie* 25.2 (1984): 283–305.

[18]Smith, "National Identity and Myths of Ethnic Descent," 99–100. Max Weber's treatment of ethnicity can be found in his *Wirtschaft und Gesellschaft*, 5th ed., ed. Johannes Winkelmann (Tübingen: J. C. B. Mohr, 1976), 1(1):234–44.

gests that *Die Abendschule*'s version of the myth of German-American identity was far more differentiated and—given the situation of conservative, Lutheran, German immigrants in the United States— far more problematical than can be accounted for solely by the examination of "German" history. "German" was simply too large a category to have contained the diversity of immigrants from the German-speaking areas of Europe. Some nineteenth-century Germans were Protestants, while others were Catholics, Jews, socialists, freethinkers, or some combination of the above. They came from places as culturally, politically, and economically diverse as Württemberg and Pomerania, to say nothing of the enormous differences that obtained between all of rural Germany and the emerging industrial cities of Silesia and the Ruhr Valley. Moreover, even though German emigration was concentrated in the second half of the nineteenth century, the five decades that followed the Revolution of 1848, punctuated as they were by the events of 1870–71, constituted an era of radical shifts in both the content and the extent of national consciousness. Thus, to have made any sense for the subgroup of German-Americans constituted in and through their reading of *Die Abendschule*, a myth of ethnic descent would have to be, at the same time, narrower and much more fully developed; a simple retelling of German and American history would not do. For the readers of *Die Abendschule*, a useable myth of ethnic descent would have to negotiate the complex and often contradictory set of relationships between those readers' identities as "Germans" and "Lutherans," as well as to link those two subject positions to a constantly shifting notion of what it meant to be "American." Yet, while there never could have been just one quintessentially German-American myth of descent, what *Die Abendschule* could offer its readers was a version of the myth tailormade to their own particular needs and aspirations.

The claim that *Die Abendschule* provided its readers with a myth of German-American descent should not be construed as an argument that its writers and editors consciously intended to fabricate a coherent and historically grounded ethnic identity for their readers. Real proof of intentionality is impossible in the best of circumstances, and in light of the fact that many of the texts published in *Die Abendschule* were actually borrowed from other sources and were written by authors who had never set foot in the United States, attempting to ascribe intent to the authors and editors would be as farfetched as the narratives themselves. I want to suggest, rather, that when taken as a whole, reading these narratives to find a myth of ethnic descent is not only a distinct possibility but also will help explain their attraction to *Die Abendschule*'s immigrant subscribers. In essence, Smith's model provides one more reason for *Die Abendschule*'s turn to history, and whatever its shortcomings the notion of an ethnic myth of descent is nevertheless useful as a heuristic device when constructing a reading of the historical narratives that were so popular in the 1870s, 1880s, and 1890s.

Having suggested a number of reasons that such texts were so widely read, the obvious next step is to explore the specific nature of *Die Abendschule*'s myth of ethnic descent using concrete texts from the magazine. The example I have chosen to begin this analysis is a version of Wilhelm Raabe's novel *Unseres Herrgotts Kanzlei* (Our Lord God's Pulpit) that appeared in the magazine in twenty-one installments in 1878–79. Because Raabe's novel was altered extensively—in fact, censored or bowdlerized are perhaps more appropriate terms—reading it side by side with the original version, which was published in volume eleven of *Westermanns Illustri[e]rte Deutsche Monatshefte* (Westermann's Illustrated German Monthly Magazine) (1861–62), also provides an opportunity to inquire into the meaning of such phrases as "revised for Die Abendschule" or "edited for Die Abendschule," which accompany so many of the texts it took from German authors.[19] However, the primary purpose of this reading is to assess the meaning of history in the discourse of German-American identity.

In a gesture that was very unusual for *Die Abendschule*, Raabe's novel was published with an accompanying introduction. There the editor, or whoever was responsible for the text, announced, "We found the following story, whose author, Wilhelm Raabe (Jakob Corvinus), is a well-known German writer, in an old volume of a German monthly magazine" (XXV, 7).[20] Although there was noth-

---

[19]I do not claim that all the texts with such "reassuring" subtitles were subject to the same degree of cleansing. Without the Herculean effort involved in reading every one of them side by side with an original, there is no way of knowing. As enlightening as the comparison of the two versions of Raabe's novel may be, I doubt that the other texts are worth the same amount of effort, for although there is much to be learned from reading the texts that German-Americans actually read, in contrast to the "canonical" texts they may have had on their shelves, the undertaking neither requires nor really warrants a "historical-critical edition" of *Die Abendschule*.

[20]Since the entire Raabe text is contained in volume twenty-five, subsequent quotations omit the volume number.

ing new in *Die Abendschule*'s "appropriation" of German material, in view of the profound religious skepticism that scholars like Jeffrey Sammons have recently rediscovered in Raabe's writings, his *Unseres Herrgotts Kanzlei* might seem like a curious choice,[21] for no matter how difficult it was to find suitable material, this particular novel presented a series of potentially grave difficulties for a magazine like *Die Abendschule*. To be sure, the plot revolved around one of the Reformation's great victories, the unsuccessful siege of Magdeburg in 1550–51, which paved the way for the Peace of Augsburg in 1555. But as the introduction warned, one of the problems with Raabe's version of those crucial events was "that one's moral or aesthetic sensibilities might be injured." As a result, the editor continued:

> Not only have we corrected individual sentences and phrases, inexact passages, and offensive material, etc., but we have reworked whole sections of the story and the characters contained there, to the extent that they are not historical, according to biblical-psychological principles. By so doing—we hope to God—we have produced a text that every Lutheran Christian can enjoy without harm. (p. 7)

The changes are, in fact, quite remarkable, but before turning to a more general analysis of those changes and their relationship to the strategies the editors admit to, it seems appropriate to look briefly at two examples from the competing versions of the text. The point of these two quotations is to demonstrate at the outset that, as it appeared in *Die Abendschule*, Raabe's *Unseres Herrgotts Kanzlei* was a very different work from the one Raabe had originally published in *Westermanns Monatshefte*. To begin at the very beginning, in *Die Abendschule*'s version of the text, the novel even acquired a new subtitle. Raabe's simple "A Story" was lengthened and specified to read "A Story from the Age of the Reformation" (p. 7), apparently lest anyone fail to see the text's appropriateness for a Lutheran audience.

The number of such changes in the rest of the text is simply staggering and in spite of the difficulty in determining a meaningful unit of measure—that is, whether a totally different paragraph should count as much or more than one altered word—to give some indica-

---

[21]Jeffrey Sammons, *Wilhelm Raabe: The Fiction of the Alternative Community* (Princeton: Princeton University Press, 1987). Sammons claims, e.g., that Raabe was "entirely devoid of religious faith" (p. 55).

tion of the extent of the changes, suffice it to say that in the first chapter alone there are at least sixty separate passages in which *Die Abendschule*'s version of the novel differs from Raabe's published text, sometimes considerably. In the novel's opening paragraph the differences range from several one-word substitutions to the substantial rewriting of the whole final sentence. For example, *Die Abendschule*'s editor changed the pejorative term "tavern" or "saloon" (*Kneipe*) to the more neutral "pub" (*Wirtshaus*) and, in what strikes me as a particularly inappropriate description of the mercenaries who are drinking and carousing there, he or she substituted "in need of refreshment" (*erholungsbedürftig*) for Raabe's repeated use of the word "thirsty" (*durstig*). Raabe's version also contains the phrase "as has been said" (*wie gesagt*), which introduces an ironic narrative voice and thereby breaks the illusion of unmediated reality. The competing versions of the paragraph's final sentence, quoted below, significantly reaccent the text's view of history. *Die Abendschule* emphasized a much more planned version of events, perhaps even divine intervention in what was one of the key events in a German Lutheran's view of world history, for the hint of luck or fate that Raabe's final sentence conveys (*Westermann*'s, [i.e., Raabe's] version is on the left [W], *Die Abendschule*'s on the right).[22]

One warlike game was over, another was about to begin, and the cards [that would determine the outcome] were already shuffled and dealt. (W, 235–36)

One war was over, another was about to begin, and everything was already prepared for the bloody dance to begin again. (pp. 7–8)

One could continue this sort of comparison almost indefinitely, but far more important than doing the philological spadework necessary for a complete history of the text is asking the underlying question: What was this "editing" all about? At first glance many of the changes seem to be little more than concessions to the contemporary (Lutheran) reader's moral sensibilities. For example, in the middle of the first chapter the editor deprived the tavern where the story

[22]The complete citation from *Westermanns Illustrirte Deutsche Monatshefte* is 11:63–66 (December 1861–March 1862), 234–73, 347–80, 467–507, 578–622; here 234–35. Subsequent quotations from the latter publication will be identified by W, plus the page number, in the text. Because the standard edition of *Unseres Herrgotts Kanzlei* contained in Wilhelm Raabe, *Sämtliche Werke*, ed. Karl Hoppe (Freiburg im Br.: Hermann Klemm, 1956), vol. 4 (ed. Karl Heim and Hans Oppermann) is based on the revised edition of 1889, no attempt has been made to correlate *Die Abendschule*'s version with it.

opens ("The Magdeburger Wreath") of its nickname "The Mag-deburger Bridal Wreath" (*Jungfernkranz*), which raises the possi-bility that not all the young women who frequented the premises were virgins (p. 9, W, 237). However, the change at the end of the first paragraph, from "a warlike game" to "war," suggests that far more was at stake than just a few "dirty" words. I contend, first, that *Die Abendschule*'s bowdlerization is a concrete empirical exam-ple of the process of reception and, second, that the glimpse it af-fords of the "editing" process is particularly interesting in the con-text of a German-American journal, because reading historical narratives was one way for German-Americans to come to grips with the past they shared with the Germans in the newly formed empire. In other words, because "history" was a significant source for the content of what it meant to be "German" in America, such texts were an important mediator and potential source of the ac-quired consciousness that we now call ethnic identity.[23] An examina-tion of the German-American version of *Unseres Herrgotts Kanzlei* can therefore not only tell us how Raabe was read in the United States but also provide an indication of what reading meant, or was supposed to mean, to Raabe's German-American audience. As the editors' introduction put it: "Our main interest in the present story is the following: by presenting our readers with magnificent exam-ples, [we hope] to strengthen them in their faith and to inspire them to imitation, but at the same time to warn against sin, no matter what guise it chooses to appear in" (p. 7).

As we shall see shortly, getting that sort of response from Raabe's text required a good deal of work. Still, the editors were well aware that the stakes involved in determining what people read and, even more important, how they read it, were extremely high—both fi-nancially and ideologically. Two-thirds of the way through Raabe's narrative, in a short essay that began on the same page as episode sixteen, *Die Abendschule* termed literature "A Much-Desired (*viel-begehrter*) Article" (XXV, 245–46).[24] The title seems to refer both to

---

[23]One could easily make the same point about the discursive role of history in the German Empire—i.e., about history's connection to German nationalism.

[24]All the subsequent quotations in this paragraph are from the same two pages. In the second half of the essay (XXV, 305–7) its author wondered "whether [for us Christians] narrative art in general and per se is not harmful and expendable." For-tunately for *Die Abendschule* he concluded: "[Narrative art] is an essential part of our earthly existence, perhaps also a very desirable element of eternal life." Having proven that narratives possess both a natural right to exist and a divine purpose, the question of whether Christians could read novels would seem to have been answered

the public's almost insatiable demand for reading material as well as to the very differently motivated needs of publishers, which combined to produce disastrous results: "Thus, constant need leads to pure fabrication and to the homogenization of the wares in question." However, the problem here was not that "a perfect work of art" might disappear under the flood of commodities, as critics and artists had feared ever since the Enlightenment, but that art itself was potentially dangerous.

For *Die Abendschule* the principal difficulty was that literary evaluation pitted two competing sets of criteria against one another. On the one hand, "bad" art could be measured by the "extent of anti-Christian and moral corruption, which can be and is . . . disseminated through those enticing channels, [namely] through belletristic works [that are] unchristian and evil in form." On the other hand: "The quality 'bad/evil' is not to be understood in this connection as if it denoted botched narratives (epics) or incompetent works that no one wants to read." Quite the contrary, the greatest danger arises precisely when the reader is "aroused and enraptured by the narrative; viewed in purely literary terms, no one can deny [such a work] his or her admiration and respect, and nevertheless it is for precisely this reason that they are utterly poisonous, as beautiful as the serpent in the Garden of Eden." In retrospect, it is easy to say that the whole dilemma could have been avoided by reframing the argument, by beginning with an interrogation of what educated readers understood under the category "viewed in purely literary terms." But without that kind of principled attack, the next best solution was the one actually adopted by *Die Abendschule*: the editors first selected what they thought was "a perfect work of art," namely, for reasons that will be discussed below, Raabe's historical novel, and then they disarmed and defused it.

Before we return to the text, a word needs to be said about Raabe's "role" in the affair—that is, about his presumably total innocence with regard to the German-American mutilation of *Unseres Herrgotts Kanzlei*. The Raabe archive in Braunschweig contains no evidence of correspondence between the author and *Die Abend-*

---

once and for all. The magazine's survival also necessitated this sort of concession to the educated members of the German-American middle class who were its readers; like it or not they certainly delved into the "profane" works of canonical authors. The only thing that remained was to launch periodic attacks against "dirty literature" (*Schmutzliteratur*), e.g., XXXVII, 625–26; XXXIX, 201–2.

schule, almost certainly because there was none. Sammons claims that Raabe "was perhaps even less amenable than most of his contemporaries to any editorial intervention, and generally he managed to hold the line." The one exception was "a hard fight" with *Die Gartenlaube* waged over the serialization of *Unruhige Gäste* (Unquiet Guests) in 1885.[25] Raabe did alter *Unseres Herrgotts Kanzlei* for the publication of a second edition in 1889,[26] but that he might have countenanced the kind of changes outlined below is simply inconceivable. Chances are that he did not even learn of their existence until two years after *Die Abendschule* had published its version of the novel. On January 4, 1880, Frieda Andreae, who was, to judge by what she says elsewhere in her letter, an aspiring writer from Erlangen, wrote Raabe to inform him:

> Since of all the forms of theft the one I *hate* most occurs in the realm of literature, where the theft of intellectual property often means that it is disfigured before it resurfaces again, I permit myself to inform you that in the German family journal "Die Abendschule," which appears in St. Louis, in North America, volume 25, no. 1 (Sept. 1878), *your* story, "Unseres Herrgotts Canzlei [*sic*]," has been printed. It has been "adapted for Die Abendschule!" and I can scarcely believe that *you* would have given your permission for this manipulation; in fact, I doubt whether you were even asked about it.[27]

There is no record that Raabe ever responded to Frau Andreae's letter. Certainly he must have seen through the rather disingenuous flattery behind her uninformed opinion: "American journals are, in such matters, literally shameless, and I would like to know if an author like you, whose reputation is so well-founded, [and] who is so widely appreciated, does not have have access to the means or avenues to thoroughly remedy these sinister doings." In fact, Raabe had no recourse. In all likelihood he was just another unwitting victim of the lack of an international copyright law, which was not enacted until 1891. By this point Raabe had also disavowed many of his youthful works, and he would have preferred directing his readers' attention to the later novels. *Die Abendschule* would have

[25] Sammons, *Wilhelm Raabe*, 37.
[26] See Raabe, *Sämtliche Werke*, 4:519ff.
[27] City Archive Braunschweig: H III 10 No. 6A. I thank Dr. Manfred Garzmann of Braunschweig for graciously providing a photocopy of Frau Andreae's letter and granting me permission to publish it. The standard edition of Raabe's works cites both the date and the name of the writer incorrectly—namely, as 6.1.80 and F. Andreae-*Erlangen*, IV, 516.

been of no use whatsoever for that purpose, and there is little reason
to believe that its editors even knew of their existence.

Even without the detailed analysis of the novel's contents that follows below, one can easily understand what must have made *Unseres Herrgotts Kanzlei* such an attractive object for *Die Abendschule*'s "theft in the realm of literature." The central figure in the
novel, Markus Horn, is a former student and sometime imperial
mercenary, who returns to Magdeburg after an absence of four years
in order to defend his hometown against the reimposition of Catholicism by his former comrades in arms. Markus has been disowned
by his father, a town councilor, and he also seems to have forgotten
his earlier affection for the neighbor's daughter Regina Lotther. Her
father, a printer whose trade was one of the reasons Magdeburg
proved to be such a thorn in the side of Charles V, is now trying to
marry her off to another soldier, Adam Schwarz. However, the elder
Lotther is unaware both that Schwarz is actually planning to betray
the city and that he was once the guilty party in a particularly sordid
case of adultery. In the end, the younger Horn is reconciled with his
father, and, once his love for "the girl next door" is rekindled, he
marries her. In the process Markus saves Magdeburg from its enemies, both inside and outside the city's walls. In Raabe's text Magdeburg survives as a monument to the freedom of the press and to
religious tolerance, both of which were exercised in the interests of
Protestantism in the middle of the sixteenth century. The specific
task of the press in the narrative, as well as the existence of a number of compelling characters there, was apparently just what the editors of *Die Abendschule* were looking for. To judge by the results,
they seem to have wanted a straightforward, readable narrative,
preferably one whose plot was set somewhere in the history of Lutheranism in Germany. The editors could then alter the text to suit
what they assumed were the needs and tastes of their readers. What
the "literary" costs were and what was at stake in the changes are
questions that the following close reading of several additional passages hopes to answer. As a means of orientation I would suggest
that three separate tasks were involved in the editing process as it
occurred in *Die Abendschule*.

First, Raabe's language was cleaned up to avoid giving offense.
Die Abendschule's soldiers never curse, and one can find dozens of
instances where a phrase from the narrator like "with a curse" (W,
237) becomes "brusquely" (*hurtig*) (p. 8) or something equally harm-

less, or is simply eliminated altogether. What the individual characters said was subject to the same kind of editing. Later in the chapter, for example, "You devil, you son of Satan!" (W, 237) becomes
"You rascal, you good-for-nothing!" (p. 9). In the eyes of the editors the first version of the passage must have been sinful in some
respect, and therefore had to be softened while still retaining more
or less the same message. What the editors wanted to avoid was
material that they regarded as "offensive," but because the narrative
had to contain enough evil to provide a plot, "sin still appears in our
story—now and again in its most hideous guise—because it would
not otherwise be possible to speak of people and their relationships
without mentioning the corruption of human nature, which occasionally breaks forth into speech" (p. 7). Why "tavern" presented a
problem in this regard is unclear, because the word appears un-
changed later in the chapter (p. 9). Similarly, "thirsty," which Raabe
used twice in his opening paragraph, appears only once in *Die
Abendschule*'s reworked version. Apparently, excessive thirst might
have led to equally excessive amounts of alcohol, and if the soldiers
are not to swear, they ought to remain sober too.

The way these soldiers were recast in *Die Abendschule*'s version
of *Unseres Herrgotts Kanzlei* raises a second issue: the changes that
were made in individual characters "according to biblical-psycho-
logical principles." A good example of the process occurs when
Markus Horn appears for the first time; the portion of the quotation
in italics was eliminated from *Die Abendschule*:

> His face had been burned by the sun and looked a bit gaunt, but his
> black eyes, which sometimes darted about and sometimes looked
> straight ahead, still glowed like coals; *and neither the strain nor the
> debauchery of his wild life in the war and the camps had been able to
> dampen that glow and that fire in the least.* (p. 18; W, 240)

Apparently, if Markus is to be the hero of this narrative, he cannot
have been guilty of a certain class of sins. In *Die Abendschule*
Markus Horn neither drinks to excess nor curses. More important,
it seems to be the case that no positive figure could recover from the
stain of an active sex life, especially one outside the confines of marriage. Even courtship is restrained to the point of its virtual disappearance. Thus, when Markus and Regina—"the moral" not "the
beautiful maiden" (p. 150; W, 379)—finally express their feelings

for one another, the two versions of the novel differ markedly (emphasis added):

<table>
<tr>
<td>

neither Markus nor the maiden could later say how they suddenly *held each other in their arms, how it happened that they embraced, that they lay heart to heart.* (W, 484)

</td>
<td>

neither Markus nor the maiden could later say how they suddenly came *to be standing next to one another, holding hands and looking intently into each other's eyes without saying a word.* (p. 194)

</td>
</tr>
</table>

In fact, *Die Abendschule* almost totally eliminates the hero's romantic motivation and allows Markus but a single flaw: the decision to forsake his parents and live the life of the prodigal son. Breaking the fourth commandment separated him not only from his father and mother but also, and more importantly, from God, and on earth from "our Lord God's pulpit." Once Markus undergoes a change of heart—that is, once God changes his heart for him[28]—his eventual success is assured. Any complications with Regina would simply detract from what was, at least for *Die Abendschule*, the central moment in the hero's life. A good example of the resulting difference is a scene late in the novel, when the reader is allowed access to the young hero's thoughts as Markus gazes upward at his father's lighted window (emphasis added):[29]

---

[28]Raabe ends chapter 9 as follows: "Regina's eyes were glued to the young man; trembling, she folded her hands in her lap. 'Markus, my son!' his mother said, in a voice filled with question and accusation. And Markus sat down at the foot of the [wounded] printer's bed, as stunned and as confused as Michael Lotther himself; his eyes were blind, his ears rang, [and] his heart pounded, as if he, rather than the brave printer, had encountered one of Duke George of Mecklenburg's battle-axes" (W, 380). *Die Abendschule*'s editors chose to use Raabe's text only up to the mention of father Lotther, and then to eliminate virtually all of the rest of the sentence, in favor of the following substitution: ". . . his eyes were moist, his heart pounded, . . . and God, the Holy Spirit was working on his heart when Magister Flacius, who had entered the chamber and asked all the others except [Markus's] mother to leave, spoke to him earnestly and kindly about God's truth and mercy. And Markus did not close his heart to God's punishing and consoling gaze. His heart was gradually still . . . and the angels in heaven rejoiced at the sinner who repented. His mother was deeply moved, and she embraced her son who had been found again, while Flacius folded his hands and said: "Oh, how many are our sins—how much more grace is there with God! Hallelujah!" (p. 150).

[29]Without making too much of the stylistic comparison, particularly in translation, it is at least worth noting that Raabe's versions are almost invariably shorter.

"If he only knew how things look inside me," he thought. "Oh, how useful it would be if we could look into each other's hearts. But often it's not necessary; you already know what the other is thinking. *Whatever happens, Regina, Regina, you are mine for all eternity! I can never lose you again. Our hearts have grown together and no one can separate them, now and forever more.*" (W, 601)

"If he only knew how things look inside me," he thought. "Oh, how useful it would be if we could look into each other's hearts. But often it's not necessary; you already know what the other is thinking. *Oh, how it depresses and torments me that my old father still seems angry. And yet I believe that he watches over what I do and where I go and that he knows more about me than he admits to himself. It often seems that he wants to test me, to see if my penitence is earnest. Oh, Father, Father, if I could only show you how much I would like to transform myself into a new person!*" (p. 307)

In *Die Abendschule* Markus's love for Regina is replaced by concern for his stubbornly unreconcilable father. The primacy of God the Father is underscored by the imposition of a virtually omniscient patriarchal authority on earth. In Raabe's version of the text, by contrast, an erotic vision is allowed to seep even into heaven. What the confrontation of these two passages ultimately produces is not only a very different rendition of the hero but also alternative eschatologies—worldly rather than divine love, even in heaven.

In a similar if less far-reaching fashion, the novel's other positive characters are also reworked until they become almost wholly good, while the evildoers are stripped of their few even partially redeeming characteristics. In *Die Abendschule*, for example, Andreas Kritzmann, a soldier from Markus Horn's company, swears revenge against Adam Schwarz, not for the villain's attempted seduction of his lover, as in Raabe's version of the novel, but for Schwarz's attention to his (as *Die Abendschule* would have it) *legal* wife. *Die Abendschule* also absolves Kritzmann's parents, particularly his father, of the woman's judicial murder.[30] And not only does Frau Johanna, the mistress of Schwarz's commanding officer, no longer help Markus foil the lieutenant's treachery, but *Die Abendschule* even

[30]Not only does *Die Abendschule* make Adam Schwarz into the real—and only—villain, but it again leaves out the erotic moment in Raabe's text, in part by transforming the unfortunate woman from Kritzmann's pregnant "fiancée" into his legal wife. Compare p. 289 with W, 593.

takes away the unfortunate woman's good looks.[31] In their revised version "the beautiful Hannah" is transformed into "the sinful female" (*Weib*); a page later she is again not "beautiful" but "wild" (pp. 227–28; W, 501–3). In short, *Die Abendschule*'s characters are anything but well-rounded or complex; they are either completely black or almost totally white—with at worst only one relatively minor and therefore relatively easily reparable flaw. For a nineteenth-century family journal, whose family orientation was thoroughly patriarchal, it is not surprising that these changes often reflect a scarcely disguised animosity toward women. The female roles are diminished almost to the vanishing point, while men, good or evil, "make" history—just as they did, and often still do, in academic historiography.

The third element in the "editing" process, which is already identifiable from the changes made in the final sentence of the novel's opening paragraph, concerns Raabe's view of history. His original version of that sentence ("One warlike game was over, another was about to begin, and the cards were already shuffled and dealt") apparently contains an attitude toward history that made *Die Abendschule*'s editors profoundly uncomfortable. Not only does the phrase "warlike game" suggest that the events in sixteenth-century Magdeburg were not of the utmost gravity, but the allusion to cards, which had already been "shuffled and dealt," adds a hint of luck or fate to what conservative Lutherans must have viewed as an obvious example of divine intervention in the course of human history, just as they saw the devil behind those who fought against Magdeburg.[32] That difference is particularly obvious in an assessment of Martin Luther's role in world history (emphasis added):

[31]A long passage explaining her role (W, 600) is simply eliminated and replaced by this explanatory phrase (ellipses and all): ". . . No! Taking advantage of this woman's help could never be acceptable to God; . . ." (p. 293).

[32]To cite another example of luck or fate that was altered by the editor: When the mayor of Magdeburg is able to flee from a disastrous defeat, Raabe explains his success by using the short phrase "as luck would have it" (W, 368), which *Die Abendschule* rendered as "God helped" (p. 132). For a note on the devil's role, see the explanatory footnote added to chapter 10, where readers of *Die Abendschule* are told: "Pay attention to this scoundrel's trick by one of Magdeburg's defenders, which is unfortunately historical, in order to see how horribly the devil and his human followers raged against the pure doctrine in those days!" (p. 162).

Once again an epoch of world history had come to a head in an *individual*, once again the struggle and the work of centuries was concentrated in a *single person*, in a focal point that would ignite the world. (W, 350)

What the constant cry during the thousand-year-long imprisonment of the whole, true church of God had [requested]: Salvation from the unbearable yoke of the Roman Antichrist, had been brought about by the Augustine monk from Wittenberg. *Awakened by God himself*, he had ignited a holy fire that was to set the whole world into bright, shining flames. (p. 99)

Here the two passages are completely different; *Die Abendschule*'s editors simply eliminated Raabe's text and replaced it with a paragraph that was entirely of their own making. As a result, the italics that have been added highlight the marked shift in emphasis rather than the substitution of individual words or phrases. For Raabe, Luther seems to have been no more than an individual actor, albeit an important one, moving about on the vast stage of world history, while for *Die Abendschule* the founder of Lutheranism, or as they put it, "the pure doctrine" (e.g., p. 34), was not so much a man as an agent of God on earth. The epochal task of fomenting and then leading the Reformation was "His"—not Luther's.

Yet, in addition to being the written record of God's active intervention in human affairs, history seems to have possessed another complete and very different layer of truth; it was also a ground or locus of direct recourse to reality. History was therefore important not just for its content but also for the position of power it conferred on those who used it as a basis for their arguments. As the editors' introduction had explained, characters would be changed only "to the extent that they are not historical" (i.e., real) (p. 7). Markus Horn was a complete fabrication; he had only to fit into the circumstances surrounding the siege of Magdeburg, but when Andreas Kritzmann is allowed to narrate his own sad story, *Die Abendschule* adds the following footnote: "Andreas (or Johann, as [the preeminent German historian Leopold von] Ranke calls him) is a historical figure, and what is related about him here has, for the most part, a sound foundation in history" (p. 164). Similarly, in a footnote appended to explain that the devil was behind a defender's treason during the siege of Magdeburg, the magazine's readers are informed: "This scoundrel's trick is unfortunately historical" (p. 162). In essence, the discursive position of history meant that certain elements of any historical fiction were essentially inviolate.

Moreover, as a close reading of these two conflicting accounts of Luther's role in the Reformation makes abundantly clear, the "editor" also seems to have disagreed with more than just Raabe's notion of historical causality. From the point of view of *Die Abendschule* there must also have been something very wrong with the actual historical content of Raabe's novel. After all, in 1550–51 the success or failure of the Reformation as a whole depended on the outcome of the siege of Magdeburg, for if that last bastion of what even Raabe sometimes termed "the pure doctrine" (p. 162) had capitulated—more important, if its presses and the writers assembled around them had fallen silent—things would have looked dark indeed for German Protestants. On the other hand, from the perspective of mid-nineteenth-century Germany, a dozen years after the less-than-auspicious end to the Revolution of 1848, it was certainly possible to reaccentuate that same history in any number of ways. Raabe's choices simply differed from *Die Abendschule*'s, often radically. To be sure, Raabe was anything but consistent in describing the stakes in the conflict over Magdeburg, whereas for *Die Abendschule* there was but a single, central issue—namely, the religious revival associated with Martin Luther. Thus, while Raabe writes of the city holding high "the banner of freedom of thought" (W, 247), *Die Abendschule* changes the phrase to read "the banner of the pure doctrine" (p. 34), and when Raabe refers to the "churches of that great, protesting city" (W, 354), the "revised" version of his narrative speaks of the "churches of the great Lutheran city" (p. 114).

The valorization of Luther's teaching is obvious and certainly not unexpected, but the substitution of "Lutheran" for "protesting" also eliminates another level of meaning. Raabe's original may well refer to the pre-1848 habit of associating Protestantism with "protest" (cf. Georg Herwegh, "As long as I am a Protestant / I'll continue to protest"), which ultimately led to the adoption of the more neutral term "evangelical."[33] In view of the sustained animosity that characterized the relationships between "reformed" and other kinds of Lutherans during the nineteenth century, *Die Abendschule*'s editors certainly might have been sensitive to the difference.

---

[33]Georg Herwegh, "Protest" (1841), *Gedichte und Prosa*, ed. Peter Hasubeck (Stuttgart: Philipp Reclam, 1975), 12. I am indebted to Jeffrey Sammons, who read an earlier version of this section of the text, for the references to Herwegh and 1848.

One could easily find dozens of other examples to document precisely this sort of change, but the point is not merely to list them or even to claim simply that *Die Abendschule* reduced Raabe's more complex version of the events in Magdeburg to a narrative that is both monocausal and, to use Bakhtin's term, monological.[34] For while it is certainly true that the magazine's "editing" did produce an essentially linear account of the triumph of Luther's teachings over the forces of evil—i.e., over Catholicism—the most interesting aspect of the differences is not how Raabe's text was changed but what the overall results of those changes were. Here is the point to return to Smith's notion of the ethnic myth of descent, because the specific elements he identifies in such myths help explain the attractiveness of narratives like *Unseres Herrgotts Kanzlei* to *Die Abendschule*. In essence, Smith's model provides a remarkably plausible answer to the question of why a conservative Lutheran magazine would go through all the trouble of rewriting Raabe's text in the first place.

Smith elaborates his concept of the ethnic myth of descent by identifying six separate submyths, three of which are to be found in Raabe's novel—especially as it was altered to suit *Die Abendschule*.[35] However, although Smith never says so explicitly, largely because his account is so general that it fails to deal with any of the temporal, spatial, or social limits on a myth's validity, there is no reason to believe that every aspect would have to be present in any single text. Indeed, one author could scarcely ever produce the kind of "grand narrative" implicit in the notion of an ethnic myth of descent. Were Smith to analyze a specific text from any of the broad range of times and places that he attempts to cover, he would no doubt see that ethnic myths of descent can exist only at the intersection of various constantly shifting sets of narratives, none of which is ever universally shared. Still, for the purpose of reading *Die Abendschule*'s historical fiction, Smith's model provides me with a useful heuristic device.

Smith begins by positing a myth of temporal and spatial origins, which for German-Americans already opens up a whole array of difficulties. For example, starting to narrate "German" history in the usual fashion—that is, with Hermann and his compatriots in the

---

[34]See Bakhtin's *Problems of Dostoevsky's Poetics*, ed. and trans. Caryl Emerson (Minneapolis: University of Minnesota Press, 1984), 78–85.
[35]See Smith, "National Identity and Myths of Ethnic Descent," 100–105.

Teutoburger Forest—would mean including everyone, Protestants, Catholics, and Free Thinkers alike. Moreover, for *Die Abendschule* the myth of Hermann, along with most everything else in "German" history, is also problematical because it simply cannot account for the specifically "American" component of its readers' experiences. But taking the Reformation as the key event in "German" history solves the problem quite neatly, and the Reformation can also help satisfy both the second and third components of Smith's model, namely, the myth of (contemporary) location and the myth of descent or ancestry. For the readers of *Die Abendschule*, for whom religion invariably constituted an extremely important site of identity formation, location was apt to be a discursive rather than a spatial metaphor. Thus the identification with the inhabitants of Magdeburg, as these sixteenth-century heroes are represented in Raabe's narrative, provided the journal's readers not only with a representation of their spiritual ancestors but also with an image of these readers' own beleaguered status in the religiously diverse society of the United States. The focus on the Reformation meant that any notion of ancestry was not strictly genealogical, for although the readers of *Die Abendschule* actually were in some sense the literal descendants both of the Germanic tribes and of the citizenry of Magdeburg, the more important "relationship" in their lives was the kinship that reading allowed them to form with participants in the religious struggles of the fifteenth and sixteenth centuries. Their symbolic family or community also helped explain the transmission of the values that held them together in their own location in the present.

The fourth element that Smith identifies is the myth of the heroic age, and the "history" of the Reformation, particularly when embodied in figures like Markus Horn, is certainly filled both with heroes and with tales of their exemplary behavior. What the Reformation cannot provide is a myth of decline and decay, nor is it able to do more than hint at the content of a myth of regeneration— except at the level of personal conduct, as *Die Abendschule*'s introduction to *Unseres Herrgotts Kanzlei* explicitly stressed. Again, while it is certainly not necessary for any single text to contain the whole of an ethnic group's myth of descent, one could easily imagine accounts of the subsequent religious history of Germany—say, the history of the Counter-Reformation or of the eighteenth- and nineteenth-century attempts at unifying the various competing Protestant groups in Germany—drawn in the bleak colors of decline and decay. With that sort of trajectory in mind, the Saxon emigration and the founding of the Lutheran Church–Missouri Synod would then be elements in the process of regeneration, connected in a straight line with the church's sixteenth-century founding fathers. In short, *Die Abendschule*'s version of Raabe's narrative makes a great deal of sense when read as part of an ethnic myth of descent. The idea of an ethnic myth of descent locates the reworked version of *Unseres Herrgotts Kanzlei* somewhere beyond the realm of mere entertainment and escape and makes it an integral part of the discourse of German-American identity.

Of course, the case of Raabe's text is particularly interesting because the "editing" process makes the stakes in its slice of the past so wonderfully clear, but *Unseres Herrgotts Kanzlei* was far from the only text to deal with the period of the Reformation. If it were, the claim that the magazine was offering its readers an ethnic myth of descent might be an obvious overinterpretation, but the very same volume of *Die Abendschule* contained a twenty-three-part narrative entitled *Olympia: Lebensbild einer auserwählten Frau aus dem Zeitalter der Reformation* (Olympia: The Life of a Chosen Woman during the Era of the Reformation), written by the same Director Lindemann whose works were at the center of the previous chapter.[36] Another favorite temporal location for the narratives favored by *Die Abendschule* was the Thirty Years' War, when "pure doctrine" was again being defended against the Roman Antichrist. In 1885–86, for example, the magazine published W. Stöber's "Aus stürmischer Zeit: historische Erzählung aus der Zeit des dreissigjährigen Krieges" (In Troubled Times: A Historical Tale from the Era of the Thirty Years' War) in seven episodes (XXXII, nos. 40–46), and volume thirty-seven (1890–91), contained Arnim Stein's sixteen-part novel, *Unter den Fahnen des Schwedenkönigs: Historische Erzählung aus dem dreissigjährigen Krieg* (Under the Banners of the King of Sweden: A Historical Tale from the Era of the Thirty Years' War).[37] In both cases the narratives contain heroes and her-

[36]Like the Raabe narrative, *Olympia* started in the first issue of volume twenty-five (7 September 1878). Lindemann was again identified only as J.C.W., and his text appeared with the bizarre subtitle "Presented, as Praise [the Price, *Preis*] for the Grace of our God, to the Female Readers of *Die Abendschule*."

[37]Although Ward identifies Stein as a German-American, the name was actually a pseudonym used by Hermann Otto Nietschmann (1840–1929). According to *Das Literarische Deutschland*, ed. Adolf Hinrichsen, 2nd ed. (1891), cited in *Deutsches Biographisches Archiv*, 900, Nietschmann was a pastor in Halle. His *Unter den*

oines whose adventures involve a defense of the true faith—that is, they redefine the origins of Protestantism in its last great military struggle against Catholicism. Specific elements of these novels need not concern us here, but it is clear that all these narratives were engaged in the task of elaborating and rearticulating *Die Abendschule*'s specific version of the ethnic myth of descent. The list of similar works of historical fiction could easily be expanded.

The preponderance of historical works among those discussed so far in this section is not meant to suggest that history was the only or even the principal locus of *Die Abendschule*'s ethnic myths. The essentially mythical world of craftsmen and farmers, which was often located nowhere in particular except vaguely in "Germany," and in a temporal space that was clearly past but seldom identifiable or specific, was clearly part of the same, larger German-American narrative. In fact, the ideology of an idealized old middle class provided the one component that was missing from the strictly historical portion of ethnic myths of descent published in *Die Abendschule*: the myth of regeneration. To be sure, the towns and villages in stories like *Ein helles Fenster* (A Brightly Lit Window) (XXVII [1881]), where a Scrooge-like bachelor uncle finally cedes his farm to the hardworking children of his impoverished sister,[38] or *Im Buchenhof* (On Beech Farm), a tale of generational conflict on a rich but somewhat rundown estate,[39] are filled with pious individuals, no doubt selected, as the introduction to *Unseres Herrgotts Kanzlei* had put it, to inspire "our readers with magnificent examples, [and] to strengthen them in their faith" (XXV, 7). But these characters' lives also carry an additional layer of meaning. Their stories represent a prescriptive response to the dangers and dislocations of modernization. To see just what the readers of *Die Abendschule* were supposed to do with their lives, consider the following account, published under the rubric of "Things Various and Sundry," on June 29, 1893:

Fahnen was first published in 1889.

[38]N. Fries, *Ein helles Fenster* 27.18–21 (1–28 January 1881). Nikolaus Fries (1823–94) was a pastor who lived and died in Flensburg; Franz Brümmer, *Deutsches Dichterlexikon*, vol. 1 (1876), describes him as follows: "Fries is an author for the people. In his popular texts he wants to represent the complete reality of human existence, in figures of flesh and blood, and to show how God's spirit triumphs over the spirit of sin" (*Deutsches Bibliographisches Archiv*, 551).

[39]Sophie von Niebelschütz, *Im Buchenhof* 41. 9–12 (11 October–1 November 1894). It is probably significant that this is one of the few texts to appear with the subtitle "An Original Story for *Die Abendschule*."

Princely Craftsmen. At the Prussian court it is an old custom that the princes acquire the skills necessary for some craft. Emperor Wilhelm I, Emperor Frederick, the present Emperor and his brother were all instructed by some master craftsman, a locksmith, a cabinetmaker, a bookbinder, etc., who had been appointed for precisely that purpose. This custom, which the Prussian court has traditionally adhered to very strictly, has at its center an ethical moment, [namely] that manual training has great pedagogical value. Perhaps the intention was also to honor the crafts and their motto: "Craftsmanship has a golden foundation [i.e., a craftman's skills guarantee him a secure income]." On the occasion of the silver anniversary of Prince Ludwig of Bavaria it was reported that the sons of that majestic man had also learned a craft. (XXXIX, 827)

It would be interesting to know just how old this tradition was— whether it was medieval or, what seems more likely, a product of the valorization of the bourgeois individual in the eighteenth century, which certainly would have meant a reinscription and reaccentuation of the values that such training represented, and how the particular crafts were selected. Princes were probably never trained as weavers or tailors, much less as brewers or butchers, although historically these trades were just as honorable as cabinetmaking and bookbinding.

"The ethical moment" in such instruction also merits a brief examination. Most commentators, no doubt in part because they were defending their own positions, thought of the *old* middle class as the moral foundation of the state and its chief bulwark against undesirable change.[40] There is finally something very "German" about these princes' education, a German component that eventually becomes an important component of *Die Abendschule*'s myth of German-American identity. Like the more "American" myth of Horatio Alger, the "German" ideology of the artisan, craftsman, and farmer represents a rejection of corporate capitalism and of large-scale production in factories, but when "Ragged Dick" and his fellow heroes and heroines from the Alger narratives climb from rags to respectability— not, as is commonly believed, to riches—they succeed in, or perhaps on the fringes of, the modern economy. Ragged Dick does not aspire to the trade of locksmith or carpenter; when Dick achieves success, as "Richard Hunter, Esq.," he is engaged as a clerk in his merchant-

[40]See Conze, "Mittelstand," esp. 73–81.

benefactor's counting-room.[41] By way of contrast, as late as the end of 1899, *Die Abendschule* reported, in another filler, this time taken from an employment agency in Chicago, that fifty-two bookkeepers and thirty-six clerks were presently unemployed, while craftsmen were still in demand. Whoever wrote the news release concluded: "The challenge contained here is to convince young men that their prospects of rewarding employment are much better if they learn a craft thoroughly, rather than bustle about behind some counter. Craftsmanship has a golden foundation" (XLVI, 81). The ideology of the old middle class was essentially a narrative of its members' success in spite of, in the face of, and in opposition to the process of modernization.

I do not mean to suggest that *Die Abendschule*'s reports were false or that modernity never intruded into the idyllic world of its ethnic myths. At times there no doubt was a strong demand for the practitioners of various trades—as there still sometimes is—but like the thoroughly modern danger of corporate capitalism that the merchant Drummond represented in *Der Schlosser von Philadelphia*, a "reaper" and a newfangled "potato harvester" are both changes to Beech Farm that the young farmer's parents are unwilling to accept. Eventually, however, they are forced to adapt, and when their grandson's life is on the line they even accede to modern medicine (XLI, 174–75). The point is that in an economic reality in which traditional vocations were increasingly threatened and irrelevant, the narrative affirmation of these premodern lifestyles was part and parcel of the myth of ethnic descent that *Die Abendschule* propagated as a model for its German-American readers. Taken as a whole, these narratives told readers who they were, they reaffirmed the readers' special destiny as a persecuted, yet ultimately victorious people, and they offered them a recipe for continuing their apparently successful accommodation with modernity into the future. In other words, these myths of ethnic descent were more important as the "imaginary" means of dealing with contemporary social, economic, and political difficulties rather than as reflections of some historical reality, however distant. In fact, unlike the mainstream authors who were developing an American "high" literature during the same time period, *Die Abendschule*'s texts made no effort to histori-

---

[41]Horatio Alger, Jr., *Ragged Dick and Struggling Upward*, ed. Carl Bode (1868, 1890; New York: Penguin Books, 1985), esp. 130–32.

cize the discourse of German-American identity.[42] Curiously enough, the past was the one space where neither history nor reality, though always present, ever intruded. In fact, it was precisely this absence of "real" history that made *Die Abendschule*'s version of the past the one place where the endings could all be happy.

It should therefore come as no surprise when Smith claims that ethnic myths tend to emerge in "periods of profound culture clash and accelerated economic and social change."[43] What was the experience of immigration and acculturation—with the latter understood as coming to terms with "American" norms and values, rather than necessarily accepting them—if not a "profound culture clash"? And when were there ever more dislocations in the lives of ordinary men and women than during the process of modernization that began to affect Western civilization so profoundly after 1880? The narratives published in *Die Abendschule* helped readers make sense of the world in which they lived, but the specific content of these narratives did more than provide an outmoded and disoriented middle class with a universally applicable world-view. From week to week and from year to year *Die Abendschule* offered its readers an opportunity to succeed vicariously through the lives of characters who championed the same threatened norms and values that, in spite of their outmoded status, still gave meaning to the readers' own lives. The appeal of such texts lay in the opportunities for identification and orientation, which provided readers with an imaginary space where they could test and reshape their identities or acquire new ones. For readers of *Die Abendschule* ethnicity—taken from all of its multiple, overlapping, contemporary, and historical sources—constituted an important component of who they thought they were.

One could almost stop at this point. Indeed, if there had been a single timeless myth of German-American descent, or even a single constant myth of conservative, German-American, Lutheran descent, the story would be over. Yet not only does the general question of German-American identity demand a multivariant analysis, but even the component parts of the myths that *Die Abendschule* offered its readers varied widely during the latter quarter of the nineteenth cen-

[42]See David W. Noble, *The Eternal Adam and the New World Garden: The Central Myth in the American Novel since 1830* (New York: Grosset and Dunlap, 1968).

[43]Smith, "National Identity and Myths of Ethnic Descent," 118.

tury. What happened was that the position of German-Americans within the oppositions they used to define their identities began to shift drastically at precisely the moment that readers of *Die Abend-schule* were first offered a coherent, well-articulated sense of who they were. The culprits, to judge from the standpoint of the German-American middle class, were working-class radicals and the "new" immigrants from southern and eastern Europe.

To understand the shift in the German-American perspective, we must take into account the altered position of immigrants in the United States in the 1880s and 1890s—that is, the resurgence of nativism and the accompanying demands for restricted entry into the country and for limits on the franchise and on the civil rights of noncitizens.[44] Such sentiments had always bubbled not far below the surface of the American political consensus, managed as it was by an all-white, male, and essentially Eastern elite, but with the arrival of yet another depression in the years 1883–86, which followed imme-diately on the heels of the record immigration of 1882, working-class agitation against immigrants, who were viewed as cheap for-eign competition for "American" jobs, increased dramatically. By the 1880s there was already a considerable history of using the most recent arrivals as strikebreakers; indeed, foreign workers were often recruited for precisely this purpose. In addition, in the eyes of the English-speaking majority, immigrants were associated with urban crime and political corruption. In fact, immigrants did populate the overcrowded tenements of the rapidly expanding, industrial cities, and they sold their votes to the unscrupulous ward bosses who con-trolled the patronage jobs that many of the immigrants relied on. "Corrupt" political machines were often the only effective way for immigrants to deal with bureaucratic difficulties on a personal level. From the perspective of their capitalist employers, however, foreign laborers soon began to seem like a mixed blessing. Not only were "foreigners" prominent in most labor unions, but the number of "radicals"—socialists, communists, anarchists—from abroad was large enough to be fairly conspicuous.

Opposition to foreigners came to a head in May 1886, when someone threw a bomb into the ranks of the policemen who were trying to break up an anarchist demonstration in Chicago. Blame

[44]For much of the information in this paragraph, see John Higham, *Strangers in the Land: Patterns of American Nativism, 1865–1925*, 2nd ed. (1955; New Brunswick, N.J.: Rutgers University Press, 1988), esp. 35–105.

was easily apportioned. For example, the *Chicago Times* declared: "The enemy forces are not American [but] rag-tag and bob-tail cutthroats from the Rhine, the Danube, the Vistula and the Elbe."[45] And in an editorial titled "The Communist Conspiracy" the *Chicago Tribune* offered the following explanation of the tragedy: "These aliens driven out of Germany and Bohemia for treasonable teachings . . . have swarmed over into this country of extreme tolerance and have most flagrantly abused its hospitality."[46] When the authorities were unable to find the actual "bombthrowers," they arrested a number of local anarchist leaders, who were then tried, found guilty, and sentenced to death for nothing more than holding "un-American" beliefs—in those days, a capital offense. Significantly, of the six men eventually executed, five were German immigrants, as was one of the two sentenced to life imprisonment.[47] When three survivors were eventually pardoned in 1893—probably not entirely coincidentally by the German-American governor of Illinois, John Peter Altgeld—yet another firestorm of criticism broke out, but antiforeign agitation had scarcely abated in any case.[48]

It would be easy to see a specifically anti-German component in this hysteria, for as the evidence cited in the previous paragraph clearly suggests, Germans were certainly among the people held responsible for labor unrest and radicalism. Not only were German immigrants, who had often had some experience in the SPD before they emigrated, conspicuous throughout the labor movement,[49] but Germany was also the home of Karl Marx, Friedrich Engels, Wilhelm Weitling, and numerous other prominent socialists. Nevertheless, John Higham, author of the classic history of nativism, argues that in the 1880s "particular targets, such as German anarchists, Irish Catholics, and Slavic contract labor, might receive the brunt of the attack, but in each case the xenophobe interpreted his particular enemy as symbolic of a generalized foreign danger."[50] Higham's

[45]Quoted in Higham, *Strangers*, 54.
[46]*Chicago Tribune*, 6 May 1886, p. 4.
[47]See Foner, ed., *Autobiographies of the Haymarket Martyrs*.
[48]See Theodore Huebener, "John Peter Altgeld: The Forgotten Eagle," *Yearbook of German-American Studies* 18 (1983): 87–90.
[49]See, e.g., Hartmut Keil, "German Working-Class Radicalism in the United States from the 1870s to World War I," in Dirk Hoerder, ed., *"Struggle a Hard Battle": Essays on Working-Class Immigrants* (DeKalb: Northern Illinois University Press, 1986), 71–94.
[50]Higham, *Strangers*, 64.

point is that both antiforeign sentiment and the related phenomenon of Anglo-Saxon racialism pre-dated the so-called "new" immigrants—most prominently, Italians and Russian Jews—who began to be viewed as a problem only in the 1890s. It is nevertheless still easy to imagine how middle-class German-Americans might well have been alarmed at the image conjured up by the adjective "German" when it was linked to the more general category of "foreign" in the English-language press.[51]

In Die Abendschule in the 1880s, there is little direct evidence of any threat posed by "outside (i.e., foreign) agitators" to the readers' identity as "Germans," and that is surprising. The Haymarket Affair, for example, did not merit a single mention in the period 1886–95. In fact, the only explicit mention that I have been able to discover is a long article entitled "The Chicago Anarchist Outrage," which appeared in 1899 for no immediately apparent reason (XLVI, 7–12). The simple if not totally satisfactory explanation for the omission is that in 1880 Die Abendschule's publisher, Louis Lange, began issuing his own twice-weekly newspaper, Die Rundschau: Nachrichten aus der Heimat und Fremde (The Observer: News from the Homeland and Abroad), which was intended to be complementary to the other, not a competitor. The appearance of the new newspaper meant that Die Abendschule ceased carrying its own weekly news summary, but also that Die Rundschau did not print the serialized fiction that was otherwise characteristic of the German-American press. Die Abendschule's subscribers were assured that the newly freed space in their "very welcome guest" would be filled with "other interesting reading material," and they were also offered an opportunity to subscribe to Die Rundschau for half price—50 cents rather than $1.00 a year, or $2.50 annually for both publications (XXVI, 544–45). Presumably, therefore, Die Abendschule's reaction to the events in Chicago was reported in Die Rundschau, but the issues of the newspaper from the 1880s and 1890s are unfortunately no longer extent.[52] Nevertheless, there is a great

[51]As quoted above, two days after the Haymarket bombing the Chicago Tribune referred to the anarchists as "aliens" from "Germany and Bohemia"; immediately following the event it had spoken only of "Anarchists, led by two wiry-whiskered foreigners" (5 May, 1886, p. 1).
[52]According to Arndt and Olson, 1:268, nothing but the first few issues, which I have seen at the Concordia Historical Institute, and a few copies from the 1920s

deal of indirect evidence of the magazine's reaction to the difficulties posed by labor unrest in general, and as we shall see, by the early 1890s *Die Abendschule* was also increasingly troubled by resurgent nativism in the hegemonic culture. Both tensions combined to produce significant ideological precipitates in the narratives published there in the last decade of the nineteenth century.

Die Abendschule had a somewhat schizophrenic view of capitalism, which should not be unexpected. A month and a half after Haymarket, one could read in "From Life—For [Your] Life," a series that dealt regularly with topics of current interest: "Honestly acquired capital is also a gift from God, and, if one has a great deal, enough to be counted in thousands and hundred thousands, it is a large gift from God" (XXXII, 689). Four issues earlier, however, the principal author of the series worried "that an increasing number of people, instead of becoming or remaining independent, are forced for better or for worse—and, oh, so unfortunately, more often for worse—to throw themselves into the arms of big business" (XXXII, 625). In essence, the ideology—or as I would also claim, the continuously rearticulated narrative—of the independent producer put *Die Abendschule* and its readers in the uncomfortably small space between the working class and those who profited, often immoderately and unjustly, from the labor of others.[53] Four articles that concerned themselves with the violent Pullman strike of 1894 illustrate the journal's dilemma quite clearly. The first article calls the strike useless and blames the bloodshed on anarchists and the "socialist sym-

---

survive anywhere. Two things are worth noting about *Die Abendschule*'s introduction of *Die Rundschau*: First, the newspaper was started for almost the identical reason that had led to the founding of the parent journal some twenty-six years earlier: "Every Christian father of a family will, however, admit to us that it is extraordinarily risky to subscribe to a daily or weekly newspaper in addition to *Die Abendschule*. Such papers, which are written and edited by unbelievers, i.e., by men directly or indirectly in the service of Satan, the lord of this world, could fall into the hands of other members of the family and cause unspeakable harm to their souls." Second, the paper's view of the "geography" of world events is interesting: "*Die Rundschau* will pay particular attention to news from abroad, namely, from Germany" (XLVI, 544–45). Thus, by 1880, the United States had become the readers' homeland.

[53]See, e.g., the discussion of the extremely unequal distribution of wealth in the United States in 1890 (XXXVII, 33) or the report on the household expenses of the Astors and Vanderbilts in 1895 (XLI, 469).

pathizing Governor of Illinois" (Altgeld) (XLI, 2). *Die Abendschule* accorded itself an important role in combating the danger:

> The strongest bulwark against subversive forces in the life of a state or a people is the Christian family. It is the cornerstone of society, and its weakening has to result in the collapse of the entire state system. Only the healthy foundation of the Christian family guarantees the future and the prosperous growth of the country. And *Die Abendschule* wants to make its small contribution to preserving Christian family ideals and a satisfying and happy form of family life. (XLI, 3)

A few months later the situation in the company town of Pullman no longer seems to have been quite so clear cut. The other three articles discuss the dependency relationship the Pullman company was able to force onto its employees, which *Die Abendschule* compared unfavorably to the more benevolent paternalism of Friedrich Krupp in Essen and to municipally financed housing in Philadelphia.[54] Along with Christianity, they wrote, "the possession of a hearth and home . . . is the surest defense against the leveling powers of the present day, against the homeless and stateless power of communism" (XLI, 397). At this point, whoever is writing the magazine's commentary, now labeled "From the Present—For the Present," quotes approvingly from an article in the *Illinois Staatszeitung* (Illinois State Newspaper), which denies the contention of the English-language press that "foreign anarchists" are responsible for the current wave of labor unrest, blaming instead "merciless and insatiable exploiters of the workers" (XLI, 469–70).

In addition to having completely reversed the magazine's original apportionment of responsibility for demonstrations, strikes, and their often bloody consequences, the final article on the Pullman unrest mentions another ingredient in the caldron of discontent brewing at most large factories and mines in the United States: the use of "foreign" strikebreakers, in this case Italians and Czechs. Like the rest of the culture, *Die Abendschule* had long since been aware that, by 1890, the character of immigration to the United States was very different from what it had been just a decade earlier, and its editors were quick to see the danger not only to the "American" way of life but also to the position that German-Americans had achieved in their new homeland. In fact, they often linked the two. For *Die*

[54]See XLI, 397–98, 433–34, 469–70.

Abendschule the fate of the United States was closely connected to the maintenance of the ethnic composition that already obtained—a result, of course, of the formerly large numbers of "Germanic" immigrants. The magazine's use of the term "Germanic" is where things first turn curious—and then get curiouser and curiouser. In August 1892, for example, "From the Present—For the Present" contained an account of the previous fiscal year's immigration, which claimed: "It is deplorable that in recent years Slavic immigration has grown far more significantly than Germanic" (XXXIX, 21). It is not particularly surprising that the latter category included both Germans from the Empire (*Reichsdeutschen*) and those from Austria, nor was the author too far off the mark when he added people from Holland, Denmark, Norway, and Sweden. But including the English and Scots in his count stretches the borders of what might be considered "Germanic" to the breaking point. Talk of the "Germanic" peoples also completely reverses the content of what *Die Abendschule* had previously labeled "German." The defining opposition was no longer "German" vs. "American," but "American" (including "German-American") vs. "immigrants of non-German blood" (XLI, 453). And, in a move that is particularly significant, the comparison was based no longer on competing sets of norms and values, but on race—disguised, in the heyday of social Darwinism and eugenics, as "science."[55]

In almost every case it was the Italians who were the preferred object of *Die Abendschule*'s scorn and abuse, and the magazine's images of Italian immigrants echo virtually all the prejudices of their nativist counterparts in the English-language press. Consider the following quotation from an editorial in 1895:

> In the large cities of our land one could tell a tale, and a sad one at that, about how the true sons of the Abruzzi [south-central Italy] live from lesser and grander larceny, and, if they do support themselves honestly, how they crowd together in such filthy neighborhoods that they are a source of constant trouble for the health department.[56] (XLI, 454)

[55] See Higham, *Strangers*, 131–57. *Die Abendschule*'s discussions were often occasioned by proposals for new laws to regulate immigration, and it is interesting to note, for example, that the magazine favored a literacy test, which it reasoned would have little effect on "Germanic" immigration (XXXIX, 22), but opposed a means test that might exclude Scandinavians, Scots, and Germans along with the Slavs and Italians against whom it was presumably aimed (XXXIX, 362).

[56] Interesting in this regard is a column published a year and a half earlier, in which

Not only are the Italians here portrayed as being responsible for crime and urban decay, but *Die Abendschule*'s identification with the United States—"the cities of our land"—has become virtually complete. By the end of the nineteenth century, attacks in the English-language press on the patriotism of German-Americans during the Spanish-American War, apparently provoked in part by some of Kaiser Wilhelm II's typically inappropriate comments, produced a number of testimonials to the contributions made by German-American soldiers ever since the Civil War, and *Die Abendschule* was quick and seemingly proud to point out that "the German-American is a loyal citizen of *our* republic, who is eager to serve" (XLVI, 1, emphasis added).[57] In short, to judge by the expressly political commentary that appeared there, the myth of ethnic identity purveyed by *Die Abendschule* had changed significantly by the end of the nineteenth century—in response to and as a means of dealing with the altered circumstances of German immigrants in the culture as a whole. I therefore propose to conclude this chapter with a brief examination of two narratives published at the turn of the century, one a historical romance and the other a Western, in which the previous version of the myth of German-American identity is drastically rearticulated. I shall also look at the ideological cost of reestablishing the myth's viability.

There are never any abrupt changes. Predictably, the volumes published around the turn of the century contain narratives set in the Reformation and the Thirty Years' War, as well as texts dealing with identifiably "German" heroes from other periods of European history.[58] These volumes are filled with precisely the texts that

---

the otherwise militantly anti-Catholic writers of *Die Abendschule* commented: "Germans, Scandinavians, Scots, and even the Irish are welcome elements who assimilate and become part of the whole—but the sunny sons of the Abruzzi, who are by and large ignorant, dirty, and criminal fellows, are a much less desirable article" (XLV, 225). See also *Die Abendschule*'s review of *How the Other Half Lives*, an account of the life of immigrants in urban tenements written by Jacob Riis, XXXVII, 680–82.

[57]See, e.g., XLV, 581–82, 822–23, and XLVI 163, 594, as well as the extensive accounts of the war itself.

[58]Volume forty-five, for example, contains a novel entitled *Die letzten Mönche von Oybin: Eine historische Erzählung aus der Reformationszeit* (The Last Monks of Oybin: A Historical Tale from the Reformation Era), by Johannes Renatus, and *Ilsalbe: Eine Erzählung aus der Reformationszeit Mecklenburgs* (Ilsalbe: A Tale from Mecklenburg during the Reformation Era), by E. von Maltzan. In addition to

readers must have come to expect from *Die Abendschule*. Concerning the magazine's version of the myth of German-American descent, however, the most important narrative—and at fifty episodes also one of the longest—is a novel that appeared in volume forty-six (1899–1900). Titled *Aethelburga: Eine Erzählung aus der Angelsachsenzeit* (*Aethelburga: A Story of Anglo-Saxon Times*), it was written by William Schmidt, a professor of history and theology in St. Paul, Minnesota.[59] The tale is set in England during the reign of Alfred the Great (871–901), but, lest there be any doubt about who its heros really are, by the second paragraph the narrator has already identified them as "our low-German cousins, the Anglo-Saxons" (p. 4).[60] Similarly, the first character to appear, a young boy named Willibrord, is described as "an authentic, curly-headed low-German," and his people, "the forebears of today's Englishmen," have prospered because they tilled the soil "with German diligence and thoroughness" (p. 4). In addition, the narrator assures us, Alfred's predecessors had had the good sense to unite "all of the German tribes of England under one government" (p. 36). And the Anglo-Saxons were also true to their roots. In Schmidt's narrative, whenever they celebrated "an authentically Germanic spirit of gaiety prevailed," in part because of "the ancient Germans' inherited, and deeply rooted love of song and saga" (p. 54). Elsewhere the text speaks of "the wild, Germanic mania for combat and games" (52), of "ancient Germanic love of truth" (150), of the ancient "loyalty of Germanic males" (197), and, when these eminently Germanic warriors need a drink, they demand "mugs filled with ancient Germanic

---

the texts discussed below, volume forty-six includes an extended biography of Johannes Gutenberg by Arnim Stein (Otto Nietschmann), mentioned above as the author of *Unter den Fahnen des Schwedenkönigs* and an anonymous short story entitled "Friedrich der Grosse und der Kandidat Linsenbart" (Frederick the Great and Candidate Linsenbart).

[59]According to *Who Was Who in America* (Chicago: Marquis, 1968), 1:1089, Schmidt was born in Hermannsburg, Hannover, in 1855, and died in St. Paul in 1931. Schmidt must have emigrated early in the 1870s, because he earned a degree from Capital University in Columbus, Ohio, in 1876.

[60]An English-language version of the novel, *Aethelburga: A Story of Anglo-Saxon Times*, was published in 1923 by Louis Lange Publishing Company in St. Louis, but I translate from *Die Abendschule*'s German version because it is precisely at those junctures where the question of ethnicity can be raised that the English edition differs substantially. For example, rather than speaking of "*our* low-German cousins," the English version refers to "*their* Germanic cousins" (p. 1). Since the quotations from *Aethelburga* are all from volume forty-six, only the page number appears in the text.

mead" (501). In short, Schmidt's Anglo-Saxons, presumably including their descendants in the United States, were "German" through
and through, but in a fashion that produces a number of noteworthy
discursive precipitates.

To begin, *Die Abendschule*'s myth of German-American descent
has now become thoroughly racist. In sharp contrast to the narratives discussed in previous chapters, "German" virtues are no longer
acquired traits, which were available also to the pious members of
other ethnic groups, but rather "inherited." "Deeply rooted" also
carries with it more than a hint of blood and the soil. Of course, the
correspondence between "Germanic" and good is not quite total.
The "Germans'" enemies, the "heathen Danes," are really no less
Germanic. Seen in this light, reading young Willibrord's comment
about their leader as an assessment of the man's racially determined
potential is not all that farfetched: "He is actually a nice fellow, this
Dane, and friendly and good as well. It's just a shame that he's a
robber and a heathen. Who knows what he could otherwise become" (p. 356). In the end, the blond, blue-eyed hero is "German"
enough to convert, and he marries Aethelburga in the bargain. Yet
exceptions and contradictions aside, the important point is that
Schmidt's Anglo-Saxons are part of the same extended "Germanic"
family as the readers of *Die Abendschule*; the location of the text's
enunciation is clearly defined in the phrase "*our* low-German
cousins." When the text then exclaims, "The raging blood of the old
pirates still coursed through the veins of that era's Anglo-Saxons"
(p. 6) and later speaks of "all the German tribes" and "the Germanic peoples" (404), its discourse can no longer be explained away
or excused as merely metaphorical. Yet, what is interesting here is
not so much a comparison with the national-racist (völkisch) ideology that was developing at the same time in Germany,[61] but the
extent to which German-American myths had appropriated a version of Anglo-Saxon racialism favored by the members of the nascent discipline of history,—that is, by precisely those people (virtually all of them white male New Englanders), whose professional
interest was in no small part linked to the definition of a historically
grounded "American" identity.

[61]See, e.g., George L. Mosse, *The Crisis of German Ideology: Intellectual Origins
of the Third Reich* (New York: Grosset and Dunlap, 1964), and, more recent, Jost
Hermand, *Der alte Traum vom neuen Reich: Völkische Utopien und Nationalsozialismus* (Frankfurt/am Main: Athenäum, 1988).

Schmidt's novel articulates and then concretizes the "germ theory" of Teutonic origins developed by Herbert Baxter Adams in the 1880s at Johns Hopkins, a university that was itself modeled on Humboldt's University of Berlin.[62] In its briefest form, Adams' theory, which was accepted as the orthodox explanatory paradigm by a whole generation of American historians up through World War I, claimed that American political institutions originated in the forests of Germany.[63] The Anglo-Saxon invaders had simply transplanted Germanic forms of local government to England, just as their descendants had carried what was otherwise thought of as the English tradition of self-government to North America. Because the "germ" or "seed" of the all-important New England town meeting was inherited, there is obviously more than a trace of biologically oriented racism at work here. Of course, the supposedly Teutonic nature of American institutions meant that "others," most important those from southern and eastern Europe, could never "melt" in, and the theory also reinforced antimodernist, antiurban biases that were so widely shared within the hegemonic culture.

The high point of Schmidt's narrative is a confrontation between two Danish chieftains. Both men claim to have won the right to Aethelburga's person in combat, but the issue is to be decided, more or less democratically, at an assembly of all the warriors in the district. The meeting, as well as the place where they are to meet, is called the "Thing," which Schmidt's narrator explains as follows:

> Even though princes and nobles had in those days already stolen many of the ancient Germanic freedoms for themselves, on particularly important occasions the *Thing* was still convened. . . . Thus one says with complete justification that the civil rights of our day have their origin in the Germanic forests. (p. 391)

[62]For a fuller account, see John Higham, *History* (Englewood Cliffs, N.J.: Prentice-Hall, 1965), esp. 160–61; and Edward N. Saveth, *American Historians and European Immigrants, 1875–1925* (New York: Columbia University Press, 1948), 16–26.

[63]Adams and his supporters were not without their critics. Frederick Jackson Turner, e.g., wrote in his well-known paper "The Significance of the Frontier in American History": "Too exclusive attention has been paid by institutional students to the Germanic origins, too little to the American factors" (*Annual Report of the American Historical Association for the Year 1893*, p. 201). See also Saveth, *American Historians*, 26–31.

Not only is this passage essentially a restatement of Adams' thesis, but, more important, it also relocates German-Americans vis-à-vis the English-speaking majority in the United States. Both Anglo-Saxon virtues and Anglo-Saxon political institutions have become "German." Schmidt, in a sense acting on behalf of the German-American middle class, is claiming the moral and intellectual high ground in the struggle to define what it really means to be "American" and to determine who should be allowed access to that status. By co-opting the elite's own definition of the United States as a social, political, and even biological entity, Schmidt's narrative attempts to situate the Germans in this country on the side of the powerful—with the excluders, rather than the excluded. Given the ongoing debate over immigration policy, the tactic was certainly understandable, but, as will become clear shortly in connection with a discussion of the other major text published by *Die Abendschule* during 1899–1900, Schmidt's strategy, which necessarily involved a thoroughgoing redefinition of German-American identity, is fraught with potentially dangerous consequences.

The appropriation of Anglo-Saxon racialism is certainly not the only instance of intertextuality in Schmidt's narrative. His text also echoes a variety of other debates from the discursive universe in which it was produced. For example, at one point, curiously enough for a "German," he seems to come down on the side of England in that country's dispute with Germany over the size of their respective fleets (pp. 38–39). Somewhat less surprising for *Die Abendschule*, but nevertheless unnecessary and in a text set in medieval England strangely inappropriate, are *Aethelburga*'s frequent anti-Catholic passages. Schmidt also takes up the perennial question of reading, this time in the form of various characters' reactions to a "classic" text from the heathen tradition. At one point a traveling bard appears among the Anglo-Saxons and, after he recites pages and pages of Christian odes—which are, curiously enough, linked both to the Catholic church's refusal to hold religious services in vernacular languages and to the tradition of Christian music that culminated in Luther (pp. 70, 55)—the assembled warriors prevail upon him to perform *Beowulf*. Because the text is deemed inappropriate for women and children, even for heroic women and children, Aethelburga is more or less sent to her room. Actually she ends up visiting her pious grandmother, who reveals that she possesses not only a "Gospel" but also a handwritten copy of the supposedly dangerous poem. The old woman then allows Aethelburga to read the forbidden verses with the following explanation: "This old warriors' song can no longer harm your Christian faith, and I have overcome my own superstitious fear of the heathen saga" (p. 86). Although the opportunity to read such texts is not to be universal ("*no longer harm*"), the text does make at least this one concession to what must have been the actual reading practices of the German-American middle class.

The question of reading also raises the issue of *Aethelburga*'s position in the overall discourse of literature in the United States, for Schmidt's novel is not just another example of historical fiction. It must be located in the tradition of dealing with medieval themes that culminated, among canonical texts, with Mark Twain's *Connecticut Yankee in King Arthur's Court* (1899).[64] Yet, unlike Mark Twain's novel, *Aethelburga* is really neither the vehicle for a critique of contemporary society by means of a comparison with an earlier, purer age, nor in any sense a celebration, however reluctant, of the advances made by civilization in the ensuing centuries. While the political gesture that it makes means that Schmidt's novel is not merely escapist—and none of the texts published in *Die Abendschule* ever were—its reassuring stance ultimately makes it little more than compensatory. Certainly there is none of the ambiguity and tension that can be found between the competing poles of Mark Twain's far darker message.

In many ways the other narrative contained in volume forty-six, *Martin Forster: Eine Erzählung aus dem wilden Westen* (Martin Forster: A Story from the Wild West), by F. J. Pajeken, is a much more ambitious work. Once again the theme is the plight of Germans in the United States, but here the message is anything but comforting.[65] For German-Americans, *Martin Forster* is essentially a

---

[64]See Lears, *No Place of Grace*, 142–81, esp. 164–67. One should perhaps point out here that by the end of the century *Die Abendschule*'s "American" writers were also very different from their "German" counterparts. For example, social conditions in the United States made it impossible to deal with the problem of a declining nobility, which was a major theme for German writers as diverse as Marlitt and Fontane, nor is there anything in *Die Abendschule* that tests the generic conventions of realism as Fontane and Raabe, among others, were doing at the same time.

[65]The 1908 edition of *Deutschlands, Österreich-Ungarns und der Schweiz Gelehrte, Künstler und Schriftsteller in Wort und Bild*, which is reproduced in the *Deutsches Biographisches Archiv*, 928, reports that Friedrich Joachim Pajeken, who was born in Bremen in 1855, "traveled as a businessman to South America. After ending up in the 'Wild West,' he built himself a log cabin high in the Bighorn Mountains. From there he wandered the countryside studying the customs of the Indians, who

story of failure, albeit in the form of a happy ending. The novel opens in 1863, on a wagon train that is under way toward California. Martin Forster, a German boy of fourteen, is about to become an orphan, and his dying father warns him: "Be careful that you don't become a burden on someone. Don't think, as I did, that happiness will find you. That's what the lazy believe. No! Work! Pray! And be true to your God! Then blessings will not fail you" (p. 28). Although another immigrant family offers to adopt him, Martin steals away from the wagon train one night because he knows that the Wollwebers are just as poor as he is. As the reader is told quite explicitly, Peter Wollweber had been forced to emigrate when the family farm proved too small. The combination of changing economic conditions and the mortgage forced on his parents by an older brother who wanted to try his luck in the United States made leaving their beloved German homeland unavoidable. At this point some readers could probably already guess that the long-lost brother would turn up by the end of the novel, but the characters must first endure a long string of misfortunes. Indeed, what the Wollwebers and their Austrian comrade Nägele experience in the United States is unmitigated misery; after they suffer a series of Indian attacks, some Americans rob them before they even reach California. There the Wollwebers are often unemployed and hungry, and they are forced to sell their few remaining possessions to keep body and soul together. Worst of all, Peter Wollweber is incredibly homesick from start to finish.

Meanwhile, Martin's decision to run away while the wagon train was in the middle of nowhere turns out to have been extremely foolish. When he stumbles into a trapper's cabin, the man decides to sell him to some Indians. Martin is little more than a slave until an Indian superstition abruptly changes his fortunes. Instead of using his good fortune to lead the life of a privileged warrior, however, Martin helps two white men escape and is almost killed for his trouble. As luck would have it, the two are from the same group of bandits who robbed his father and the Wollwebers, and they try to trick him into joining their band. Instead Martin warns the merchant they intend to rob and ends up nursing the unfortunate man (later revealed to be Peter Wollwebers' elder brother) back to health while working

---

were then [1879] still warlike." Since all twenty-five episodes of *Martin Forster* are contained in volume forty-six, the quotations in the text will only be identified by page number.

as a blacksmith on a railroad construction site. Yet even here the idyll of master craftsman and apprentice is only temporary. Once the tracks are laid, the community will have to disband as the "free" space of the American West recedes in the face of technological progress.

In a sense, then, Martin fails by succeeding, for unlike the Wollwebers his failure is not the result of a lack of opportunity but, curiously enough, the tragic consequence of having accepted his father's advice. Before every mistake he invokes that memory in the form of the word "progress" (*vorwärts*). To cite but one example, when Martin refuses to rely solely on his skill as a hunter, he explains: "I want to progress, to do something useful in the world. I can certainly only do that by working, which means, first of all, that I have to earn my own bread, and I can't ask if I like it or not" (p. 251). His goal here is what Marxists would term alienated labor, a job in which he has no control over the process of production and no real stake in its results; he is to earn his wages, but at the cost of giving up his personal freedom. Not only can such a job never make him truly happy, but, perhaps not surprisingly, given the novel's overall message, that form of work is also identified as quintessentially "American." Already in the opening chapter Martin's inner conflict is staged as a choice between "German" and "American" values. As uncertain as their own fate might be, the Wollwebers realize that they dare not abandon the young orphan: "We certainly cannot entrust him to our traveling companions? There are a couple of bad characters among them—for example, the Americans Billy Clark and James Morgan. Yes, I believe the two of them are in fact evil" (p. 27). But it is nevertheless the Americans who echo Martin's misbegotten dream: "We want progress. *Time is money!* The Germans apparently don't think so, and they stick together like glue" (p. 27. Emphasis in the original; the italicized words were also originally English, i.e., linked explicitly to their American origin). Even toward the end of the novel, when Martin is finally reunited with the Wollwebers, he still believes in the "American dream": "What I was searching for then, when I ran away from you, was what I have now found: work, wages, and bread" (p. 396). Yet it is only when the two long-lost brothers are finally united that the possibility of a truly happy ending emerges, and Martin, whose adventures have dominated the novel, is suddenly reduced to little more than the unwitting instrument of their accidental reunion.

Of course, the "German" values of family, community, and unalienated production triumph, and in the final paragraph of Pajeken's narrative Martin, the adopted son of the elder Wollweber and husband of the other brother's daughter, is the respected proprietor of a model farm and about to be elected to represent his home district in the local parliament. So far the happy ending is nothing extraordinary for *Die Abendschule*—except for the fact that the final idyllic scene takes place not in the United States, where it was apparently no longer possible, but in Germany! At the elder brother's suggestion they have all reemigrated: "Back to our beloved, precious homeland? Oh, [dear] brother! Brother! Do I dare believe it? Back to the precious plot of ground that was already cultivated by our great grandparents?" (p. 411). The Wollwebers and their young charge have thereby rejected not only "American" values but also the prospect of realizing "German" dreams on American soil. To no small degree, these characters and their individual narratives deny the whole project of German-American identity.

At this point the next task should be to attempt to connect *Martin Forster* with *Aethelburga*, but first two other aspects of Pajeken's representation of "America" merit some comment. They should also help clarify the novel's almost total rejection of what the discourse of "America" must have meant to many of its readers—at least to his German readers, for the following passage, like much of the novel, somehow seems curiously out of place in *Die Abendschule*. Pajeken takes particular pains to discount various novelistic legends about American Indians, specifically those contained in Cooper's *Last of the Mohicans*:[66]

> He remembered the books he once thought had made him familiar with the Indians with a disparaging grin. Where were the noble, selfless, loyal, thankful, brave heroes who were depicted there? The men with whom he was forced to eke out a meager existence possessed none of these virtues; in fact, he had often had the opportunity to observe that the red people [*das rote Volk*] were disgustingly dirty, as well as deceitful, thieving, underhanded, thankless, disloyal, violent, and extremely selfish. (p. 156)

[66]Before Martin finds out that he is to be sold to the Indians, the narrator explains the boy's interest: "With what fascination had he read stories about Indians, and now the heroic figures they contained began to appear before his mind's eye. . . the loyal Mohican Chingachgook, called the Great Snake, or his son Unkas . . . " (p. 124).

As the narrator explains the problem: "The writers who are the first to make Indians into the heroes of their novels were artists (*Dichter*), and they never became thoroughly acquainted with the red people" (p. 331). Pajeken had spent a considerable amount of time in the United States, but Cooper lived his whole life there, so one cannot help but wonder if other authors—say Karl May—were not his real targets. In a more general sense, the destruction of the myth of the noble Indian—and the invective that he heaps on Native Americans amounts to a kind of literary overkill—certainly would have eliminated much of the fascination with the American West that was just beginning to become fashionable among novelists in the United States. In fact, by 1900, the genre of the Western was just barely into its infancy in the United States, although as May demonstrates the chronotope of the American West was already available to German authors.[67]

The other aspect of the discourse of America that *Martin Forster* represents in an extremely critical yet ultimately ambiguous fashion is the treatment of immigrants, specifically the Chinese immigrants, who were brought in to do the dirty work involved in building a transcontinental railroad. In contrast to the rabid attacks directed against Native Americans, the narrator limits his criticism of the Chinese to his perception that "the pig-tailed sons of the heavenly kingdom, who were content to live on rice, depressed wages" (p. 332). As a result, they are regularly mistreated by the "Americans" in the novel, except for one incident when Martin rescues a group of four Chinese laborers from some ruffians, only to see them pack up and leave anyway. And although he repeatedly tries to mend his relationship with the "American" miscreants, Martin barely speaks to the Chinese, who are portrayed as somewhat less than fully human. Unlike the Wollwebers' companion, whose Austrian dialect lends him a certain charm, the one Chinese laborer who does speak can explain the four men's departure only by mumbling ungrammatically, "Not good work here" (p. 347). Not only is this the language of the other—far more negative than the novel's representation of Indians and, for present-day readers, reminiscent of the "reported" speech of German "guest workers" (*Gastarbeiter*)—but it is also not too farfetched to hear the very real echoes of an almost global rejection of "America" in the unfortunate man's "here." Again, the discursive interest is that the reality of the United States—

[67]See Schulte-Sasse, "'Culture' for the Masses," 101–5.

and, in this case a fairly accurate version of that reality—has been brought face to face with the myth of "America," much to the latter's detriment.

As intrinsically interesting as *Martin Forster*'s treatment of Native Americans and of Chinese immigrants is, for the purposes of the present study the important question is what Pajeken's narrative reveals about the discourse of German-American identity. Although I do not intend to argue that volume forty-six of *Die Abendschule* presents a coherent, fully articulated version of the myth of German-American descent, it is true that the two narratives examined here spoke to essentially the same set of fears and aspirations. For example, if *Aethelburga* was to no small degree concerned with proving that Germans were the real source of Anglo-Saxon—that is, "American"—virtues and institutions then what links Schmidt's narrative to *Martin Forster* is the latter's contention that German immigrants were not just the real heroes of the American West but also the only people capable of understanding that absolutely essential ideological space. In short, the "Germans" in these two novels are the only *real* "Americans"; they are both the origin and the sole legitimate embodiment of what "America" stood for. Yet, it is precisely this gesture of seemingly triumphant appropriation that exposes the contradictions and gaps inherent in *Die Abendschule*'s attempt to specify a "German-American" identity at the end of the nineteenth century. In that sense "1871" was not just a memory that the "Germans" in the United States could invoke; it was also the sign of their continued identity crisis.

The chief difficulty was that, in accepting the arguments of Anglo-Saxon racialism and in staking their own claim to "American" history—all the way from its murky English origins to its so recently closed Western frontier—these two texts essentially eliminated every conceivable reason for the continued survival of a separate German-American identity and of a separate German-American culture. *Aethelburga* and *Martin Forster* presented the readers of *Die Abendschule* with someone else's past; the history they chose to represent was no longer exclusively "German." The two texts' rearticulation of the myth of German-American descent is perfectly understandable as a defensive gesture intended to parry both the hegemonic culture's continued attacks on immigrant radicalism and, for want of a better term, the new immigrants' excess of "otherness." However, the new identity that these texts offered *Die Abendschule*'s German-American readers also radically undermined their demands for a special dignity, for cultural autonomy, and for their own distinct identity, which Smith argues is the real point of articulating a myth of ethnic descent in the first place.[68] In effect, the German-American middle class was done in by its own success. By positioning themselves on the side of the powerful, German-Americans had almost completely undercut themselves ideologically. Long before America's entry into World War I made the continued maintenance of an overtly self-confident German-American identity virtually impossible, *Die Abendschule*'s version of German-American identity was already crumbling and hollow.[69]

Moreover, despite the magazine's continued outward success, by 1900 the whole project behind *Die Abendschule* was coming unglued. Throughout the 1890s the magazine had added various special sections and features, each aimed at different segments of its readership. In 1892, for example, subscribers began to receive the biweekly *Beiblatt für Frauen und Mädchen* (Supplement for Women and Girls), which was subsequently retitled *Frauenfleiss* (Woman's Work), no doubt because its pages were filled with the recipes and knitting instructions intended to keep middle-class women busy while the patriarch was gainfully employed and therefore absent from what had become the separate sphere of the home and family.[70] In addition, since 1886, the main body of the magazine contained a regular, one- or two-page section, *Für die Jugend* (For Young People). And by the end of the century, readers who were interested could also turn to pages devoted to male-oriented crafts (*Für die Werkstatt* [For the Workroom]) and medical advice (*Unser Hausarzt* [Our Family Doctor]). Starting in 1899, readers could even get advice on building a house from *Unser Architekt* [Our Architect]). Yet it is precisely in the face of this new richness that questions arise about the original goals of this German family journal published in

[68]See Smith, "National Origin and Myths of Ethnic Descent," 105–7.

[69]In a similar fashion, as Hartmut Keil has argued, the German-American working class had probably already subjected their own "German" identity to the same kind of ethnically destructive rearticulation as early as the 1890s. For German socialists the unity of the working class, particularly at the level of the trade union movement, demanded an end to the separate organizations of German craftsmen and laborers. See Keil, "German Working-Class Radicalism."

[70]The fact that the advertisements for patent medicines, assorted household devices, and church furniture, which had previously been located in a special supplement, apparently because such mundane matters were deemed unsuitable for *Die Abendschule* itself, were now banished to the women's pages also says a good deal about the actual status of women in German-American society.

the United States. By offering something for everyone, *Die Abend-schule* may have won new readers or maintained the otherwise flag-ging loyalty of its regular subscribers, but the magazine could no longer claim to be a force uniting the otherwise disparate members of the family that was still nostalgically portrayed in its masthead. No matter how interesting these new features may have been, few of them were designed to be read aloud, certainly not to young and old alike.[71] So while circulation remained high until 1917, and re-bounded significantly in the 1920s, when judged in terms of layout and orientation, by the turn of the century *Die Abendschule* as a whole was suffering from the same malaise that had crept into the narratives. Undone in large part by its own success, *Die Abend-schule* was little more than the tattered remnant of a dream that had never come true.

Thus, throughout German-American culture, for resolutely practi-cal as well as for vaguely political or ideological reasons, the only acceptable identity had come to be "American"—even if that "American" identity was articulated in the German language. Claiming to be more "American" than the English-speaking major-ity in the United States was kind of a last-ditch attempt to preserve an identity that was rapidly becoming little more than a linguistic curiosity. By 1900, the discourse of German-American identity had simply become an attempt to guarantee the survival of a language, which had neither a supporting culture nor any reason other than nostalgia to justify its continued use. German-Americans no longer possessed the fundamental core of "German" norms and values that would have been necessary to sustain anything like the vision ini-tially put forth by *Die Abendschule*. And although the magazine continued to be published in German, there was no longer anything "German" left in it. The label "German" even disappeared from the magazine's subtitle; after 1881 *Die Abendschule* was no longer "A German Family Journal" but rather "An Illustrated Family Journal." For just as immigration from Germany was drying up, so too was the once vibrant culture of the German-Americans increasingly

---

[71]The announcement of the new section *For Young People* is interesting in this regard: "A family journal also has to pay particular attention to the members of the family who are growing up" (XXXII, 828). The telltale "also" suggests both that the magazine had not previously concerned itself with its younger readers and that the "members who are growing up" constituted a separate interest group. Not only are those implications demonstrably false for the earlier years of *Die Abendschule*, but they would have appalled the journal's founders.

threatened by Americanization. It was in this respect more than prescient pessimism in 1898 when the leaders of 150 German-American organizations warned that the restrictive immigration measures then before the American Congress would hasten the already alarming decline in German-American culture:

> If, in particular, the now comparatively feeble stream of German immigration is completely cut off, then they [the nativists] will succeed in oppressing Germans in this country, and ruin the German element politically and industrially. To the great satisfaction and delight of the English-American press, many a German newspaper, whose competition is a thorn in their flesh, will be forced to the wall. No German church building will then be erected anymore, or conserved; no German school could exist, and the German language will disappear from the public schools.[72]

Of course, the problem also ran far deeper. Although it had never really been possible to establish an idyllic community of "German" craftsmen and farmers in the United States, the impossibility of that dream was painfully obvious by 1900. So it is probably not accidental when *Martin Forster* attempts to retransplant the ideologically open space of the American West to Germany, where by 1900 dislocations in the agrarian sector of the economy were in fact proceeding more slowly than in the United States. Of course, all the other versions of the myth of German-American identity offered to the readers of *Die Abendschule* had also proven themselves untenable in the face of American reality, fundamentally because they were all responding to a contemporary crisis with answers that were rooted in the past, indeed in purposely fanciful reconstructions of the past. This is not to argue that, for a long time, the narratives examined in the course of this study did not actually perform the essential function of helping readers cope with the disorienting new environment in which they found themselves. Nor should the invocation of implacable history be construed as an indictment. Given the resolutely conservative nature of the political stance that underlay *Die Abendschule*'s regressive visions, their failure was anything but tragic. From my perspective, if there was a tragedy it was in the extent to which such myths answered readers' immediate needs and thereby prevented them from changing their lives in a more progressive di-

[72]Quoted in Prescott F. Hall, *Immigration and Its Effects upon the United States* (New York: Henry Holt, 1907), 268. See also Higham, *History*, 107.

rection. Whether they might have done so within the confines of a German-American identity is a question that belongs in the realm of pure speculation. For the purposes of this study, it is enough to note how necessary some form of identity actually was. In other words, had someone wanted to present the "German" population of the United States with an alternative vision, *Die Abendschule*'s decade-long preoccupation with the myth of German-American descent suggests that a purely political program, however logical and persuasive, could never have answered the deeper needs of the magazine's ordinary readers. Unrealizable as it may have been, the dream of community offered up by *Die Abendschule* was nevertheless powerful. For German immigrants, who were often unsure of who they really were, popular narratives were an important means of dealing imaginatively with an otherwise intractable reality.

From "German-Americans" to "Americans (Who Read German)"

The death knell the previous chapter sounded for German-American culture was of course premature. Not only does a considerable proportion of the population of the United States still identify itself as "German," but the German-American institutions that seemed so threatened in 1900, and even more so in 1918, actually enjoyed a kind of renaissance in the 1920s and 1930s. It was, after all, not until December 1940 that *Die Abendschule* finally suspended publication, not, I suspect, because of the impending war but rather because its subscribers, who were no longer being replenished by successive waves of immigration from Germany, were simply dying off. In any case, the magazine had largely fulfilled the task it had set for itself and its readers in the "Prospectus" issued in 1854: "We do not want to be American Germans but rather Americans, German Americans; we do not want something complete and particular for ourselves alone, we want rather to be a particularly noble part of the whole."[1] In fact, it was precisely the magazine's success in defining this "particularly noble part of the whole" that also sowed the seeds of its readers' eventual demise as an identifiable ethnic group—or, at the very least, that prefigured the meager remnants of Germandom that remain with us today. Ultimately there was not enough Germanness left in *Die Abendschule* to provide the next generation of readers with a distinctly "German-American" identity. By 1900, *Die Abendschule*'s representations of "German Americans" consisted of little more than embellishments on roles for people who could otherwise "melt" into the mainstream of middle-class culture

[1]"Prospectus der Illustrirten Abendschule," CHI, A & HL 1052.

in the United States. Once "German-American" had come to denote *the* particularly valuable version of an "American" identity, which was itself defined as not being foreign, there was no longer any reason save nostalgia for maintaining the "German" portion of the identity.

Does this mean that the constitution of ethnic identity through popular narratives was somehow a failure? Hardly. As this study has demonstrated, becoming "German Americans" would have been a difficult undertaking in any circumstances, but acquiring the complex set of narratives that constituted German-American identity in the context of a culture that was itself undergoing profound social, cultural, political, and demographic changes meant that German immigrants were confronted with a constantly shifting set of demands, all of which necessitated different subject positions for the individual readers of *Die Abendschule*. And while the present work has stressed the ethnic component of those readers' identities, it could just as easily have concentrated on the impact of urbanization or, as the first chapter did in part, on evolving gender roles within the German segment of the American population, to name but two examples of the available variables. Yet, as the texts examined above clearly indicate, ethnicity—both its content and its constitution— was an extraordinarily important part of immigrants' lives, one that has unfortunately been overlooked for far too long because of the persistent misreading or, more accurately, nonreading of German-American popular narratives. This study is an attempt to redress the balance. It takes a first step in adding the hopes and aspirations that were represented in the narratives read by German immigrants to the social and political histories of immigration that have already been written.

Because most of the people who emigrated from Germany left under the threat of industrialization and modernization, it is hardly surprising that the idyllic world of craftsmen and farmers was repeatedly thematized in the texts *Die Abendschule* published. But the move to the United States also introduced a number of other tensions into the lives of the particular group of German immigrants that formed the journal's core audience. As conservative Lutherans from Germany, although that country did not yet formally exist, *Die Abendschule*'s readers were initially torn between three conflicting but also always overlapping subject positions: "German," "Lutheran," and "American." To judge by the narratives they read in the 1850s, 1860s, and 1870s, these immigrants were often forced—

or, put more positively, were frequently able—to shift from one identity to another as their circumstances demanded. Although they might have longed for a single, unified subject position, even the echo of German unification that reverberated through the German immigrant population of the United States after 1871 was not strong enough to produce *one* German-American identity. In the context of a society that was itself changing as rapidly as the Germany that the immigrants had left, there was simply too much at stake in any final choice.

By 1880 the emerging triumph of corporate capitalism in the United States must have made it obvious that immigrants would not be able to recreate an untroubled version of the Old World in their new homeland in the present. It is not surprising therefore, that the texts published in *Die Abendschule* were increasingly historical fiction. Not only did the past provide a space where the idyllic and therefore compensatory life of the precapitalist small town could continue, but by gradually articulating an "ethnic myth of origins," history, particularly the history of the Reformation and the religious wars in seventeenth-century Germany, could also offer *Die Abendschule*'s readers the ground on which to constitute and justify their special destiny as German Protestants in the United States. In the process, one of the defining oppositions in their search for an identity shifted from "German" vs. "American" to one particular type of middle-class "German-American" vs. "new immigrants" or even "ethnics," which were pejorative terms for the recent largely working-class arrivals from southern and eastern Europe. As it was represented in *Die Abendschule* during the final two decades of the nineteenth century, "German-American" was no longer oppositional within the framework of the hegemonic culture. In fact, *Die Abendschule* would increasingly take up the Anglo-Saxon elite's defense of its own threatened dominance. In essence, the "German-American" identity that the magazine had struggled to articulate for so long was increasingly being replaced by an American myth with only a few German overtones. In *Die Abendschule*'s version of the past, Germans were the only *real* Americans. Yet having become "a particularly noble part of the whole," there was no longer any compelling reason for German immigrants to be "German." To be sure, among the few remnants that remained was the language, but it too had been stripped of much of its cultural content. While the magazine's readers still read and presumably still spoke German, the German-language texts published in journals like *Die Abendschule* had ceased to provide them with an exclusive framework around which they could construct their identities.

So while the popular literature published in *Die Abendschule* between 1854 and 1900 played an important role in the constitution of various German-American identities, the magazine was never really able to forge the kind of "German" community in "America" that its narrative voices had constantly thematized. In helping German immigrants cope with the dislocations of migration and modernization, *Die Abendschule* had indeed performed a valuable service, but the magazine's nostalgically utopian vision could never have provided a lasting answer to the quest for a "German" identity in the United States. However, the ideal communities represented by master craftsmen and their happy apprentices triumphing in the face of industrial competition and by the village made up of independent farmers do go a long way toward explaining why the costumes and customs of rural Bavaria are now almost universally accepted as symbols of German ethnicity. Stripped of any real content by the relentless pressures of a developing economy, the "German" portion of the identity of those people in the United States who still call themselves Germans or German-Americans has basically been reduced to a few external signs—*Lederhosen, Dirndls*, bratwurst, and beer—that would have struck their Prussian, Westfalian, or Saxon forebears as wildly inappropriate. Certainly, there is little left of the richness and diversity that once characterized "German" culture in the United States. The traditions that remain were, to use Terence Ranger's and Eric Hobsbawm's term, "invented" as part of a much larger response to social and economic change.[2]

Perhaps the decline was inevitable, but it was certainly hastened by the unfortunate choices made in *Die Abendschule*'s version of the German-American myth. Thus if there was a German-American tragedy, it might be characterized as the loss of some of the cultural pluralism that once existed here. If we want to understand and learn from that experience—if we want to know more about the hopes and aspirations of the millions of ordinary people who emigrated to the United States and then lived and died here, to say nothing of the millions of immigrants who are again arriving from the diverse cul-

[2]Hobsbawm and Ranger, *The Invention of Tradition*. See also Stuart Hall, "Notes on Deconstructing the 'Popular,'" in Raphael Samuel, ed., *People's History and Socialist Theory* (London: Routledge and Kegan Paul, 1981), 227–40.

tures of Africa, Asia, and Latin America—then, taking full advantage of the ambiguity available in English punctuation, we ought to turn to the stories they read(,) to find out who they were. For German-Americans, one way to find what they found is to read journals like *Die Abendschule.*

Bibliography

Albares, Richard P. "The Structural Ambivalence of German Ethnicity in Chicago." Ph.D. Diss., University of Chicago, 1981.

Alger, Horatio Jr. *Ragged Dick and Struggling Upward.* New York: Penguin, 1986 (1868 and 1890, respectively).

Allen, James Smith. "History and the Novel: Mentalité in Modern Popular Fiction." *History and Theory* 22.3 (1983): 233–52.

Althusser, Louis. *Lenin and Philosophy and Other Essays.* Trans. Ben Brewster. New York: Monthly Review Press, 1971.

Anderson, Benedict. *Imagined Communities: Reflections on the Origin and Spread of Nationalism.* London: Verso, 1983.

Arndt, Karl J. *German-American Newspapers and Periodicals, 1735–1955.* Heidelberg: Quelle and Meyer, 1961.

Arndt, Karl J., and May E. Olson, eds. *The German-Language Press of the Americas.* New York: K. G. Sauer, 1980.

Bakhtin, M. M. *The Dialogic Imagination: Four Essays.* Trans. Caryl Emerson and Michael Holquist. Austin: University of Texas Press, 1981.

———. *Problems of Dostoevsky's Poetics.* Ed. and trans. Caryl Emerson. Theory and History of Literature 8. Minneapolis: University of Minnesota Press, 1984.

Barth, Dieter. "Das Daheim und sein Verleger August Klasing: Eine kultur- und zeitgeschichtliche Untersuchung über ein deutsches Familienblatt des XIX. Jahrhunderts." *Jahresbericht des Historischen Vereins für die Grafschaft Ravensburg* 66 (1968–69): 43–111.

———. "Das Familienblatt—Ein Phänomen der Unterhaltungspresse des 19. Jahrhunderts: Beispiele zur Gründungs- und Verlagsgeschichte." *Archiv für Geschichte des Buchwesens* 15 (1975): cols. 122–315.

———. *Zeitschrift für Alle: Das Familienblatt im 19. Jahrhundert: Ein sozialhistorischer Beitrag zur Massenpresse in Deutschland.* Arbeiten aus dem Institut für Publizistik, 10. Münster, 1974.

Benjamin, Walter. *Illuminations.* Ed. Hannah Arendt. Trans. Harry Zohn. New York: Shocken Books, 1969.

Bennett, Tony, and Joan Wollacott. *Bond and Beyond: The Political Career of a Popular Hero.* New York: Methuen, 1987.

Bergquist, James. "The German-American Press." In *The Ethnic Press in the United States: A Historical Analysis and Handbook*, ed. Sally M. Miller, 131–59. Westport, Conn.: Greenwood Press, 1987.

Berman, Russell A. *The Rise of the Modern German Novel: Crisis and Charisma.* Cambridge: Harvard University Press, 1986.

Bishoff, Robert. "German-American Literature." In *Ethnic Perspectives in American Literature: Selected Essays on the European Contribution*, ed. Robert J. Di Pietro and Edward Ifkovic, 43–64. New York: Modern Language Association, 1983.

Blackbourn, David, and Goeff Eley. *The Peculiarities of German History: Bourgeois Society and Politics in Nineteenth-Century Germany.* Oxford: Oxford University Press, 1984.

Bodner, John. *The Transplanted: A History of Immigrants in Urban America.* Bloomington: Indiana University Press, 1985.

Boelhower, William. *Immigrant Autobiography in the United States (Four Versions of the Italian American Self).* Verona, Italy: Essedue edizioni, 1982.

———. "The Immigrant Novel as Genre." *MELUS* 8 (Spring 1981): 3–13.

———. *Through a Glass Darkly: Ethnic Semiosis in American Literature.* New York: Oxford University Press, 1987.

Börnstein, Heinrich. *Fünfundsiebzig Jahre in der Alten und Neuen Welt: Memoiren eines Unbedeutenden.* Ed. Patricia A. Herminghouse. 1881. Reprint. Bern: Peter Lang, 1984.

———. *Die Geheimnisse von St. Louis oder Die Raben des Westens.* 1851. Reprint. St. Louis: G. Witters Buchhandlung, 1874.

———, ed. *Haus-Bibliothek des Anzeiger des Westens.* St. Louis: Office des Anzeigers des Westens, 1855ff.

Brewster, Philip James. "Wilhelm Raabes historische Fiktion im Kontext: Beitrag zur Rekonstruktion der Gattungsproblematik zwischen Geschichtsschreibung und Poesie im 19. Jahrhundert." Ph.D. Diss., Cornell University, 1983.

Brooks, Peter. *Reading for the Plot: Design and Intention in Narrative.* New York: Vintage, 1984.

Burbank, David T. *Reign of the Rabble: The St. Louis General Strike of 1877.* New York: Augustus M. Kelly, 1966.

Bürger, Christa, et al., eds. *Zur Dichotomisierung von hoher und niederer Literatur.* Frankfurt am Main: Suhrkamp, 1982.

Cawelti, John F. *Adventure, Mystery, and Romance: Formula Stories as Art and Popular Culture.* Chicago: University of Chicago Press, 1976.

Certeau, Michel de. "On the Oppositional Practices of Everyday Life." *Social Text* 3 (Fall 1980): 3–43.

Chambers, Ross. *Story and Situation: Narrative Seduction and the Power of Fiction.* Theory and History of Literature 12. Minneapolis: University of Minnesota Press, 1984.

Chametzsky, Jules. "Some Notes on Immigration, Ethnicity, Acculturation." *MELUS* 11 (Spring 1984): 45–51.

Cohn, Jan. *Creating America: George Horace Lorimer and "The Saturday Evening Post."* Pittsburgh: University of Pittsburgh Press, 1989.

Condoyannis, George. "German-American Prose Fiction from 1850–1914." Ph.D. Diss., Columbia University, 1953.

——. "German-American Prose Fiction: Synopsis of Works." *German-American Studies* 4 (1971): 1–126.

Conze, Werner. "Mittelstand." In *Geschichtliche Grundbegriffe: Historisches Lexikon zur politisch-sozialen Sprache in Deutschland,* ed. Otto Brunner, Werner Conze, and Reinhart Koselleck, 4:49–92. Stuttgart: Klett-Cotta, 1978.

Conzen, Kathleen Neils. "German-Americans and the Invention of Ethnicity." In *America and the Germans,* ed. Frank Trommler and Joseph McVeigh, 1:131–47. Philadelphia: University of Pennsylvania Press, 1985.

——. "Historical Approaches to the Study of Rural Ethnic Communities." In *Ethnicity on the Great Plains,* ed. Frederick Luebke, 1–18. Lincoln: University of Nebraska Press, 1980.

——. *Immigrant Milwaukee, 1836–1860. Accommodation and Community in a Frontier City.* Cambridge: Harvard University Press, 1976.

Davis, Lennard J. *Resisting Novels: Ideology and Fiction.* New York: Methuen, 1987.

Deleuze, Gilles, and Félix Guattari. *Kafka: Toward a Minor Literature.* Trans. Dana Polan. Theory and History of Literature 30. Minneapolis: University of Minnesota Press, 1986.

Denkler, Horst. "Die Schule des Kapitalismus: Reinhold Solgers deutsch-amerikanisches 'Seitenstück' zu Gustav Freytags 'Soll und Haben.'" In *Amerika in der deutschen Literatur: Neue Welt—Nordamerika—USA,* ed. Sigrid Bauschinger, et al., 108–23. Stuttgart: Reclam, 1975.

Denning, Michael. *Mechanic Accents: Dime Novels and Working-Class Culture in America.* London: Verso, 1987.

Detjen, David W. *The Germans in Missouri, 1900–1918: Prohibition, Neutrality, Assimilation.* Columbia: University of Missouri Press, 1984.

Dirlik, Arif. "Culturalism as Hegemonic Ideology and Liberating Practice." *Cultural Critique* 6 (Spring 1987): 13–50.

Dobbert, Guido A. *The Disintegration of an Immigrant Community: The Cincinnati Germans, 1870–1920.* New York: Arno Press, 1980.

——. "German-Americans between New and Old Fatherland, 1870–1914." *American Quarterly* 19 (Winter 1967): 663–80.

Dobert, Eitel Wolf. *Deutsche Demokraten in Amerika: Die Achtundvierziger und ihre Schriften.* Göttingen: Vandenhoeck and Ruprecht, 1958.

Doerries, Reinhard R. "The Americanizing of the German Immigrant: A Chapter from U. S. Social History." *Amerikastudien* 23.1 (1978): 51–59.

——. "Church and Faith on the Great Plains Frontier: Acculturation Problems of German-Americans." *Amerikastudien* 24.2 (1979): 275–87.

——. "Immigrant Culture and Religion: Church and Faith among German-Americans." In *Germans in America: Retrospect and Prospect,* ed. Randall M. Miller. Philadelphia: German Society of Pennsylvania, 1984.

——. *Iren und Deutsche in der Neuen Welt: Akkulturationsprozesse in der amerikanischen Gesellschaft im späten neunzehnten Jahrhundert. Vierteljahrsschrift für Sozial- und Wirtschaftsgeschichte,* suppl. 76. Stuttgart: Franz Steiner, 1986.

Donaldson, Ronald Paul. "Robert Reitzel (1849–98) and his German-American Periodical *Der arme Teufel.*" Ph.D. Diss., Johns Hopkins University, 1976.

Dorpalen, Andreas. "The German Element and the Issues of the Civil War." *Mississippi Valley Historical Review* 29 (June 1942): 55–76.

Draeger, Hartmut. "Vom Kulturasketismus zum geistlichen Biedermeier: Protestantisch-konservative Literaturkritik im preussischen Vormärz." D. Phil. Diss., Freie Universität, Berlin, 1981.

Eco, Umberto. *The Role of the Reader: Explorations in the Semiotics of Texts.* Bloomington: Indiana University Press, 1979.

Engelsing, Rolf. *Analphabetentum und Lektüre: Zur Sozialgeschichte des Lesens in Deutschland zwischen feudaler und industrieller Gesellschaft.* Stuttgart: Metzler, 1973.

——. "Die Perioden der Lesergeschichte in der Neuzeit: Das statistische Ausmass und die soziokulturelle Bedeutung der Lektüre." *Archiv für Geschichte des Buchwesens* 10 (1970): cols. 945–1002.

Evans, Richard J. *In Hitler's Shadow: West German Historians and the Attempt to Escape from the Nazi Past.* New York: Pantheon, 1989.

——. *Rethinking German History: Nineteenth-Century Germany and the Origins of the Third Reich.* London: Unwin Hyman, 1987.

Faust, Albert B. *The German Element in the United States with Special Reference to Its Political, Moral, Social, and Educational Influence.* Boston: Houghton Mifflin, 1909.

——. "Non-English Writings I: German." In *The Cambridge History of American Literature,* ed. William Trent, 5:572–90. New York: Putnam, 1914.

Fischer, Fritz. "Der deutsche Protestantismus und die Politik im 19. Jahrhundert." *Historische Zeitschrift* 171.3 (1951): 473–518.

Foner, Philip S., ed. *The Autobiographies of the Haymarket Martyrs.* New York: Humanities Press, 1969.

——. *The Great Labor Uprising of 1877.* New York: Monad Press, 1977.

Forster, William O. *Zion on the Mississippi: The Settlement of the Saxon Lutherans in Missouri, 1839–1841.* St. Louis: Concordia Publishing House, 1953.

Freund, Elizabeth. *The Return of the Reader: Reader-Response Criticism.* New York: Methuen, 1987.

Fullerton, Robert. "Creating a Mass Book Market in Germany: The Story of the 'Colporteur Novel,' 1870–1890." *Journal of Social History* 10 (Fall 1976): 265–83.

——. "Toward a Commercial Popular Culture in Germany: The Development of Pamphlet Fiction, 1871–1914." *Journal of Social History* 12 (Summer 1979): 489–511.

Gillhoff, Johannes. *Jürnjakob Swehn der Amerikafahrer.* 1917. Reprint. Munich: DTV, 1978.

Glazer, Nathan, and Daniel Patrick Moynihan. *Beyond the Melting Pot: The Negroes, Puerto Ricans, Jews, Italians, and Irish of New York City.* Cambridge: MIT Press, 1963.

Gleason, Philip. "American Identity and Americanization." In *Concepts of Ethnicity,* ed. William Peterson, et al., 57–143. Cambridge: Harvard University Press, 1982.

Grimminger, Rolf, ed. *Hansers Sozialgeschichte der deutschen Literatur,* vol. 3: *Deutsche Aufklärung bis zur Französischen Revolution, 1680–1789.* Munich: Hanser, 1980.

Gruppe, Heidemarie. *"Volk" zwischen Politik und Idylle in der Gartenlaube, 1853–1914.* Bern: Peter Lang, 1976.

Hammer, Carl Jr. "A Glance at Three Centuries of German-American Writing." In *Ethnic Literatures since 1776: The Many Voices of America,* ed. Wolodymyr T. Zyla and Wendel M. Aycock. Proceedings of the Comparative Literature Symposium, No. 9. 1976, Part 1, 217–32. Lubbock: Texas Tech University Press, 1978.

Hampton, Margaret. "The *Wächter am Erie*: A Study of the Newspaper for the Years 1852–1853 and 1860–1864." Ph.D. Diss., Case Western Reserve, 1978.

Handlin, Oscar. *The Uprooted: The Epic Story of the Great Migrations That Made the American People.* 1951. Reprint. Boston: Little, Brown, 1973.

Hanson, Marcus Lee. "The Third Generation in America." *Commentary* 14 (November 1952): 492–500.

Häntzschel, Günter. "Lyrik-Vermittlung in Familienblättern am Beispiel der 'Gartenlaube' 1885 bis 1895." *Literaturwissenschaftliches Jahrbuch,* n.f. 22 (1981): 155–85.

Hausen, Karen. "Die Polarisierung der 'Geschlechtscharaktere': Eine Spiegelung der Dissoziation von Erwerbs- und Familienleben." In *Sozialgeschichte der Familie in der Neuzeit: Neue Forschung,* ed. Werner Conze, 363–93. Stuttgart: Klett, 1976.

Hawgood, John A. *The Tragedy of German America: The Germans in the United States of America during the Nineteenth Century and After.* New York: Putnam, 1940.

Helbich, Wolfgang, ed. *"Amerika ist ein freies Land . . ." Auswanderer schreiben nach Deutschland.* Darmstadt: Luchterhand, 1985.

Helbich, Wolfgang, Walter D. Kamphoefner, and Ulrike Sommer, eds. *Briefe aus Amerika: Deutsche Auswanderer schreiben aus der Neuen Welt.* Munich: Beck, 1988.

Hering, Christoph. "Otto Ruppius, der Amerikafahrer, Flüchtling, Exilschriftsteller, Rückwanderer." In *Amerika in der deutschen Literatur: Neue Welt—Nordamerika—USA,* ed. Sigrid Bauschinger, et al., 124–34. Stuttgart: Reclam, 1975.

Hermand, Jost. *Der alte Traum vom neuen Reich: Völkische Utopien und Nationalsozialismus.* Frankfurt am Main: Athenäum, 1988.

Herminghouse, Patricia. "German-American Studies in a New Vein: Resources and Possibilities." *Die Unterrichtspraxis* 9 (1976): 3–14.

Higham, John. *History*. Englewood Cliffs, N.J.: Prentice-Hall, 1965.
———. *Strangers in the Land: Patterns of American Nativism, 1865–1925*. 1955. Reprint. New Brunswick, N.J.: Rutgers University Press, 1988.
Hobsbawm, E. J. *The Age of Capital, 1848–1875*. New York: Scribner's, 1975.
Hobsbawm, E. J., and Terence Ranger, eds. *The Invention of Tradition*. Cambridge: Cambridge University Press, 1983.
Hoerder, Dirk, ed. *"Struggle a Hard Battle": Essays on Working-Class Immigrants*. DeKalb: Northern Illinois University Press, 1986.
Hofacker, Erich P. *German Literature as Reflected in the German-Language Press of St. Louis Prior to 1898*. St. Louis: Washington University, 1946.
Holub, Robert C. *Reception Theory: A Critical Introduction*. New York: Methuen, 1984.
Horkheimer, Max, and Theodor W. Adorno. *Dialectic of Enlightenment*. Trans. John Cumming. New York: Continuum, 1972.
Horovitz, Ruth. *Vom Roman des Jungen Deutschland zum Roman der Gartenlaube: Ein Beitrag zur Geschichte des deutschen Liberalismus*. Breslau: M. und H. Marcus, 1937.
Howe, Daniel Walker, ed. *Victorian America*. Philadelphia: University of Pennsylvania Press, 1976.
Huebener, Theodore. "John Peter Altgeld: The Forgotten Eagle." *Yearbook of German-American Studies* 18 (1983): 87–90.
Iser, Wolfgang. *The Act of Reading: A Theory of Aesthetic Response*. Baltimore: Johns Hopkins University Press, 1978.
———. *The Implied Reader: Patterns of Communication in Prose Fiction from Bunyan to Beckett*. Baltimore: Johns Hopkins University Press, 1974.
Jameson, Fredric. "Ideology, Narrative Analysis, and Popular Culture." *Theory and History* 4 (Winter 1977): 543–59.
———. "Magical Narratives: Romance as Genre." *New Literary History* 7 (Autumn 1975): 135–63.
———. "Reification and Utopia in Mass Culture." *Social Text* 1 (1979): 130–48.
JanMohamed, Abdul R., and David Lloyd. "Minority Discourse—What Is to Be Done?" *Cultural Critique* 7 (Winter 1987): 5–17.
Jockers, Ernst. "Deutschamerikanische Dichtung." *Der Auslandsdeutsche* 12 (1929): 321–26.
Joeres, Ruth-Ellen, and Annette Kuhn, eds. *Frauenbilder und Frauenwirklichkeit*. Düsseldorf: Schwann, 1985.
Joeres, Ruth-Ellen, and Mary Jo Maynes, eds. *German Women in the Eighteenth and Nineteenth Centuries: A Social and Literary History*. Bloomington: Indiana University Press, 1986.
Johnson, Hildegard Binder. "The Election of 1860 and the Germans in Minnesota." *Minnesota History* 28 (March 1947): 20–36.
Jones, Maldwyn Allen. *American Immigration*. Chicago: University of Chicago Press, 1960.
Kamphoefner, Walter. "Transplanted Westfalians: Persistence and Transformation of Socioeconomic and Cultural Patterns in the Northwest German Migration to Missouri." Ph.D. Diss., University of Missouri, 1978.

Kappeler, Susanne. *The Pornography of Representation*. Minneapolis: University of Minnesota Press, 1986.

Keil, Hartmut, ed. *German Workers' Culture in the United States, 1850 to 1920*. Washington: Smithsonian Institution Press, 1988.

Keil, Hartmut, and Heinz Ickstadt. "Elemente einer deutschen Arbeiterkultur in Chicago zwischen 1880 und 1890." *Geschichte und Gesellschaft* 5 (1979): 103–24.

Keil, Hartmut, and John B. Jentz, eds. *German Workers in Industrial Chicago, 1850–1910: A Comparative Perspective*. DeKalb: Northern Illinois University Press, 1983.

Kelley, Mary. "The Sentimentalists: Promise and Betrayal in the Home." *Signs* 4 (Spring 1979): 434–46.

Kellner, George K. "The German Element on the Urban Frontier: St. Louis Germans, 1830–1869." Ph.D. Diss., University of Missouri, 1973.

Keyl, Theo. S. "The Life and Activities of Pastor Stephanus Keyl: The First Immigrant Missionary of the Missouri Synod, 27 June 1838–15 December 1905." *Concordia Historical Institute Quarterly* 22 (July 1949): 65–77.

Kienzle, Michael. *Der Erfolgsroman: Zur Kritik seiner poetischen Ökonomie bei Gustav Freytag und Eugenie Marlitt*. Stuttgart: Metzler, 1975.

Klein, Karl Kurt. "Auslandsdeutsches Schrifttum." In *Reallexikon der deutschen Literaturgeschichte*, ed. Paul Merker and W. Stamler, 4 Berlin: DeGruyter, 1931.

Klemm, Frederick A. "Four German-American Novelists of New World Adventure." *American-German Review* 7 (August 1941): 26–29.

Knoche, Carl Heinz. *The German Immigrant Press in Milwaukee*. New York: Arno Press, 1980.

Kocka, Jürgen, ed. *Bürgertum im 19. Jahrhundert: Deutschland im europäischen Vergleich*. 3 vols. Munich: DTV, 1988.

———, ed. *Bürger und Bürgerlichkeit im 19. Jahrhundert*. Göttingen: Vandenhoeck and Ruprecht, 1987.

Kocka, Jürgen, and Thomas Nipperdey, eds. *Theorie und Erzählung in der Geschichte*. Theorie der Geschichte 3. Munich: DTV, 1979.

Köllmann, Wolfgang, and Peter Marschalk, eds. *Bevölkerungsgeschichte*. Cologne: Kiepenheuer und Witsch, 1972.

Kraul, Margret. *Das deutsche Gymnasium, 1780–1980*. Frankfurt am Main: Suhrkamp, 1984.

Kreidke, Peter, Hans Medick, and Jürgen Schlumbohm. *Industrialization before Industrialization: Rural Industry in the Genesis of Capitalism*. Trans. Beate Schempp. Cambridge: Cambridge University Press, 1981.

Kulas, John. "*Der Wanderer* of St. Paul: An Overview of the First Years." In *A Heritage Fulfilled: German-Americans*, ed. Clarence A. Glasrud, 64–93. Moorhead, Minn.: Concordia College, 1984.

Kurth-Voigt, Lieselotte E., and William H. McClain. "Louise Mühlbach's Historical Novels: The American Reception." *Internationales Archiv für Sozialgeschichte der deutschen Literatur* 6 (1981): 52–77.

LaCapra, Dominick. *History and Criticism*. Ithaca, N.Y.: Cornell University Press, 1985.

——. *Rethinking Intellectual History: Texts, Contexts, Language.* Ithaca, N.Y.: Cornell University Press, 1983.

Lang, Barbara. *The Process of Immigration in German-American Literature from 1850 to 1900.* Munich: Fink, 1988.

Laplanche, J., and J.-B. Pontalis. *The Language of Psychoanalysis.* Trans. Donald Nicholson-Smith. New York: Norton, 1973.

Lears, Jackson. *No Place of Grace: Antimodernism and the Transformation of American Culture, 1880–1920.* New York: Pantheon, 1981.

Luebke, Frederick C. *Immigrants and Politics: Germans of Nebraska, 1880–1900.* Lincoln: University of Nebraska Press, 1969.

Lukács, Georg. *The Historical Novel.* Trans. Hannah and Stanley Mitchell. Lincoln: University of Nebraska Press, 1983.

Lundgreen, Peter. "Analyse preussischer Schulbücher als Zugang zum Thema 'Schulbildung und Industrialisierung.'" *International Review of Social History* 15 (1970): 85–121.

Marschalk, Peter. *Deutsche Überseewanderung im 19. Jahrhundert.* Stuttgart: Ernst Klett Verlag, 1973.

Marsden, George M. *Fundamentalism and American Culture: The Shaping of Twentieth-Century Evangelicalism, 1870–1925.* New York: Oxford University Press, 1980.

Maurer, Heinrich H. "The Fellowship Law of a Fundamentalist Group: The Missouri Synod." *American Journal of Sociology* 31 (July 1925): 39–57.

Mayer, Arno J. *The Persistence of the Old Regime: Europe to the Great War.* New York: Pantheon, 1981.

Maynes, Mary Jo. *Schooling in Western Europe: A Social History.* Albany: State University of New York Press, 1985.

McCormick, E. Allen, ed. *Germans in America: Aspects of German-American Relations in the Nineteenth Century.* New York: Brooklyn College Press, 1983.

Merrill, Peter C. "Recent Doctoral Dissertations in German-American Studies." *Society for German-American Studies Newsletter* 8 (March 1987): 6.

——. "The Serial Novel in the German-American Press of the Nineteenth Century." *German-American Studies* 12 (Winter 1978): 16–22.

Meyer, Carl S. *Moving Frontiers: Readings in the History of the Lutheran Church–Missouri Synod.* St. Louis: Concordia Publishing House, 1964.

Miller, Edmund E. "Das New Yorker Belletristische Journal, 1851–1911." *American-German Review* 8.2 (1941): 24–27.

Miller, Wayne Charles. "Toward a New Literary History of the United States." *MELUS* 11 (Spring 1984): 5–25.

Mitterauer, Michael, and Reinhard Sieder. *Vom Patriarchat zur Partnerschaft: Zum Strukturwandel der Familie.* Munich: Beck, 1984.

Modleski, Tania. *Loving with a Vengeance: Mass-Produced Fantasies for Women.* New York: Methuen, 1982.

Moi, Toril. *Sexual/Textual Politics: Feminist Literary Theory.* London: Methuen, 1985.

Möller, Horst. *Vernunft und Kritik: Deutsche Aufklärung im 17. und 18. Jahrhundert*. Frankfurt am Main: Suhrkamp, 1986.

Mosse, George L. *The Crisis of German Ideology: Intellectual Origins of the Third Reich*. New York: Grosset and Dunlap, 1964.

——. "Was die Deutschen wirklich lasen: Marlitt, May, Ganghofer." In *Popularität und Trivialität*, ed. Reinhold Grimm and Jost Hermand, 101–20. Frankfurt am Main: Athenäum, 1974.

Müller-Salget, Klaus. *Erzählungen für das Volk: Evangelische Pfarrer als Volksschriftsteller im Deutschland des 19. Jahrhunderts*. Berlin: Erich Schmidt, 1984.

Naumann, Manfred, et. al. *Gesellschaft—Literatur—Lesen: Literaturrezeption in theoretischer Sicht*. Berlin: Aufbau-Verlag, 1976.

Noble, David W. *The Eternal Adam and the New World Garden: The Central Myth in the American Culture since 1830*. New York: Grosset and Dunlap, 1968.

Nollendorfs, Valters. "History of Teaching German in America." *Monatshefte* 79 (Fall 1987): 289–91.

Novak, Michael. *The Rise of the Unmeltable Ethnics: Politics and Culture in the Seventies*. New York: Macmillan, 1975.

Olson, Sister Audrey Louise. "The Nature of an Immigrant Community: St. Louis Germans, 1850–1920." *Missouri Historical Review* 64 (1971): 342–59.

——. "St. Louis Germans, 1850–1920: The Nature of an Immigrant Community and Its Relation to the Assimilation Process." Ph.D. Diss., University of Kansas, 1970.

Ostendorf, Berndt, ed. *Amerikanische Ghettoliteratur: Zur Literatur ethnischer, marginaler und unterdrückter Gruppen in Amerika*. Darmstadt: Wissenschaftliche Buchgesellschaft, 1983.

——. "Literary Acculturation: What Makes Ethnic Literature 'Ethnic.'" In *Le facteur ethnique aux Etats-Unis et au Canada*, ed. Monique Lecomte and Claudine Thomas, 149–61. Lille: Université de Lille, 1983.

Park, Robert E. *The Immigrant Press and Its Control*. New York: Harper, 1922.

Peterson, Brent O. "The 'Political' and the German-American Press." *Yearbook of German-American Studies* 23 (1988): 41–48.

Plax, Martin. "Towards a Redefinition of Ethnic Politics." *Ethnicity* 3 (1976): 19–33.

Pochmann, Henry A. "The Mingling of Tongues." *Literary History of the United States*, ed. Robert E. Spiller, 676–93. New York: Macmillan, 1948.

Poore, Carol J. *German-American Socialist Literature, 1865–1900*. Bern: Peter Lang, 1982.

Prüssmann, Hartwig. "Deutsche Immigranten in Missouri von Gottfried Duden zu Heinrich Börnstein, 1830–1860." Master's thesis, Washington University, 1983.

Radhakrishnan, R. "Ethnic Identity and Post-Structuralist Differance." *Cultural Critique* 6 (Spring 1987): 199–220.

Radway, Janice A. *Reading the Romance: Women, Patriarchy, and Popular Literature*. Chapel Hill: University of North Carolina Press, 1984.

Rapping, Elayne. "PBS Meets Knot's Landing." Review of Meredith Tax, *Union Square. The Nation*, 10 April 1989, pp. 492–94.

Reilly, John M. "Criticism of Ethnic Literature: Seeing the Whole Story." *MELUS* 5 (Spring 1978): 2–13.

Riedel, Walter E., ed. *The Old World and the New: Literary Perspectives of German-Speaking Canadians*. Toronto: University of Toronto Press, 1984.

Rippley, La Vern J. *The German-Americans*. Boston: G. K. Hall, 1976.

Rischke, Anne-Susanne. *Die Lyrik in der "Gartenlaube," 1853–1903: Untersuchungen zu Thematik, Form und Funktion*. Frankfurt am Main: Peter Lang, 1982.

Ritter, Alexander. "Die deutschsprachige Literatur des Auslands: Zwischen literarischem Vorbehalt und kulturpolitischer Empfindsamkeit." *German-Canadian Yearbook* 6 (1981): 149–66.

——, ed. *Deutschsprachige Literatur im Ausland. Zeitschrift für Literatur und Linguistik*, suppl. 13 Göttingen: Vandenhoek and Ruprecht, 1985.

Roberts, James S. *Drink, Temperance, and the Working Class in Nineteenth-Century Germany*. Boston: Allen and Unwin, 1984.

Rollko, Bodo. *Die Belletristik in der Berliner Presse des 19. Jahrhunderts*. Berlin: Colloquium, 1985.

Rowan, Steven. "The Cultural Program of Heinrich Börnstein in St. Louis, 1851–1861." *In Their Own Words* 3.2 (1986): 187–206.

Rowan, Steven, and James Neal Primm. *Germans for a Free Missouri: Translations from the St. Louis Press, 1857–1862*. Columbia: University of Missouri Press, 1983.

Rücktäschel, Annamarie, and Hans Dieter Zimmermann, eds. *Trivialliteratur*. Munich: Fink, 1976.

Said, Edward. *Orientalism*. New York: Pantheon, 1978.

Sammons, Jeffrey L. *Wilhelm Raabe: The Fiction of the Alternative Community*. Princeton: Princeton University Press, 1987.

Saveth, Edward N. *American Historians and European Immigrants, 1875–1925*. New York: Columbia University Press, 1948.

Schach, Paul. "German Language Newspapers in Nebraska, 1860–1890." *Nebraska History* 65 (1984): 84–107.

Schenda, Rudolf. *Die Lesestoffe der Kleinen Leute*. Munich: Beck, 1976.

Schulte-Sasse, Jochen. "Literarischer Markt und ästhetische Denkform: Analysen und Thesen zur Geschichte ihres Zusammenhangs." *Lili Zeitschrift für Literaturwissenschaft und Linguistik* 2.6 (1972): 11–31.

——. *Literarische Wertung*. Stuttgart: Metzler, 1976.

——. "Toward a 'Culture' for the Masses: The Social-Psychological Function of Popular Literature in Germany and the U.S., 1880–1920." *New German Critique* 29 (Summer 1983): 85–105.

——. "Trivialliteratur." In *Reallexikon der deutschen Literaturgeschichte*, ed. Werner Kohlschmidt and Wolfgang Mohr, 4:562–83. Berlin: Walter de Gruyter, 1981.

Schulte-Sasse, Jochen, and Renate Werner. "E. Marlitts 'Im Hause des Kommerzienrates': Analyse eines Trivialromans in paradigmatischer Absicht." In Eugenie Marlitt, *Im Hause des Kommerzienrates*, 389–434. Munich: Wilhelm Fink Verlag, 1977.

Schwab, Gabriele. "Genesis of the Subject, Imaginary Functions, and Poetic Language." *New Literary History* 15 (Spring 1984): 453–74.

Sengle, Friedrich. *Biedermeierzeit: Deutsche Literatur im Spannungsfeld zwischen Restauration und Revolution, 1815–1848*. Stuttgart: Metzler, 1971.

Siedler, Reinhard. *Sozialgeschichte der Familie*. Frankfurt am Main: Suhrkamp, 1987.

Silverman, Kaja. *The Subject of Semiotics*. New York: Oxford University Press, 1983.

Skårdal, Dorothy. *The Divided Heart: Scandinavian Immigrant Experience through Literary Sources*. Lincoln: University of Nebraska Press, 1974.

Smith, Anthony D. "Ethnic Myths and Ethnic Revivals." *Archives Européennes de Sociologie* 25.2 (1984): 283–305.

———. *The Ethnic Revival*. Cambridge: Cambridge University Press, 1981.

———. "National Identity and Myths of Ethnic Descent." *Research in Social Movements, Conflict and Change* 7 (1984): 95–130.

Smith, Paul. *Discerning the Subject*. Theory and History of Literature 55, Minneapolis: University of Minnesota Press, 1988.

Smith, Timothy L. "Religion and Ethnicity in America." *American Historical Review* 83 (December 1978): 1155–85.

Sollors, Werner. *Beyond Ethnicity: Consent and Descent in American Culture*. New York: Oxford University Press, 1986.

———. "Literature and Ethnicity." In *Harvard Encyclopedia of American Ethnic Groups*, ed. Stephan Thernstrom, 647–65. Cambridge: Harvard University Press, 1980.

Spuler, Linus. "Von deutschamerikanischer Dichtung." *German-American Studies* 1.1 (1969): 8–16.

Spuler, Richard. *"Germanistik" in America: The Reception of German Classicism, 1870–1905*. Stuttgart: Akademischer Verlag Hans-Dieter Heinz, 1982.

Starcher, B. K. "Ernst Keil und die Anfänge der 'Gartenlaube.'" *Seminar* 17.3 (1981): 205–13.

Steiger, Ernst. *Dreiundfünfzig Jahre Buchhändler in Deutschland und Amerika: Erinnerungen und Plaudereien*. New York: E. Steiger, 1901.

———. *Vertrieb deutscher Bücher und Zeitschriften in den Vereinigten Staaten*. New York: n.p., 1868.

Steinberg, Hans-Josef. "Workers' Libraries in Germany before 1914." *History Workshop* 1 (Spring 1976): 166–80.

Steinberg, Stephen. *The Ethnic Myth: Race, Ethnicity, and Class in America*. Boston: Beacon Press, 1981.

Stellhorn, A. C. "J. C. W. Lindemann: First Director of the Evangelical Lutheran Teachers' Seminary in Addison, Illinois." *Concordia Historical Institute Quarterly* 14 (October 1941): 65–92.

Stuecher, Dorothea Diver. "Double Jeopardy: Nineteenth-Century German American Women Writers." Ph.D. Diss., University of Minnesota, 1981.

Suelflow, August. "*St. Louiser Volksblatt.*" *Concordia Historical Institute Quarterly* 18 (January 1946): 108–10.

Suhr, Heidrun. "*Ausländerliteratur*: Minority Literature in the Federal Republic of Germany." *New German Critique* 46 (Winter 1989): 71–103.

Taylor, Philip. *The Distant Magnet: European Emigration to the U.S.A.* New York: Harper and Row, 1971.

Teraoka, Arlene Akiko. "*Gastarbeiterliteratur*: The Other Speaks Back." *Cultural Critique* 7 (Fall 1987): 77–101.

Tilly, Charles. "Did the Cake of Custom Break?" In *Consciousness and Class Experience in Nineteenth-Century Europe*, ed. John M. Merriman, 17–44. New York: Holmes and Meier, 1979.

Tolzmann, Don Heinrich. "The German Language Press in Minnesota, 1855–1955." *German-American Studies* 5 (1972): 169–78.

———, ed. *German-American Literature*. Metuchen, N.J.: Scarecrow Press, 1977.

Tompkins, Jane. *Sensational Designs: The Cultural Work of American Fiction, 1790–1860*. New York: Oxford University Press, 1985.

Trommler, Frank. "Vom Vormärz zum Bürgerkrieg: Die Achtundvierziger und ihre Lyrik." In *Amerika in der deutschen Literatur: Neue Welt—Nordamerika—U.S.A.*, ed. Sigrid Bauschinger, et al., 93–107. Stuttgart: Reclam, 1975.

Trommler, Frank, and Joseph McVeigh, eds. *America and the Germans: An Assessment of a Three-Hundred-Year History*. Philadelphia: University of Pennsylvania Press, 1985.

Turner, Frederick Jackson. "The Significance of the Frontier in American History." In *Annual Report of the American Historical Association for the Year 1893*, 199–227. Washington, D.C.: Government Printing Office.

Uhlig, Walter D. "Our Unforgettable Fick," *Concordia Historical Institute Quarterly* 36 (January 1964): 101–14.

Vecoli, Rudolf J. "Ethnicity: A Neglected Dimension of American History." In *The State of American History*, ed. Herbert J. Bass, 70–88. Chicago: Quadrangle Books, 1970.

———. "The Resurgence of American Immigration History." *American Studies International* 17 (Winter 1979): 46–66.

———. "Return to the Melting Pot: Ethnicity in the United States in the Eighties." *Journal of Ethnic History* 5 (Fall 1985): 7–20.

Walker, Mack. *Germany and the Emigration, 1816–1885*. Cambridge: Harvard University Press, 1964.

Ward, Robert E. *A Bio-Bibliography of German-American Writers, 1670–1970*. White Plains, N.Y.: Kraus International Publishers, 1985.

———. "The Case for German-American Literature." In *The German Contribution to the Building of the Americas*, ed. Gerhard K. Friesen and Walter Schatzberg, 373–89. Worchester, Mass.: Clark University Press, 1977.

———. Review of Barbara Lang, *The Process of Immigration in German-American Literature from 1850 to 1900*. In *Yearbook of German-American Studies* 24 (1989): 170–72.

Warner, Charles Dudley. "Studies of the Great West, VIII: St. Louis and Kansas City." *Harper's New Monthly Magazine* 77 (October 1888): 748–62.

Wehler, Hans-Ulrich. *Entsorgung der deutschen Vergangenheit: Ein polemischer Essay zum "Historikerstreit."* Munich: Beck, 1988.

Weisheit, Eldon. *The Zeal of His House: Five Generations of Lutheran Church–Missouri Synod History, 1847–1972.* St. Louis: Concordia Publishing House, 1973.

Weiss, Gerhard H. "The German Language Press in Minnesota." In *A Heritage Fulfilled: German-Americans,* ed. Clarence A. Glasrud, 47–63. Moorhead, Minn.: Concordia College, 1984.

White, Hayden. *Metahistory: The Historical Imagination in Nineteenth-Century Europe.* Baltimore: Johns Hopkins University Press, 1973.

Wilson, Christopher. "The Rhetoric of Consumption: Mass-Market Magazines and the Demise of the Gentle Reader, 1880–1920." In *The Culture of Consumption: Critical Essays in American History, 1880–1980,* ed. Richard Wightman Fox and T. J. Jackson Lears. New York: Pantheon Books, 1983.

Wittke, Carl. *The German-Language Press in America.* Lexington: University of Kentucky Press, 1957.

——. *Refugees of Revolution: The Forty-eighters in America.* Philadelphia: University of Pennsylvania Press, 1952.

Wright, Will. *Sixguns and Society: A Structural Study of the Western.* Berkeley and Los Angeles: University of California Press, 1975.

Zinn, Howard. *A People's History of the United States.* New York: Harper and Row, 1980.

Zucker, A. E. "*Die Abendschule,* 1853–1940: A Pioneer Weekly." *The American-German Review* 8 (February 1942): 14–17.

Index

269

McVeigh, Joseph, 85
Marlitt, E., 109
Martin Forster, 239–44, 247
Marx, Karl, 103, 229
Marxism, 70, 119–21
mastheads, 10–37, 87, 98, 99, 100, 139,
    153, 188–89
May, Karl, 243
Meergeusen, Die (The Water Beggars),
    134–35
"Meineid, Der" (Perjury), 136
Melanchthon, Phillipp, 42–43
"melting pot," 48–50
middle class, 27, 191–92. *See also* "mid-
    dle class, old"
"middle class, old" 33, 113, 132, 189–90,
    195–96, 201–2, 225
"minor literature," 70–75
Missouri Synod. *See* Lutheran Church–
    Missouri Synod
modernization, 2, 35, 40, 57, 224, 250
Modleski, Tania, 124–26
moral authority, 3, 99, 102, 172–74, 177,
    184
moralische Wocheschriften (moral week-
    lies), 19, 173
"moralische Zustand des Volkes der Ver-
    einigten Staaten, Der" (The Moral
    Condition of the People of the United
    States), 35–36, 147–49, 180–81. *See
    also* assimilation
Moynihan, Daniel Patrick, 49
Mühlbach, Louise, 95, 134n, 205
Müller-Salget, Klaus, 12n, 63n, 174
Mysteres de Paris, Les (The Mysteries of
    Paris), 109
"mystery novels," 109, 121–22
"myth of ethnic descent." *See* ethnicity:
    and "ethnic myth of descent"

Native Americans, 242–43
nativism, 228, 229–31
Neidner, Moritz, 140
*New Yorker Kriminalzeitung und Bel-
    letristisches Journal* (New York
    Crime Reporter and Belletristic Jour-
    nal), 88
nobility, narrative function of, 114, 198
Novak, Michael, 49

Oertel, Wilhelm, 12, 135. *See also* Horn,
    W. O. von
Olson, Audrey Louise, 54
"other," 23, 50–51, 66, 104

Pajeken, F.J., 239, 244
Park, Robert Ezra, 48, 89
Pfarrhaus im Harz, Das (The Parsonage in
    the Harz Mountains), 177

Pfau, Gustav, 45
Pfennig-Magazin, Das (Penny Magazine),
    19
Pichler, Luise, 197, 199, 204
Poore, Carol, 83, 85–88
postmodernism, 5
poststructuralism, 69
press, German-American
    question of (political/real) content in,
    88–93
    literature in, 79–80, 88–93
proto-industrialization, 40, 114

Raabe, Wilhelm, 208–23
racism 107–8n, 148–49, 233–36. *See
    also* nativism
Radhakrishnan, R., 73
Ranger, Terence, 252
Rapping, Elayne, 121n
reading
    as a dangerous practice 151–53, 156,
    211–12, 238–39 (*see also* dancing;
    theater)
    as family activity, 5, 10–14, 23–25,
    27–34, 99–100, 245–46
Reformation, 43, 164, 168, 171, 209, 234
Reitzel, Robert, 92
"rettende Bible, Die" (The Saving Bible),
    136
Revolution of 1848, 41, 85–86, 97, 117,
    134, 138–39, 149n, 207, 220
Richardson, Samuel, 111
Richter, Ludwig, 29
Riehl, Wilhelm Heinrich, 13, 35
Rischke, Anne-Susanne, 166
Rollka, Bodo, 92–93
Romanticism, 173
Rüdiger, Otto, 202, 205
Rundschau, Die (The Observer), 230
Ruppius, Otto, 77

Sabbartarianism. *See* temperance
Said, Edward, 23
Sammons, Jeffrey, 209, 220n
Saxer, Alexander, 26, 137, 138
Schiller, Friedrich, 80, 202n
"Schlosser von Philadelphia, Der" (The
    Locksmith from Philadelphia), 192–
    97, 199–200, 226
Schmidt, William, 235, 237, 238, 239,
    244
Scott, Sir Walter, 200–201
Sealsfield, Charles, 63, 78
secularization 3, 19, 35, 99, 102, 103,
    172–74, 199
Sedan, battle of, 144
Sedan Day, 47
Sengle, Friedrich, 174

Library of Congress Cataloging-in-Publication Data

Peterson, Brent Orlyn.
   Popular narratives and ethnic identity: literature and community in Die Abend-
schule/Brent O. Peterson.
      p. cm.
   Includes bibliographical references and index.
   ISBN 0–8014–2548–4 (alk. paper)
      1. German Americans—Ethnic identity. 2. German-American literature—19th cen-
tury—History and criticism. 3. German fiction—United States—History and criticism.
4. Popular literature—United States—History and criticism. 5. Abend-Schule. 6. German Americans—Books and reading—History—19th century. I. Abend-Schule. II.
Title.
E184.G3P48 1991
305.831′073—dc20   91–17895